DESIGN FOR RESILIENCE

DESIGN FOR RESILIENCE

Making the Future We Leave Behind

STUART WALKER

The MIT Press
Cambridge, Massachusetts
London, England

The MIT Press would like to thank the anonymous peer reviewers who provided comments on drafts of this book. The generous work of academic experts is essential for establishing the authority and quality of our publications. We acknowledge with gratitude the contributions of these otherwise uncredited readers.

This book was set in Adobe Garamond Pro by New Best-set Typesetters Ltd. Printed and bound in the United States of America.

Library of Congress Cataloging-in-Publication Data

Names: Walker, Stuart, 1955– author.
Title: Design for resilience : making the future we leave behind / Stuart Walker.
Description: Cambridge, Massachusetts : The MIT Press, [2023] | Includes bibliographical references and index.
Identifiers: LCCN 2022028156 (print) | LCCN 2022028157 (ebook) | ISBN 9780262048095 (hardcover) | ISBN 9780262374453 (epub) | ISBN 9780262374460 (pdf)
Subjects: LCSH: Engineering design—History. | Technological forecasting. | Sustainable design. | Material culture. | Sustainable living. | Human ecology. | Environmental protection—Citizen participation. | Future, The.
Classification: LCC TA174 .W263 2023 (print) | LCC TA174 (ebook) | DDC 620/.0042—dc23/eng/20221006
LC record available at https://lccn.loc.gov/2022028156
LC ebook record available at https://lccn.loc.gov/2022028157
ISBN: 978-0-262-04809-5

10   9   8   7   6   5   4   3   2   1

The firm, the enduring, the simple, and the modest are near to virtue
—Confucius

Contents

Preface

Human societies are full of variety, with different languages, customs, and ways of life. Over tens of thousands of years, societies have evolved in places with markedly different climates, geographies, plants, and animals. But despite all this variety and all this history, we have yet to find a perfect society—one in which there is peace and justice, where people live in harmony with nature and are happy and content. In truth, there is no such thing as a perfect society and no such thing as a stable society—the world is in a continual state of flux.

Consequently, whatever society, time, and place we happen to be born into, we are always confronted with the same question, which each generation must try to answer for itself: "How should we live?" This question has been asked down the ages. Many have tried to answer it, and some, from very different contexts and eras, have arrived at the same answer. Even so, we have yet to live in ways that heed their teachings.

Today, more than at any other time in human history, the clock is pressuring us to change our lifestyles, to live more gently on the planet. And once again, the question "How should we live?" is uppermost in our minds, and many are trying to answer it. Predictably, given the times in which we live, the answers are now dominated by technological innovations—clean-energy production by harnessing the sun, the wind, and the waves; clean transport; and genetically altered plants and animals. Such answers are far from those offered by earlier generations, which are by and large ignored, and so we are uninformed by history and our heritage of philosophical and spiritual teachings, which have addressed this question so thoughtfully.

Can technology save us? It seems unlikely, especially when we recognize that it is the development of industrialized, technological society that has brought us to this point and is largely responsible for the current state of the planet. But if our faith in modern technology is misplaced, what other avenues are open to us? What should we do? *How should we live?*

With these questions in mind, I embarked on a journey of discovery to find out what kinds of artifacts and activities have been present in human cultures from very early times, irrespective of language, belief systems, or geography. What has been found to be essential to how we live? The answers are many and varied, they are associated with home, food, culture, and recreation as well as with deeper spiritual aspects of being human. Taken together, they tell us much about what is necessary, what is important, and what is not. And they offer tangible examples, and a wide variety of insights into the complex, interrelated facets of the question "How should we live?"

Stuart Walker
Lancaster, England

1 INTRODUCTION

We are living the exception rather than the rule, a burst of profligacy that will burn itself out, perhaps literally. It hasn't always been this way, and it need not be this way. We have made it so—we have designed it so. But it cannot hold.

New technologies, new products, and new systems are the fuel of modern societies—new at any cost. We seek ceaseless change, ceaseless growth. Existing products and practices are freely discarded in favor of the latest fashions, the most up-to-date devices. Such extravagant lifestyles expose the fact that we do not value material things; we value newness, and the environmental toll is immense.

In this world of obsessive change, the raisons d'être of businesses, universities, and governments have become originality and innovation. But as we shall see in chapter 7, the true meanings of these words are far more congruent with the resilient ways of tradition than with the reckless extravagances of today.

For the longest time in human history, the rapid, unrestrained creation of novelty was neither sought after nor celebrated. Traditional societies valued continuity, kept to practices that had stood the test of time, and lived within the parameters of their local environment.[1] They practiced conservation and respected the contributions of their predecessors. And by and large, they were resilient.

Adaptability, robustness, and being able to endure are essential to resilience and are commensurate with thoughtful approaches to originality and innovation. Accordingly, design is in a position to make constructive contributions to resilient ways of living. Fundamentally, it is a creative discipline, which means that when a project begins, we do not know where it will lead. If we knew the outcome beforehand, we would not be allowing the creative process to unfold. Also, to progress a project toward resolution, a whole series of design decisions have to be made. We must consider and perhaps question the basis of these decisions. Many will be steered by business priorities, while others will be more subjective, related to values and aesthetic preferences. We can ensure these decisions are grounded in sound principles, and we can draw on experience. To achieve resilience, we should also look at the values, priorities, and practices of our predecessors, as well as reflect on how they wrestled with the question "How should we live?" And when we do this, we find the answer is typically based in values of benevolence, care for other people and the natural environment, and attention to the traditions and teachings that have been handed down over generations. Together, these represent the accumulated wisdom of humankind about how we can live in harmony with each other and the natural world. Essentially, they boil down to moderation and compassion.

We also have precedents—manifestations of these values—in the form of artifacts and activities that have been present in human cultures for centuries, even millennia. By examining a wide range of such precedents, we see that meanings can be delineated that transcend any specific era, belief system, or economic structure. In one form or another, all the precedents discussed in the following pages have endured in their purpose and value, and they have been continually adjusted to suit changing circumstances. As a result, they hold important lessons about the meaning and manifestation of resilience. By considering them, we can perhaps develop a more complete picture of resilience and its critical relationship to sustainable, ethical living. Their continual presence in human culture over such long periods of time means that they represent something of deep significance and value, something permanent.

I will begin by examining how we have arrived at our present, highly precarious state and the gross inadequacies of the modern era's answer to the question "How should we live?" I discuss alternative paths, the need for greater discernment and critique in design, and how we might take a more appreciative design approach. I look at precedents related to home, food, culture, play, and spirit. And from these I cautiously offer a constructive, and what I trust is a reasonably comprehensive, interpretation of *design for resilience*.

Contrary to the approaches being advocated by some leaders today,[2] the interpretation of resilience that emerges here will be attained neither by relying on yet-to-be-invented technologies nor by expecting little change in our current ways of life. A far more fundamental shift is needed, but this can be positive, leading to less acquisitive but more meaningful, rewarding, and enriching ways of life that are also healthier for people and planet.

The selection of precedents was informed by a variety of factors—utility, social function, spiritual role, presence across time and culture, relationship to the natural environment, and personal preference. The criteria for selection were not defined too rigidly, so as to enable ideas and examples to be mutually informing, to allow cases to arise during the process, and to keep open opportunities presented by chance encounters. This looser approach seems to me to be in keeping with the serendipitous nature of the design process itself. As a result, the precedents come from a wide variety of cultures and times—and even though many are rooted in *particular* cultures, their multilayered meanings transcend any individual worldview, belief system, or economic structure.

Similarly, grouping the artifacts and activities into particular areas of endeavor, such as home, food, and culture, will inevitably be rather loose and porous and is used here simply to arrange things in a reasonable order. The precedent of "correspondence," for instance, is both an artifact, in the form of a letter or postcard, and a practice, which could take the form of a composition written by hand, an email, or a quick reply on WhatsApp.

Nowadays, considerable amounts of time, energy, and money are put into producing design guidelines, toolkits, and frameworks—all developed through perfectly logical, analytical processes of data collection and classification. But such systematic approaches can never get to the heart of the matter because they lack vital facets of creative practice—imagination, intuition, uncertainty, experience, and skill. Design embodies all of these, and, consequently, design outcomes will implicitly express beliefs, values, priorities, and preferences. Design combines rational thinking based on empirical data with imagination and creative interpretation.

All the precedents express values and qualities consistent with resilient behaviors. And, as will become apparent, they tend to embody values of humility and kindness. On the whole, they are quiet designs that are appropriate to people and place.

Perhaps especially today, design has the potential to be a force for the good by challenging the constant production of novelty and the accompanying societal atomization and disruption that characterizes contemporary society. It can look again to the wisdom, gentleness, and inherent qualities of community building and environmental stewardship common to many traditional practices, and reinterpret them for today, thereby giving them renewed relevance and potency. Through such means, we will perhaps be able to refind and revalue many of those things that, in recent times, we have too readily swept aside.

The chapters are arranged in three parts and, in keeping with the above thoughts on the nature and spirit of design, include rational, systematic approaches; discussions about values and perspectives that are more personal and interpretive; and some sections that are more imaginative, including short lyrical pieces, fictions, and satires. All these help convey ideas about the state of design today; the magnitude of revision and improvement that is required to effectively address resilience; and the benefits of adopting less consumptive, more meaningful ways forward.

Part I: Resilience introduces and discusses resilience from a variety of angles, including materialism, production, appreciation, critique, and potential.

Part II: Precedents includes numerous examples of artifacts and activities that, in some form, have been present in human societies for centuries. They are grouped into five chapters: "Resilient Home" includes discussions of such basic artifacts as chair, table, lamp and pot; "Resilient Food" considers the growing of produce, the catching of fish, and the practices and artifacts these activities involve; "Resilient Culture" looks at the abiding place of music, dance, and theater, as well as bodily adornment and forms of communication; "Resilient Play" examines artifacts that encourage the imagination, as well as the origin and role of indoor games and field sports; and finally, "Resilient Spirit" looks at, among other things, ritual, shrine, and sanctuary. These loose groupings provide the book with a convenient sense of order, but, in reality, there are no distinct boundaries. Artifacts enable activities and convey meanings that may be at once utilitarian, cultural, recreational, and/or spiritual. Each of these chapters begins with a discussion of the main theme followed by the various precedents and their relationships to resilience. Taken together, they reveal a rich picture of possibilities and wide-ranging forms of expression that are, and have always been, fundamental to being human.

Part III: Resilience by Design begins with a reflection called "Design for Good" and the paradox of civilized societies coexisting with inequality and even barbarism—tendencies that are at odds with sustainable futures. Both the role of the creative arts within such a milieu and whether design can truly be a force for the good are considered. In response to the disruptions to our modes of living and working caused by COVID-19, rather than returning to these norms, "Design after a Pandemic" explores design options for building a fairer, more environmentally responsible "normal." The final chapter, "Design for Resilience," brings together insights and ideas from all the earlier chapters to identify factors for substantive and lasting change, which include challenging current norms; developing a new outlook; recognizing the importance of tradition; identifying the key attributes of resilient living; and, finally, developing Ten Principles of Design for Resilience.

PART I RESILIENCE

2 THE DRAGROPE OF THE SOUL

In this chapter, I discuss the lineage of modern design; its connection to utilitarianism; and the particular, even peculiar, way of perceiving the world that has emerged from this relationship. It has spawned much technological innovation but has also repressed critical aspects of our humanity. These developments may have had many positive effects, but there have always been notable critics whose misgivings, in hindsight, are proving all too prescient. It is important for us to look at this history, because instead of learning from this past, we are in danger of simply reinforcing directions that have long been recognized as both philosophically problematic and severely damaging.

Any background to modern design naturally includes at least some discussion of the Industrial Revolution, which had its beginnings in Great Britain and continued in the United States. The British phase set the foundations of industrial-scale production, but it was America that pioneered mass production for mass markets. In turn these developments laid the groundwork for today's consumer society. The industrialization of society created wealth and improved the material standards of living for millions of people around the world. However, the longer-term effects of this system—which is based on science, technology, and innovation and linked to ideas of progress and economic growth—are inseparable from major environmental destruction and a host of social ills, including exploitative labor practices and gross economic inequities.

Two world wars in the twentieth century saw science and technology being redirected toward the development and production of weapons. In

World War I, chlorine, phosgene, and mustard gas were used in trench warfare, with devastating effects. In World War II, industrial-scale killing was used in the Nazi death camps, and the United States dropped atomic bombs on civilian populations in the Japanese cities of Hiroshima and Nagasaki. Unsurprisingly, in the years following these events, there was growing disillusionment with the promise of science and technology. Along with other concerns, this disillusionment contributed to mass protests and social changes in Europe and North America during the latter half of the twentieth century. The Universal Declaration of Human Rights was proclaimed by the United Nations General Assembly on December 10, 1948, and the 1960s saw major developments in the civil rights movement in the United States, as well as the rise of women's rights and gay rights. This period also saw the beginnings of the environmental movement, though its roots lay in the late 1800s, particularly in the United States, with writers such as Henry David Thoreau, John Muir, and the poet Walt Whitman. The publication of Rachel Carson's *Silent Spring* in 1962, which documented the damaging environmental effects of pesticide use, is often seen as marking the birth of modern environmentalism. Awareness grew during the 1960s, and in the 1970s numerous environmental organizations were founded, including Friends of the Earth in the United Kingdom and Greenpeace in Canada.

However, to understand why these developments occurred, their relevance to today, and their relationship to contemporary design, we have to go back further. We have to know something of the early developments of industry and the effects they had on society and on design education.

A CRITICAL VIEW OF THE FOUNDATIONS OF DESIGN

Typically, the history of the Industrial Revolution has been written in very positive terms. As one might expect, this is a history penned largely by those who saw it as a triumph of British ingenuity, industrial might, and supremacy. But even at the time, some were contesting this view and the rationalism, materialism, and utilitarianism on which it rested. Now that we are at some distance from it, we can attempt a more balanced telling, one that not only recognizes its achievements but also its less-positive consequences. We can consider the wheels it set in motion, the changes in outlook it fostered, and the impacts these have had.

The 150 years between the mid-eighteenth and the late nineteenth centuries set the context for some of the major issues affecting design and society today, including design conventions and the relationships among contemporary manufacturing, social injustices, and the state of the natural world.

Two of Britain's major schools of applied arts, the Royal College of Art in London and the Manchester School of Art, were founded, under earlier designations, in 1837 and 1838 respectively. The Great Exhibition was held in London's Hyde Park in 1851 and was followed in 1862 by the International Exhibition in South Kensington. Both fairs were dedicated to the achievements of industry, especially British industry. They were the crowning events of the British phase of the Industrial Revolution and were instrumental in setting the scene for British design education during the latter part of the nineteenth century. In South Kensington, close to the site of the Crystal Palace exhibition, the Victoria and Albert Museum, now the world's largest museum of applied arts, was established in 1852, the Science Museum in 1857, and the Natural History Museum in 1881—all of which became major resources for the nearby Royal College of Art.

These two major exhibitions were not only celebrations of industry but also powerful demonstrations of the ascendency of practical reason and utilitarianism—as advocated by English philosophers Jeremy Bentham and John Stuart Mill. Utilitarianism is concerned with the pursuit of happiness and the maximization of pleasure together with a due respect for liberty. The goals of happiness and pleasure are seen as self-evidently true and therefore in need of no further justification. Actions that maximize happiness and pleasure are judged to be right and important, while those that don't are of little interest. It follows from this that practical reason is concerned with the means to happiness and pleasure, which according to the utilitarian philosophy is entirely objective.[1]

The Great Exhibition was effectively a grand showcase for the tangible results of this way of looking at the world and was a bold statement of confidence and pride in Britain's technological prowess.[2] Queen Victoria, writing to her uncle, described its opening as "the *greatest* day in our history, the most *beautiful* and *imposing*."[3] The writer William Makepeace Thackeray created an "Exhibition Ode," published in *The Times*, that directed readers to pay proper attention to the British products on show:

> Look yonder where the engines toil;
> The trophies of her bloodless war:
> Brave weapons there.
> Victorious over wave and soil,
> With these she sails, she weaves, she toils,
> Pierces the everlasting hills
> and spans the seas.[4]

This sense of triumphalism, however, was only one view; others, in Britain and abroad, saw these developments rather differently. Creative people often take a dim view of such insistently rationalistic, supposedly objective approaches, with their theoretical abstractions and brute utilitarian efficiencies. Artistic creativity tends to work in other ways, which involve quite different modes of thinking and are by no means entirely objective. It also draws on and values intuition, imagination, interpretation, experience, human skill, tacit knowledge, spontaneous insights, and spiritual sensibilities. One writer at the time wrote: "Despite the Utilitarians, and their fine spun theories, and subtle arguments, we delight in painting and the kindred arts. Man was not created to spend his whole existence in toil."[5] The unadorned functional forms of mechanically reproduced products might be tolerable for tools and the necessities of work, but decoration and ornament, and a harmonious combination of utility and beauty, were regarded as the refinements of a better life. Consequently, the utilitarians were vilified by some for producing "useful ugliness."[6]

The prominent nineteenth-century philosopher, commentator, and social thinker John Ruskin was a critic of Mill and the philosophy of utilitarianism, and while Ruskin was not opposed to the use of machines, he advocated caution in their use to ensure that human work did not become unskilled and servile and that the world did not become reduced to a polluted bedlam. In his essay "Ad Valorem," presaging today's environmental crisis and the air pollution experienced in many modern cities, he wrote, "All England may, if it so chooses, become one manufacturing town; and Englishmen, sacrificing themselves to the good of general humanity, may live diminished lives in the midst of noise, of darkness, and of deadly exhalation."[7] Designer and socialist William Morris, a key name in the Arts and Crafts Movement, believed that the processes of design and production should be fully integrated, as they are in craft practices. This differs from factory-based mechanical production methods, where the designer defines the product but is not intimately involved in its production. Morris argued that good work provides people with a sense of accomplishment and hope. Expressing views similar to those of Ruskin, Morris also said that so-called labor-saving machines have the effect of eliminating skills and reducing working people to the ranks of unskilled laborers.[8]

Similarly, not all foreign visitors to these exhibitions saw them in a positive light. Fyodor Dostoyevsky, who attended the International Exhibition and had read about the Great Exhibition, was a severe critic of the rising dominance of rationalism in European society, which these exhibitions epitomized. Unlike his compatriot and fellow author Ivan Turgenev, who was Western-leaning in temperament, Dostoyevsky was a passionate Slavophile. He argued that all the abstract schemes and theories of utilitarianism and rationalism, which supposedly advance humanity's interests, are just idle exercises in logic. He suggested that the kind of civilization they produce serves only to develop our capacity for an increasing variety of sensations, nothing more. What many thought of as cause for celebration and pinnacle events of the Industrial Age, he saw as monstrosities of Western civilization and its addiction to materialism.[9] To him they represented a corrupting ideology and a form of cultural hegemony that "offer material abundance while demanding the sacrifice of spirit, autonomy, and authenticity"; he saw this as the path to "cultural homogenization that promised brotherhood while inevitably producing atomization and alienation."[10] Some years later, Jean-Paul Sartre similarly argued that all materialist philosophies result in the objectification of people, rather than treating them as subjects, which echoed Georg Wilhelm Friedrich Hegel's view that a person's identity is based solely on mutual recognition in an interpersonal context.[11]

While these two exhibitions represent the Industrial Revolution's culminating events, its beginnings were 150 years earlier. A look at some of the major developments in Britain between the early 1700s and the mid-1800s, reveals the beginnings of conventions and expectations that still dominate design and society today.

Science, technology, industry, and commerce do not exist in a bubble but are instead part and parcel of developments and events in other spheres. As the Industrial Revolution was progressing, there were also major developments in politics, society, the arts, and philosophical understandings. A parallel development to the growth of industry was the intellectual and artistic movement known as Romanticism, which had its origins in continental Europe. It lies at the opposite end of the philosophical spectrum to materialism and utilitarianism and is in many ways a reaction to them. Romanticism extolled the beauties of nature but had a tendency to create an idealized view of rural life and see the rural worker in heroic terms. This movement was represented by such figures as William Wordsworth, William Blake, and Mary Shelley in Britain; Johann Wolfgang von Goethe and Friedrich Schiller in Germany; and Jean-Jacques Rousseau in France. Communism also developed during these years—Karl Marx and Friedrich Engels published the *Communist Manifesto* in 1848. It defended the interests of ordinary working people and challenged the inequities of a class-based system in which the majority endured unending labor, poor conditions, and anxiety.[12]

There are also the perspectives of those who were colonized by the European powers during these years. In Africa, India, the Americas, and Australasia, peoples with their own cultures and beliefs were profoundly affected by both colonization and the consequences of industrialization. They were frequently subjugated, abused, driven from their lands, and in some cases enslaved or systematically killed. And the legacy of these traumatizing events lives on. As recently as the 1990s, in the former British colonies of Canada and Australia, Indigenous peoples were being prevented from speaking their own language and practicing their traditional beliefs. Tragically, too, their children were still being taken from them and placed in residential schools, often far from their families. This was all part of a deliberate policy to eradicate the languages, stories, and cultures of Indigenous peoples and to "Europeanize" them. And in the twenty-first century, the Black Lives Matter movement arose to eradicate enduring issues of discrimination, abuse, and inequity of opportunity.

Ironically and rather belatedly, today's Western scientists are turning to Indigenous peoples to learn more about their deep traditional knowledge of the natural environment and their local ecosystems in an effort to address issues of sustainability, which is a concern largely created by industrialization, Western lifestyles, and immoderate levels of consumption and energy use.[13] As Nicholas has pointed out: "These knowledge systems, developed over countless generations, are based on individual and collectively learned experiences and explanations of the world, verified by elders, and conveyed and guided by experiential learning, and by oral traditions and other means of record keeping. . . . Traditional Knowledge has today become a highly valued source of information for archaeologists, ecologists, biologists, ethnobotanists, climatologists and others."[14]

FROM COUNTRYSIDE TO TOWN

In the mid-eighteenth century, England was already the leading manufacturing nation in the world, but this was based predominantly on craft or cottage industries, which were spread all over the country, not just in urban centers. Production was carried out in small workshops or in the home, and this is where the Industrial Revolution had its roots. It began with craftspeople—millwrights, watchmakers, canal builders, carpenters, and blacksmiths.

Up until this time, a major part of the British economy had been the slave trade, which was a highly lucrative business because of the triangular route between Britain, Africa, and the Americas. Profits were made on each leg of the journey. In the outward passage, ships would leave Britain with their holds filled with manufactured goods, such as tools, housewares, and munitions. In Africa, these were exchanged for slaves. In the Middle Passage, the slave ships crossed the Atlantic to the Americas—a journey of up to two months in which many died. Profits from the slave markets meant the ships could return to Britain loaded with sugar, rum, tobacco, rice, and coffee, and, in later years, cotton.

By the second half of the eighteenth century, however, international trade was becoming more competitive and cottage industries were no longer sufficiently productive. Consequently, the organization of labor radically changed, and by 1820 it had become the norm for people to go to work in the new factories or mills. As this was before the advent of motorized transport, they had to live near their place of work, which resulted in rapid urbanization. This massive social upheaval led to widespread urban deprivation, squalor, and the darker consequences of industrial advancement.

The early machines of the Industrial Revolution were windmills and watermills, which had been around for hundreds of years. The millwrights, who were the nascent engineers of this new age, began making practical improvements to these ancient machines. These early years also witnessed a nationwide building of canals for carrying coal, iron ore, and manufactured goods all over the country.

One of the most famous ironmasters of the early 1700s was Abraham Darby, who set up his ironworks in Coalbrookdale in the Severn Valley in Shropshire, which became a major center of early industry. Major advances in iron- and steelmaking led to their use in the construction of boats, the manufacture of armaments and industrial machinery, and the building of bridges—the first iron bridge, across the River Severn, was completed in 1779.

The steam engine was invented by Thomas Newcomen in 1712, and it was this machine that accelerated the pace of industrial development, especially after its design had been improved by James Watt. By the 1790s, Watt's steam engines were powering textile mills—especially in the northwest of England around Manchester—and foundries, flour mills, and workshops throughout the country. The location of a windmill or waterwheel is constrained by topography, but with the advent of the steam engine, power could be generated anywhere it was needed. Besides factories, it was used in agriculture for ploughing and threshing and in mining for hauling ore. The steam engine led the way for major industrial expansion. It also heralded a revolution in transportation through the development of transatlantic steamships and the building of railways. All this, of course, was accompanied by huge increases in the use of coal. The age of steam saw the large-scale burning of hydrocarbons to produce power. This we are continuing to do—through coal-fired power stations; the use of petroleum and diesel in vehicles; and the burning of coal, oil, and gas for the heating of homes. These early developments, therefore, set the foundations of our contemporary environmental crisis.

SCIENTIFIC RESEARCH AND DISCOVERY

The second phase of the Industrial Revolution took place in the United States from around the middle of the nineteenth century. It is characterized by major technical advances that were essentially scientific in nature. They required a knowledge of pure science and a systematic process of scientific experiment and testing. Their commercial success also depended on the establishment of working relationships between industrialists, technologists, and scientists.

The last quarter of the nineteenth century saw a host of inventions, innovations, and discoveries that collectively heralded the beginning of the modern way of life. They included Bell's telephone; Edison's phonograph, which recorded the human voice and was the precursor to the recorded music industry; Edison's electric light bulb; the motor car by Daimler and Benz in Germany and Levassor in France; vaccines by Pasteur; the pneumatic tire by Dunlop; and the discovery of radioactivity by Marie Curie.

Systematic developments in the factory system in the United States included the division of manufacturing into a large series of simple processes, each carried out by a specialized, power-operated machine. In the twentieth century, this evolved into the manufacture of small-scale machines for the home, or "durable consumer goods." One of the first of these was the electric dishwasher, invented by Josephine Cochran in 1886 and commercially manufactured a few years later. These developments, which were both technical and organizational, came to be known as mass production.

By 1900, therefore, the foundations of large-scale industry and consumer society had been laid. Marconi sent the first transatlantic radio message in

1901, which marked the start of broadcasting and mass home entertainment. The first motorized airplane flight by the Wright brothers in 1903 led to developments in international air travel. Henry Ford's assembly line for producing affordable automobiles began with the Model T Ford in 1908. With these rapid and widespread developments, the years that followed saw an ever-increasing variety of consumer products and household appliances. This, in turn, led to the new discipline of design for industry and the arrival of the industrial designer. Professional product designers were employed to develop new consumer goods, both for efficient, economical production and to be attractive and distinctive in the marketplace. One of the most famous of these early designers was Raymond Loewy (1893–1986), who has often been referred to as the father of modern industrial design.

A SOBERING LEGACY

The pursuit of happiness, on which utilitarianism rests, became strongly linked to the pursuit of pleasure and engaging in sensory-pleasure-seeking activities. When these are combined with a consumption-based, growth-oriented economy, it is easy to see why adherence to this philosophy quickly led to self-indulgence, decadence, and a culture of waste. It produced not only a system that lacks moderation but also one that is based on an incomplete and entirely inadequate understanding of the nature of being human. The modern period was dominated by this partial perspective. Science and technology gained such a dominant role because they are so well-suited to addressing utilitarian concerns through the endless development of all manner of appliances, devices, and gadgets. As a consequence, other spheres of human endeavor, including the visual arts, humanities, music, and religion, came to be seen as less important. These different areas, however, should not be regarded as mutually exclusive—the arts and humanities complement the sciences and are equally necessary if we are to attain a broad understanding of the world. We can acknowledge the importance of science and technology while still recognizing that they cannot provide for all our needs. In addition to physiological and essentially extrinsic, utilitarian needs, we also have social needs and are constantly faced with ethical questions about how we ought to act toward others. Furthermore, human beings have always been concerned with larger existential questions—we ask why and search for meaning; we seek the good and have deeper, spiritual needs. These more profound questions involve human values, social relationships, and qualitative interpretations of the world. Answers to these questions are not necessarily to be found "out there" through so-called objective analysis or through an abundance of sensory experiences and pleasures. These deeper questions are related to our inner sense of purpose and intrinsic aspects of who we are as individuals.

With its emphasis on rationalism and utilitarianism, the modern period's foundational philosophy is clearly incapable of providing for this variety of complex and interrelated human needs, especially when pursued primarily through science and technology. Scientific investigation seeks to understand the natural world and natural phenomena through systematic inquiry. It is a disciplined field of activity that develops theories and principles and prizes objectivity and repeatability; consequently, acquired skills, tradition, qualitative considerations, and personal intuition tend to play little or no part. The discoveries that emerge from such investigations are frequently developed into technologies, which essentially use scientific knowledge for practical applications. However, when we only understand a thing analytically, we suspend our judgments of value about it. We reduce it to an object, a quantity, and it then becomes all too easy for us to dominate the natural world and use, abuse, and waste it for our own purposes. In doing so, we are effectively repressing aspects of ourselves that would otherwise enable us to perceive the natural world and respond to it in a more holistic manner. C. S. Lewis argues that when we treat living things in this way, they "resist the movement of the mind," and we pay a price "for our analytical knowledge and manipulative power, even if we have ceased to count it."[15] But, importantly, he goes on to say: "It is not the greatest of modern scientists who feel most sure that the object, stripped of its qualitative properties and reduced to mere quantity, is wholly real. Little scientists, and little unscientific followers of science may think so. The great minds know very well that the object, so treated, is an artificial abstraction, that something of its reality has been lost."[16] Thus, modernity's priorities and preoccupations foster a worldview that is incapable of dealing with a broad swathe of critical human needs. But it is this impoverished worldview that has driven such enormous developments in technology and industry, and these, in turn, continue to feed our insatiable, consumption-based economic system.

The discipline of design has been intimately involved in these developments from the earliest stages of mass production. What is more, the foundations of modern design, which were developed to serve this system, turn out to have little substantive basis. The minimalist designs of the modernists were, in reality, not based on a robust philosophical position but were more a reaction to the ornamental forms of design that had preceded them. There was no coherent link to the affordances and constraints of mechanized production, and the *form follows function* principle turned out to be just another style.[17]

The second half of the twentieth century saw a questioning of the modern project, and new design directions began to be explored. Some late-modern or postmodern experiments sought to consciously leave behind the dominantly rationalistic, minimalist trends that had characterized design and design education for decades. The most notable were carried out in Italy in the 1970s and 1980s by Studio Alchimia[18] and the Memphis group with designers such as Ettore Sottsass and Andrea Branzi.[19] The brightly colored laminate surfaces of their furniture pieces announced a clear break from modernism and the possibility of a new direction for design. Their work was a conscious attempt to depart from the functionalist forms and neutral colors of modernism.

Yet despite these developments and a greater awareness of the effects of human activities on the natural environment, the imbalanced legacy of modernity remains dominant to the present day. In recent times, successive British governments have preferentially championed and supported education in science, technology, engineering, and mathematics (STEM) over other areas, including the arts, the humanities, and religion. While STEM subjects are obviously of great value, they provide only part of the picture.

Hence, the government's position is firmly grounded in ideas that remain partial, that have proved to be inadequate in addressing a wide variety of concerns, that are retrograde, and that pay little regard to a large sector of human activity. In a highly politicized move, those in power have chosen to designate as "low quality" many courses offered by university departments that fall outside the STEM subject areas. These courses are not considered to be of sufficient value to the country, at least when measured against such criteria as graduate earnings and the perceived potential of graduates to contribute to economic growth. Recently, it allocated ten thousand more places at education institutions in England for subjects "of strategic importance."[20] Understandably, concerns were expressed that the criteria used to allow institutions to bid for these extra places were "deeply subjective and closed-minded."[21] In a further blow, the UK government has approved a 50 percent funding cut to higher education arts and design courses in England, with savings being redirected to support STEM subjects.[22]

It is sobering to realize that despite the world being brought to the brink of environmental disaster and being torn apart by division and social inequity, as well as a pervasive sense of disillusionment and fear, we still stick to the same old materialistic ways and appear incapable of instigating more creative and more fundamental reform. This applies equally to the field of design, where the ethos of modernity remains strong even with its destructive record of focusing on extrinsic, physical phenomena and creating endless functional novelty and sensory pleasures. This remains the case despite experiments in continental Europe and new insights being gained from research into traditional knowledge and Indigenous design, which are often quintessentially sustainable. Much professional design, perhaps especially in the United Kingdom and the United States, remains wedded to its determinedly pragmatic and prosaic, almost anti-intellectual, utilitarian roots. Consequently, the designs often seem to lack the flair and qualitative depth that characterizes work founded on broader philosophical underpinnings and a more meaningful sense of purpose. A primary aim of a leading British product designer, for example, is "to achieve pleasure for the user," attained through the design of the product's physical qualities—its style, visual appeal, feel, and weight.[23] And we just have to look at a smartphone to know that modernism's minimalist aesthetic is alive and well.

In an attempt to counter these overly narrow understandings, the British Academy, Arts Council England, and the London School of Economics recently came together to launch SHAPE. This initiative draws attention to the value and importance of social sciences, humanities, arts, people, and the economy and aims to champion these subjects. Quite rightly, it is presented as being complementary to science and technology, not in opposition to them.[24] One can but hope that it will build sufficient momentum to make a real and lasting difference, for, as Alice Walker has said, "materialism is the dragrope of the soul."[25]

3 SMALL *IS* BEAUTIFUL

In 1973, E. F. Schumacher published *Small Is Beautiful: A Study of Economics as if People Mattered*, in which he challenged the purpose of business and laid out a basis for socially and environmentally responsible enterprise. One of his main premises, as the title suggests, was that smaller-scale businesses are better for people, place, and the creation of resilient economies. He also argued that small-scale, relatively nonaggressive technologies can give people the chance to enjoy their work, instead of just working for a wage and only enjoying themselves in their time off. He wanted industry to become a force for the good in modern life by developing collaborative partnerships between management and employees as well as forms of common ownership that would help ensure common wealth. The way to achieve this, he said, was to have methods and equipment that are affordable, thereby making them accessible to virtually everyone; that are suited to small-scale applications; and that allow people to express their creativity. With these three elements, he believed we could develop a harmonious relationship with nature that facilitates a culture of permanence, but if just one of the three is neglected, things will inevitably go awry.[1]

I first read *Small Is Beautiful* shortly after it was published, in an under-graduate economics class. It came to mind again during a recent visit to Tintern, in the southeast corner of Wales. This beautiful spot on the River Wye, with its picturesque abbey ruins and wooded hillsides, had once been a center of industry. Two centuries before the Industrial Revolution, the area had been home to small-scale metalworking. Products were exported all over the world and thousands of jobs were created. The area's eventual decline was brought about by the widespread adoption of an innovative new technology—one that was inherently polluting and whose effects are still being felt today through subsequent developments based on the same fundamental idea.

In contrast to Schumacher's thesis, the immense scale of mass production today, and its associated environmental impacts, are unprecedented and can be largely attributed to a system in which technological progress and economic growth are virtually sacrosanct. Driven primarily by individual levels of consumption, this system churns out vast quantities of short-lived products that are constantly promoted by highlighting only their attributes and putative benefits but none of their deficits. It is a system that creates enormous profits for the few while relying on exploitative labor practices and ignoring or even deliberately obfuscating the evidence of long-term harm. In the 1920s, R. H. Tawney warned that economic ambitions can be good servants but bad masters. He advised us to give greater consideration to the purpose of industry and the goal of our economic ambitions.[2]

Many of the problems with our current system are related to scale—the scale of industrialization, resource acquisition, production, consumption, and waste; the scale of greed and the size of profits sought; the scale of environmental destruction and pollution and of socioeconomic inequities; and, on an individual level, our own personal scale of material expectations. We are all involved in the inexorable advance of this system, which, on so many levels, is harmful and quite obviously unsustainable.

The irony is that we already know the features of more sustainable, socially equitable, and environmentally responsible lifestyles and forms of industry—from historical precedents and from the writings of visionaries such as Schumacher—but, seemingly, we do not wish to consider them, or we too readily dismiss them as unrealistic, idealistic, or backward-looking. However, our failure to take sufficient account of more benign ways of living is foolish, for there is much to learn. Looking to the past does not imply that we should try to return to some previous state, nor does it mean pretending modern technologies do not exist. Rather, it suggests that we are prepared to learn from history in order to develop more caring and more responsible ways forward.

Here, I will consider an example of early manufacturing that tells us about the relationship of industry to place, environmental stewardship, social responsibility, lack of waste, and human-scale operations. It is an example of pre–Industrial Revolution production that created thousands of jobs over the course of several centuries, until a highly polluting technological innovation triggered its demise.

A PAST EXAMPLE OF SMALL-SCALE INDUSTRY

During the reign of Elizabeth I, British government policy encouraged less dependence on imported goods. To that end, the Company of Mineral and Battery Works was established in 1566. It set up an iron- and wire-making industry in the small, steep-sided Angidy Valley above Tintern on the River Wye.

The assistance of mechanical power was at a very early stage at this time. The process of wire-making involved pulling a thin rod of metal through a series of holes of diminishing diameter in a metal die plate. To increase the speed and power of the "pull," the wiredrawer was strapped into the seat of a swing that was fixed to a beam and powered by a waterwheel—he would be pulled back and forth with considerable force in a regular swinging motion. At each swing forward and using large tongs, he would grab the wire protruding from the die plate. As he was swung back, the wire would be drawn through the hole of the die, thereby reducing its width and extending its length. This power-assisted method was used only for making wire from harder metals, especially brass and iron; softer metals such as gold, silver, and copper could be drawn by hand.

The first brass wire to be made in Britain was created in this works in 1566, but there was particular demand for its iron wire.[3]

Employment: The wire-making operation created a wide range of jobs. It was a skilled activity that involved a number of processes. There were also furnace operators, founders, power-hammer operators, blacksmiths, bellows makers, and carpenters, and laborers were employed to keep the water channels and millponds clear. The industry also supported various ancillary jobs.

To supply fuel for the furnaces, people were employed in the surrounding woodlands, especially in the coppicing of oak for charcoal-making, and as charcoal burners.[4] A secondary industry was the harvesting of oak bark, used in the tanning of leather. It was taken to the tanneries on shallow-bottomed sailing barges called trows. Consequently, trow-building enterprises were also set up a few miles upstream at the village of Llandogo. And people were employed in boat hauling—essentially teams that pulled the trows up the river against the current. The wire-making industry also supported shopkeepers, suppliers, publicans, and boarding-house keepers.

Exports for Product Manufacture: Large quantities of wire were taken by river to Bristol, where wire was the source material for a vast array of useful products including buckles, fishing hooks, sieves, mousetraps, nails, knitting needles, pins, hook-and-eye fasteners, priming wire for guns, and birdcages. Wire was also used in the wide, structured skirts and bodices of fashionable Elizabethan clothing. One of the principal uses was in the manufacture of carding combs for the wool industry. At this time, wool cloth was Britain's main export commodity, and there was great demand for carding combs. Their manufacture employed thousands of people. As the works at Tintern had an iron-making furnace, cooking pots and other cast iron goods were also manufactured, and in the 1780s, cannons were cast here to supply British forces during the American War of Independence. Wire from this works is also said to have been used to make the first transatlantic telegraph cable.[5]

Industry Tied to Place: The reason the industry grew at this particular location was intimately related to the natural attributes of the place itself. All the key ingredients needed for iron-making and wire-drawing were in plentiful supply in the local region. There was fast-flowing water for power as well as woodland for the production of charcoal to fuel the furnaces and forges. When the operations began, iron was brought to the site from nearby Monkswood and Pontypool. In the mid-1600s, to better control the quality of iron, smelting facilities were installed on site, with a blast furnace and water-powered bellows. Iron ore was available locally from the nearby Forest of Dean, but by the late-1700s, it was more economical to ship in higher-grade ores from the recently developed Lancashire-Cumbria ore field.[6]

Another important aspect of the Angidy works was its proximity to the navigable tidewaters of the Wye, which facilitated the export of its goods. A tidal dock was created at Tintern, so that the trows could be loaded and unloaded even at low tide. Wire and other goods were taken down the Wye to the Severn Estuary and the sea. This was by far the least expensive form of transport at this time, which predated the railway. Its favorable geographical location allowed products to be economically shipped to ports around Britain and Ireland and to mainland Europe, North Africa, and Turkey.

A SUSTAINABLE FORM OF INDUSTRY?

In many ways, this form of industry was reasonably sustainable. It was place-specific and provided thousands of productive jobs over centuries, even though, by today's standards, the manufacturing was on a very small scale. Initially at least, the iron ore was available from local sources, and the charcoal fuel for the furnaces, which is relatively clean-burning, was made from local, renewable resources. Waterpower was used in the production process, and resources were imported and goods exported using sail-powered water transportation. In addition, the industry's waste products were shipped out for use in other forms of manufacturing.

Despite the relatively low environmental impacts of the manufacturing process, a number of authors in the twentieth century claimed that Wordsworth had painted a false picture of a rural idyll when he wrote,

> how oft—
> In darkness and amid the many shapes
> Of joyless daylight; when the fretful stir
> Unprofitable, and the fever of the world,
> Have hung upon the beatings of my heart—
> How oft, in spirit, have I turned to thee,
> O sylvan Wye! thou wanderer thro' the woods,
> How often has my spirit turned to thee![7]

The reality, they argued, was that the industry had despoiled the area—hillsides had been deforested because of the high demand for charcoal, the river was heavily polluted and filled with noisy boat traffic, and there were homeless indigent workers and beggars living in the woods and among the abbey ruins, as well as much destitution. However, by meticulously examining the writings of contemporary authors and taking into account the industrial processes involved, C. J. Rzepka refutes these claims. He concludes that there is "absolutely no evidence of industrial 'despoilation' at or in the immediate vicinity of Tintern Abbey, either on shore or in the woods nearby or flowing past the ruins." He argues that, while the surrounding woodland did provide the wood for charcoal, far from deforesting the hillsides, designated areas were set aside for charcoal production from managed coppices. Clear-cutting would not have made sense. Moreover, tour information from the period mentions the lush woodland along the banks of the river, including the area around Tintern,[8] confirming Wordsworth's description:

> The day is come when I again repose
> Here, under this dark sycamore, and view
> These plots of cottage-ground, these orchard-tufts,
> Which, at this season, with their unripe fruits,
> Among the woods and copses lose themselves.
> Nor with their green and simple hue, disturb
> The wild green landscape[9]

While greenhouse gas emissions are produced in the charcoal-making process, there are also socioeconomic and environmental advantages to using a locally available fuel rather than an imported alternative, and, if properly managed and regulated, charcoal production can make a significant contribution to sustainability through income generation and environmentally responsible forestry practices.[10]

Claims of river pollution and noisy boat traffic are also questionable. The "ouzy tide of pollution" suggested by some authors as being caused by the ironworks is more likely to have been due to natural causes. The low reaches of the Wye at Tintern are affected by the tide, and the so-called pollution was most likely naturally occurring flows of mud brought upriver on the tide from the Severn Estuary—an effect that can still be seen today. Writings from 1786 and 1831 attest to the Wye at Tintern being an excellent spot for salmon fishing, a major source of income for local people (figure 3.1). And as for noisy boat traffic, the steam engine had not yet been invented, so the boats on the Wye would have been rowed, sailed, or hauled—all of which are near silent activities.[11]

A further element of the sustainable nature of the operations was the fact that little was discarded. The works produced tons of furnace slag as a by-product of the iron-making. The slag was crushed to a fine powder and shipped to Bristol, where it was used as a source material for glassmaking. As already mentioned, oak bark was sent to tanneries—oak-bark tanning is a traditional craft that is far less toxic than using harmful chemicals. It is a slow process, but the resulting leathers are especially hard-wearing; sadly, it is now an endangered British craft.[12]

Social equity is another important ingredient of sustainability, and here, too, we find positive practices, often led by socially responsible heads of industry. Wiredrawers at Tintern received sick pay and pensions and benefited from tax concessions and voting rights. The company also paid for a schoolteacher and a priest and offered its workers an annual feast, at which it paid for ale and tobacco. And when the plague came to the area, the company put measures in place to care for the sick and the dying.[13]

While some authors suggested the place was home to many beggars, vagrants, and indigent charcoal makers living in the woods, these accounts are not borne out by an understanding of the processes involved or by writings of the time. First, charcoal-making was a skilled process and was so vital to the industry that it is hardly likely that it would have been left to an unreliable, unskilled workforce. Second, of sixteen surviving accounts by visitors to Tintern Abbey between 1770 and 1798, none mention beggars, vagrants, or indigent workers in the abbey grounds, on the village streets, or living in the woods. We also find that tourists flocked to the area, which supports the idea that, as the industry flourished, Tintern remained a pleasant place to live and work; a visitor of 1802 wrote of "woody hills" and "a pleasing retreat."[14] In fact, far from being regarded as a place of despoliation, tourists came to see the industry as much as the abbey. They were fascinated by the glowing furnaces that lit up the night sky and the sounds of the forge

Figure 3.1 *Bread and Cheese Stones*
"Wordsworth's Walk" above Llandogo
His stay at the village, it is believed, inspired his famous *Lines Composed a Few Miles above Tintern Abbey on Revisiting the Banks of the Wye during a Tour, July 13, 1798*

hammers. They left various accounts that tell of their wonder and delight at the colors, heat, and noise of the works.

SMALL, DISTRIBUTED, AND COSMOPOLITAN

Although small by today's standards, the industries at Tintern were the largest in Wales, and led the way in Britain's industrial development for over three hundred years. As Tawney tells us, much that later became mechanical was, at this time:

> personal, intimate, and direct, and there was little room for organization on a scale too vast for the standards that are applied to individuals, or for the doctrine which silences scruples and closes all accounts with the final plea of economic expediency.
>
> Such an environment, with its personal economic relations, was a not unfavourable field for a system of social ethics.[15]

Hence, this small-scale, localized form of earlier manufacturing seems, in many ways, to have been environmentally and socially responsible and caring. It used water-based power; water-based transport; and local, natural, renewable fuels. It was also a form of distributed industry, in that a wide variety of interrelated small-scale concerns employed many people in useful, productive work. A significant proportion of the jobs were skilled, and employers looked after their workers through a variety of social benefits. These kinds of distributed systems in which production processes and technological components cannot be separated from the social elements align precisely with Tawney's analysis.[16]

This approach to production compares favorably with Schumacher's arguments in *Small Is Beautiful*, in which he counsels against growing one industry until it is enormous, unmanageable, and "too big to fail." Instead, he advocates that, above a certain size, the operation should branch off and create another small industry in another location. Such a policy keeps industry human-scale and helps create a distributed economy. It also means people can live close to their work, reducing the need for commuting, saving time, and eliminating the associated environmental impacts.[17]

We also find that, far from being insular and inward-looking, the operations at Tintern practiced an early form of cosmopolitan localism whereby wider sociocultural awareness fosters local-global connections and interactions. During the early stages of production at Tintern, expertise was needed in the art of wire-making, so specialists were brought over from Germany, initially to make brass wire. And as we have seen, its location allowed business connections to ports in Britain, Ireland, and further afield. E. Manzini and M. K. M'Rithaa have argued that this is precisely the kind of outward-looking, small-scale, distributed, and networked approach that is needed for more resilient and sustainable societies.[18]

DECLINE AND DEMISE

As I discussed in chapter 2, the steam engine had been widely adopted by the late 1700s. It relied on the burning of coal to convert water into steam that, in turn, drove the pistons and wheels of this new powerful machine. And, of course, this reliance on the burning of hydrocarbons has continued to the present day and is linked to potentially catastrophic global heating.

The steam engine replaced the waterwheel as the main source of power and, in so doing, eliminated the advantages of topography and the place-dependent nature of industry. It also heralded the demise of specialisms and designs that were distinctive to a particular location and eroded the traditional bonds between people, place, and craft, which typically relied on local knowledge. In addition, by the 1850s, thousands of miles of rail tracks had been laid, connecting most parts of the country.

Wire-making at Tintern carried on until the late nineteenth century but it had been in decline for some years. In 1876, a rail connection was built over the Wye, heralding the end of the wind-powered trows. The steam engine led to the widespread industrialization of Britain and was quickly adopted in other countries in Europe and in the United States. While many historians have written of these developments in positive terms, less attention has been paid to the loss of place-based culture and the sense of identity, community, and belonging that is anchored in locale, topography, and climate. All these things help forge a connection between people and the natural environment—a tangible relationship to place that may be unspoken, perhaps even unacknowledged, yet is palpable. It is a tie that helps foster respect and stewardship, creates a sense of rootedness, and provides a foundation for common purpose and networks of interdependencies. In the example of iron- and wire-making at Tintern, we see this in the links between the interrelated specialisms, the ancillary opportunities that the industry created, and the company's provision and social care for its employees.

RECOVERY AND RENEWAL

The nature and scale of the wire-making industry at Tintern meant that once the works closed, the natural environment was able to quickly recover, without the need for major expenditure on demolition or large-scale landscaping—as was the case in later and much larger industrial operations, such as nearby Ebbw Vale, where a huge steelworks was closed in the 1970s.

In Tintern today, most of the former industrial buildings have been demolished—their stone being used for houses and walls in the vicinity—and the traces of the former industries are hidden among the recovered woodlands. The remains can still be seen, stretching for two miles along the Angidy, which once powered twenty-two waterwheels.

New types of small-scale enterprise have developed in the area—including a vineyard producing award-winning Welsh wines; a brewery producing a variety of craft beers, including one named Llandogo Trow Ale; fisheries and sports fishing; craft practices; honey production; farming; and software development. As in the days of Wordsworth, there also remains a thriving tourist trade, which supports local shops, pubs, hotels, and holiday accommodation. Tourists come to visit the picturesque abbey ruins, walk in the footsteps of the poet, and follow the heritage trails through the former industrial sites.

The question of scale is fundamental to this area's continuing ability to support livelihoods in ways that are environmentally responsible, fulfilling, and enduring. More generally, the transition to more sustainable ways of living will not be achieved by simply eliminating polluting technologies and replacing them with vast arrays of cleaner alternatives, such as wind- and solar-farms. We also have to consider the scale of our operations and pay far greater attention to small, context-based development and the creation of enterprises that are committed to people, place, and environmental stewardship. Through such means, businesses not only become a force for the good but also contribute to the development of a diversified and resilient enterprise economy, one that is far more robust than large-scale industries, which effectively create highly precarious monocultures. When the steelworks at Ebbw Vale closed, the whole town was devastated, with mass unemployment lasting for decades, and it has never fully recovered. This scale of dependence does not occur in a diversified, small-scale enterprise model.

Working with small enterprises, designers can make a real difference, becoming involved in a variety of projects and all stages of the process, while simultaneously developing their own small-scale design business that itself is committed to people and place. And rather than looking back and thinking we have to somehow recreate a lost past, we can intelligently embrace the opportunities offered by digital communications and applications to develop new kinds of distributed, small-scale enterprises that accord perfectly with the benefits of cosmopolitan localism.

4 THE NATURE OF THE MATERIAL

A sudden sharp pull on a taught nylon string sets it in motion and creates an audible sound. Changing the length alters the speed and amplitude of the vibration and hence the pitch. If a number of such strings are stretched over a hollow shell of thin wood or other material, the volume is increased, the shell serving as a monopole source that radiates the sound uniformly in all directions. Acoustic amplification is caused by the creation of resonating vibrations of the air inside the hollow shell. Finite-element and modal-analysis measurement techniques can provide detailed information about the vibrational states, but it appears that the particulars of the shape of the hollow shell are relatively unimportant in determining the nature of the acoustics.[1]

This kind of explanation about a familiar aspect of material culture may be factually correct, but it entirely fails to capture the nature and meaning of the activity being described. By comparison, descriptions by those who care about this activity as an artform tend to use words such as *beautiful, elegant,* and *gentle.* If the sound is light and airy, they might describe it as *summery* or *whimsical.* If it is more decorous, as *ornamental* or *flamboyant,* and if it is altogether darker in tone, as *atmospheric, moody, tense,* or *portentous.* They may also make appraisals about the standard of the performance, describing it as well-judged and full of melodic instinct or as workaday, lacking in lightness, or demonstrating insufficient dynamic control. All these words and phrases attempt to describe the aesthetic experience of listening to a performance of this activity—they convey something of the atmosphere conjured and the emotions felt.

While both forms of description may be true, the difference between them is that the first is a straightforward statement of the physical facts, while the second is concerned with listeners' experiences and their impressions about the artistic value of the performance. The first tells us about the mechanics of sound production and amplification but nothing about the music thus created, its artistic proficiency, or its cultural contribution. It is a stark description of the physical process but does not touch us emotionally, nor does it provide any clues as to why this activity has been highly valued for centuries.

Our material culture has meanings that extend far beyond mere facts, utility, and the austere logic of physical functionality. And because aesthetic experience and assessments of value are to a certain extent personal and subjective, not only are these descriptions very different from the factual language of science, but commentators may also vary widely in their views and judgments. This is because these kinds of accounts are primarily *interpretive* in nature.

Critical interpretation of creative works does not just involve sensitivity and knowledge of the field. Appreciation of a work and evaluation of its significance also depend on how we relate it to our own lived experience. And this has temporal components—the time when the work was created, the time when we are responding to it, the stage we are at in our lives, our openness to the relevance of the past and its traditions, and whether or not we feel the work has something to say to the present.[2]

The difference between factual explanations and values-based interpretations is perhaps most obvious when applied to artistic works. The phenomena of vibrating strings provide the physical basis for creating both excruciating discord and beautiful music. Colored substances spread on a stretched canvas can result in an ugly mess, a masterpiece, and everything in between. While the differences may be most apparent in the arts, these two kinds of descriptions—and their interrelationships—apply to *all* aspects of our human-made material culture. Both are necessary and ultimately inseparable. In terms of our own personal reality, outer physical phenomena and inner, meaning-seeking interpretations are fused within one holistic experience—a lived experience through which we interpret, respond to, and appreciate the world around us.

Consequently, the nature of our design endeavors matters much more than merely achieving functional effectiveness and economic viability. The human-made world contributes to our aesthetic experiences and thus to the quality of our lives. Cumulatively, the outputs of design can create everything from dissonant ugliness to timeless beauty.

We therefore have to ask ourselves how our individual design projects might contribute to a sense of harmony and continuity when they are added to the ever-accumulating whole. This raises a further concern—if we are driven by a search for originality, innovation, and a wish to stand out from the crowd, our contributions are unlikely to fit within the greater scheme of things. If we are all working as individuals and all trying to be novel, we will inevitably create a collective material culture of disharmony. And arguably this is precisely what we have been doing for some time.

If we are to steer a different, more intelligent course, we have to include facts *and* values, objective rationalizations *and* more intuitive, subjective interpretations. Fundamentally, a different course must involve not only originality, innovation, and individualism but also tradition, orthodoxy, continuity, and community. Design for resilience has to recognize the importance of all these facets of human understanding and cultural development. Our drive to be creative and innovative does not mean we have to turn our back on our own history. The pursuit of originality can also seek continuity and harmony with what already exists. And our need to express our own individuality can draw on and fit in with community. In recent times, society has tended to become increasingly individualistic and atomized, but there are many signs today that we are refinding and reasserting the importance of community, as well as ideas about authenticity, place, heritage, and tradition. All these things have to work together if we are to create designs that are at once beautiful, life affirming, and in harmony with the natural world.

When we design a chair, a lamp, an appliance, or a digital product, its form, finishes, fastenings, colors, and materials emerge from a variety of interrelated creative decisions. Together, these not only define the nature of the physical thing but also reflect the awareness, responsiveness, and sense of moral responsibility of the designer, for, as we will discuss in chapter 5, ethics and aesthetics are closely tied. How we create our material culture is intimately related to who we are and our sense of what is good, right, and true. And conversely, once present in and normative to our everyday world of things, it affects us and molds our understandings, attitudes, and ideas. As is the case when we listen to a piece of music or gaze at a painting, the things with which we surround ourselves *affect* us, we interpret them, and we attribute them with value based on judgments that may fluctuate over time.

When things do not last, when they are readily disposed of and replaced, there is both a shallowing of meaning and an ethical implication. When the primary driver of design is commercial rather than the search for a fitting result, the process will reflect this imperative—development time is shortened, surface appearance begins to trump creative integrity, corners are cut, and design as a discipline becomes compromised. To evaluate the durability of an object, we can measure and thoroughly quantify its physical and performative specifications. But as we have seen, the success of the object as a piece of creative work cannot be quantified, because such an assessment is always interpretive and temporal. Ultimately, designers and, more broadly, creative people of all kinds have to be true to their work and have to maintain their own inner sense of truth and ethical coherence. To again quote Alice Walker, "I suppose I am left with a project that will be a private one whose success will be largely immeasurable, but since I don't believe success must be measurable I don't mind at all."[3]

5 ATTAINMENT

"Alas," he cried, "is there anything in life so disenchanting as attainment?"
—Robert Louis Stevenson[1]

In all aspects of modern life, we have come to esteem ambition and an immoderate desire for achievement, advancement, and *more*. We take pride in aspiration, seeking wealth, and raising our sights and our standing in society. As individuals we want to be richer, more attractive, and noticed; as institutions we want to be at the top of the pile. An alternative to this way of looking at the world is not mediocrity but sufficiency. This, however, with its connotations of moderation, humility, and contentment, is seen as unenterprising and lacking in vision. And regardless of how much we already have, our consumption-driven market system constantly encourages us to wish for more.

Too Much of the Right Stuff: Amsterdam claims to offer visitors first-class shopping opportunities with a multitude of "ethical, sustainable and local products [that] tell a story from some of Amsterdam's finest social enterprises."[2]

So goes the persuasive publicity, in which "ethical," "environmental," and "local" have been commandeered as catchwords for driving sales and shifting product. Reading on, we find we can buy "pillows for guilt-free sleep" produced by a social enterprise that provides jobs for women who have few other employment opportunities. The decorative patterns feature old-style Dutch houses, and the filling is made from recycled clothing. A different outlet offers "beautiful, versatile and sustainable" vase covers. These are made by women in Mumbai, and, through our purchase, we will be helping to lift them out of poverty. The vase covers, we are told, are not just available in Amsterdam but are also sold in "high-end'" stores around the world (figure 5.1). Other products include "craft beer with a conscience," "bicycles with a story," and "bread and textiles made with love."[3]

Such businesses can make a valuable contribution, and many are genuinely striving to be socially responsible. But it is also worth noting that, in this kind of marketing, members of the public are implicitly being asked to consider not just the *product* but also the *process*. The information we have about both is primarily dependent on what the enterprises and associated stakeholders are prepared to tell us, which is hardly objective. How they convey this information can also be revealing.

A pillow is, of course, a useful product and, if made from recycled materials by a social enterprise that creates jobs for disadvantaged women, we may feel inclined to buy it. But we may be put off by *how* it is being sold to us. The enterprise claims that the product is ethical, but for this to ring true, the same approach must extend to the marketing. We are told that the pillow offers customers "guilt-free sleep," which suggests that by *not* purchasing it, we are simultaneously depriving ourselves and morally culpable. People are placed in a no-win situation where the only positive way forward is consumption. There is nothing new here—these tactics are the very lifeblood of advertising: make prospective customers feel guilty, inadequate, or discontented and suggest that "this product" will be the solution.

The vase cover is equally problematic. The world is surely not ready for vase covers, versatile or not, and their very production and alleged global availability makes a mockery of claims to be "sustainable" and "local." The accompanying blurb that tells us they are being sold in high-end stores internationally is also questionable because it fosters notions of prestige and status through consumption choices—the very same techniques used by multinational corporations to push product, inflate prices, and stimulate sales, seemingly with no upper limit.

It is vitally important for enterprises today to be socially responsible and abide by sustainable principles. But the products they produce must be genuinely worth producing. There are dangers, also, in explicitly marketing

Figure 5.1 *Paper "Vase Cover"*

the product and enterprise on credentials of "social responsibility" and "sustainability," especially when techniques are employed that make people feel censured, thereby nurturing a "holier than thou" backlash. Such claims can stick in the craw because they make a big thing out of acting ethically, which we should be doing anyway, simply because it is the right thing to do.

Our behavioral norms have to change from always wanting more to questioning the social acceptability of continual consumption. Social enterprises can help in this endeavor by not only producing more responsible products but also developing other ways of creating value, via a service or an artistic or spiritual contribution, and by rejecting the dubious rhetoric of mainstream consumerism. In doing so, they would be fostering new ways of doing business and new ideas about success and attainment and pointing the way toward a more responsible, ethical, and truly guilt-free future.

Big Sky and Big Stuff: For many years, I lived in Alberta in western Canada, where the prairies meet the Rockies. On weekends, we'd invariably head west to go hiking in the foothills or the higher mountains of Banff and Jasper National Parks. We seldom went east into the prairies—where there were no parks of such majesty and where hiking was more restricted, for, unlike Britain, Canada has no extensive rural footpath system through farmlands.

On the occasions we did venture into the prairies, however, there were other kinds of gems to be discovered. In the east of the province, there is a region known as the Badlands—a dramatic landscape of narrow river valleys, dry gullies, and strangely eroded "hoodoos," like giant rock mushrooms. Here, in the small town of Drumheller, is the Royal Tyrrell Museum, with a remarkable collection of dinosaur remains and wonderful displays of ancient life on earth. An hour south of Edmonton is the Reynolds Museum, with vintage cars, trucks, agricultural equipment, and aircraft, including small, flimsy-looking floatplanes that once took mail, supplies, and people to the remotest parts of northern Canada. In the little town of Mundare, there is the Basilian Fathers Mission and Museum, which owes its foundation to a French-Canadian priest but commemorates the Ukrainian settlement of Canada as well as the Basilian Fathers' contribution to Ukrainian cultural and spiritual heritage. The mission was especially important to the settlers of the region, when, for many years, contact with their homeland was cut off by the Communist regime.

After the first pioneers mapped North America, the Canadian prairie became a place of immigration, homesteading, farming, and small towns. Curiously, many of these settlements nowadays seek to lay claim to the biggest something-or-other in the world. They achieve this by featuring giant, ersatz confections executed with varying degrees of competence. Drumheller predictably boasts the world's largest dinosaur. It is twenty-five-meters high, twelve people can fit in the mouth at the same time, and it cost over a million dollars to construct. Mundare is home to the world's largest sausage—a thirteen-meter-long Ukrainian kielbasa built to celebrate the town's meat processing and sausage factory. There are many such creations dotted over Canada's prairies—the world's largest cookie jar; a massive fire hydrant; the biggest piggy bank; a giant cowboy boot; a UFO landing pad; and all manner of people, animals, and plants. There is also a huge painted Easter egg, an enormous axe, and even the world's largest paperclip. They may be humorous, bizarre, and perhaps intriguing. They are invariably very literal and brash, and their conception and construction are not always what they could be. But they are also celebrations of people, place, culture, and story; they are visual statements about community and identity. Collectively they give a sense of commonality and neighborliness to the small communities scattered across the prairies.

Another purpose of these constructions is to attract visitors, who may eat at the restaurant, stay at the hotel, and buy local produce, thereby boosting the local economy. The big paperclip has been featured in magazines, the news media, and a Spanish commercial for cars. It has also been included in the *Guinness Book of Records* and *Ripley's Believe It or Not!* Its origin celebrates the story of Kyle MacDonald who swapped a paperclip for a pen, the pen for a doorknob, and so on, until he made a swap to spend an afternoon with rock singer Alice Cooper, which he then swapped for a snow globe, to add to his extensive collection. His story led to a movie, in which he negotiated a role and which brought revenues and unforeseen fame to the small settlement of Kipling, Saskatchewan.[4]

Fascinating as the various sights may be, as we travel through the endless fields of wheat, other thoughts come to mind. For there is a whole other side to these developments and the changes set in motion by those who came here in a search for *more*.

For millennia, First Nations peoples had traveled these vast plains following the buffalo herds—the Stoney, Tsuut'ina, and Blackfoot near the mountains; the Cree, Dene, and Dakota, and further east the Assiniboine and Ojibwe. The costs to them have been incalculable—the annihilation of the buffalo, the parceling off of their lands with barbed wire, and their relocation to small, disconnected areas designated as "reservations."

Against this backdrop, the world's biggest sausage, cookie jar, and fire hydrant seem incongruous impositions.

Cutting-Edge and World-Leading: A recent but not untypical announcement from a provincial university states its plans to build a new addition to its engineering faculty with the words: "Work on a new engineering building is set to begin this spring! With cutting-edge facilities and a 3D lecture theatre, it will support world-leading research and teaching." Cutting-edge! World-leading! Before a clod has been turned. Such pompous proclamations by the modern, market-led university have become commonplace. The phrase "proof of the pudding" comes to mind.

This type of language may be de rigueur nowadays, but it is also self-aggrandizing, unimaginative, and mostly untrue. They all say it, but they can't all be it. Such puffery is especially unseemly when it emerges not from some corporate marketing department trying to flog us a new digital thing-amajig but from an institution of higher learning in which critical self-reflection and more moderate tones are essential. The use of such hyperbole in an attempt to increase the institution's perceived standing and attract more students has the effect of legitimizing unproven claims and normalizing overstatement.

Striving to be seen as special, even when we have earned it, is immodest and undignified; when we have not, there is the whiff of dishonesty about it. Either way, it is a discreditable route to self-attainment that reveals at its heart a sense of inadequacy and vulnerability. Any academic worthy of the name cannot help but feel a sense of loss and sadness about these kinds of assertions and the effects this marketization of public education has had on our universities. Bombast, however, is just the more visible symptom of a deeper malaise in higher education that is being driven by an ideological agenda of privatization and competition and characterized by such phrases as "leveling up the playing field" and "consumer choice."[5] Conducting such an experiment on a nation's public system of higher education is hazardous, not least because the evidence is simply not there to suggest that marketization, competition, and, essentially, the commodification of knowledge improves learning. Indeed, it may well damage quality because it regards students in increasingly instrumental terms and can result in a lowering of quality due to grade inflation, which British universities have been repeatedly accused of in recent years.[6] It can also lead to resources being diverted away from teaching and learning and directed toward promotion, marketing, and student recruitment, in order to boost revenues from student fees. And it also leads to outlandish increases in the salaries of vice chancellors and substantial premiums being paid for so-called brand assets, such as membership of the self-selected association of "world class" British universities known as the Russell Group.[7] But perhaps worst of all, it inexorably couples education with avarice.

These marketing techniques and psychological hooks—whether they concern products, communities, or education establishments—are all redolent of exaggeration, inflation, and self-interest, and they demean both the purveyor and the recipient. Time-honored teachings from many cultures warn against broadcasting our accomplishments and good deeds in public, else they become testaments to pride and self-absorption. The wise tell us both that we ought to weaken our ambitions and control our desires and that true fulfilment arises from selfless actions.[8]

6 PASQUINADE

As a society, we have long had a love affair with ratings, rankings, and awards—the top of the music charts, the Booker Prize, the Oscars, the ten best movies, hikes, holiday destinations, and so on. In education, schools have performance tables[1] and universities have the Research Excellence Framework (REF), the Teaching Excellence Framework (TEF), and, more recently, the Knowledge Exchange Framework (KEF).[2] These ranking systems are needed to identify and reward excellence, thereby showing our appreciation for people's efforts, achievements, and contributions.

Yet, as Z. I. Podpolya has pointed out, such rankings have not yet been applied to individuals.[3] Doing so would allow each of us, through our various roles and activities, to be rated in terms of our overall value and contribution to society. Today's ubiquitous digital culture gives us the ability to do just this and, in the process, holds the potential to boost individual aspiration and productivity and with it the national economy and material standards of living.

To be fair and comprehensive, rankings would have to be based on the cumulative results of a range of measures that would effectively rate an individual's performance and value, not just in their chosen occupation but also in their community, region, and country, and even internationally. To be consistent across sectors and regions, the most effective basis for doing this would be through a set of categories that are measurable and in a form that is both universal and as objective as possible. A system shaped by softer, qualitative criteria would have to be discounted because this would inevitably introduce a subjective element that would be dependent on interpretation, thereby producing ambiguity and jeopardizing both impartiality and accuracy. For these kinds of systems, facts are required, not values or personal moral judgments. A ranking system based on a straightforward set of numerical ratings would ensure an internally consistent and comprehensive set of measures that are quantifiable and could be compared and contrasted within and between sectors and regions.

In contemporary society, the measure of value employed in virtually every country in the world is that of money—monetary worth is easily gauged and universally understood. Moreover, international exchange rates and analogous cost-of-living indexes are readily available to ensure this Personal Excellence Framework (PEF) can be applied in different contexts and be compared internationally. At the occupational level, ratings could include categories such as salaries, and funds raised for the organization in terms of profits, investments, dividends, grants acquired, and so on. At the community/societal level, it could include donations to good causes, fundraising, and in-kind contributions of time and expertise appropriately calculated to a monetary equivalence.

This kind of PEF would be entirely in keeping with the values and priorities of contemporary society and their predominant modes of governance. Importantly, it would be a way of showing our appreciation for people. Implementing it would add to this already burgeoning sector, expanding bureaucracies by creating jobs in middle management and administration. Such a scheme would undoubtedly appeal to a considerable echelon of our political and corporate elites, being seen as a major incentive to boost individual ambition. It would help identify and eliminate unproductive or unprofitable occupations, education courses, and charitable causes and increase individual efficiency, productivity, and wealth. What could possibly be wrong with that?

7 APPRECIATIVE DESIGN

Our appreciation of someone or something is a reflection of ourselves and our knowledge, understanding, and magnanimity. A condition of appreciating is paying attention—we have to "attend to," and try to see and understand—with the heart as well as the head. When we become acquainted with and learn about other people, the natural world, or material things, we gain a heightened sense of responsibility toward them. Only then will we care for them.

How we think about others and the world is often tellingly revealed in the language we use. To appreciate people, we have to see others not as "them"—not through some collective label such as consumers, foreigners, illegals, or the herd but as individuals with lives, loves, worries, and aspirations that are probably not so very different from our own. The language we use matters. It reflects our outlook, and, to a significant degree, it determines how we respond to the world and formulate our activities. When we resort to stereotypes, we erect a cognitive barrier that prevents us seeing the reality that lies beyond our damaging, preset categorizations. Individual faces and individual lives disappear into an aggregate blur. Similarly, natural habitats and the all too fragile beauty of complex ecosystems become just so many square miles of real estate ripe for development.

Seeing, understanding, and appreciating are critically important. Only by seeing others as individuals can we hope to become fully rounded human beings ourselves. Looking into the eyes of another is the basis of empathy, compassion, and charity. And in our attitudes toward the natural environment, we have to get to know and really *see* if we are to appreciate. Here, too, language matters. When we talk of aspects of the natural world using words like *pests*, *weeds*, *resources*, *stocks*, and *acreage*, we are implicitly saying that the natural environment is something we can subdue, exploit, and own. As has become patently evident in recent times, this is not the language of appreciation and stewardship but of control, abuse, and desecration. Another kind of language is possible—a language that speaks of recognition, obligation, gratitude, even reverence.

A particular type of grass, called sweetgrass, grows on the Great Plains of the United States and the prairies of southern Canada. The Potawatomi people consider it sacred. Their name for it is *wiingaashk*, which means the sweet-smelling hair of Mother Earth. For the Potawatomi, it is a spiritual plant that is also valued for its medicinal properties. It is woven into braids and baskets and given as gifts; but to retain its sacred qualities, it should not be sold.[1] This same plant is also considered sacred in Britain, where it is called holy grass since it is usually found near ancient religious sites.[2] In times past, it was scattered in front of church doors on festival days.[3]

The language we use is telling—it reflects how we think and affects how we act. Names that suggest a plant is holy or sacred help us respond in ways that are mindful and respectful. If we need to use plants or animals or minerals, this kind of language encourages us to do so with thoughtfulness and moderation.

When we are respectful of other people and the natural environment, those things we create from the earth's abundance to serve our needs will be expressions of gratitude. By necessity, they will be produced with care and attention to the impacts on others and nature. We will be more concerned about what and how much we produce so as to avoid excess and waste, which would be squandering the earth's provision and would therefore be immoderate and unappreciative.

Hence, if designers are to make a positive contribution and help overcome some of the social and environmental ills of our age, they must gain a deeper knowledge and understanding of the people and places affected by their decisions. There is a need for inquiry and awareness—these are necessary ingredients of appreciation. This applies at all stages of the process, from the initial concept through the ideation and design development to the making, using, maintaining, and eventual disposing of manufactured things.

Attitudes and Actions: Changing our attitudes and actions is dependent on changing our outlook. Design has a responsibility to take a more sensitive, benevolent, and conciliatory approach, one that is capable of overcoming the destructive tendencies that have characterized it for too long. A new realization is needed and from this a new ethos toward people and the world. This is at the very core—the conditio sine qua non—of meaningful and substantive change, change that becomes realized in the intimate act of creativity.

We saw in chapter 2 that Dostoyevsky was a severe critic of the philosophy of utilitarianism, its abstract schemes and rationalizations and its corrupting effects on the human spirit and culture. Similarly, we need to be far more circumspect about adopting many of the methods and approaches that are commonly cited today in design, such as seemingly endless frameworks and guidelines, Double Diamonds and Venn diagrams. These types of rationalized but ultimately inadequate conventions are merely utilitarian constructs. More fundamental, positive change lies beyond the reach of formulaic approaches; true creativity involves very different modes of thought.

The intimate act of creativity—that solitary, silent, sometimes wrenching struggle to find purchase—is nonprescriptive and always unfamiliar. Fundamentally, it is an imaginative act—an appropriate response to which ought to be gratitude for its mysterious, life-giving wonder. This wonder-full ability should not be led astray by the multitude of barren rules, recipes, and codes that seem to be generated ad nauseam in our institutions of higher education. Their rationalized austerity and imaginative paucity do a disservice to the reality of the creative act.

The kind of change we are talking about here is the adoption of an attitude that has nothing to do with rules or formulas. The creative act can be understood as a kind of spiritual contemplation—a conscious, voluntary act of love that involves the intimate revealing of one's innermost thoughts, imaginings, emotions, and aesthetic sensitivities. Together, these coalesce into some form of nascent expression—an initial manifestation of intention, articulated but still rudimentary and contingent. For positive change, thankfulness, empathy, and virtue must suffuse this intention, thus directing and characterizing the nature of the creative act. No methodology, structure, or measurement system is capable of capturing this profoundly subject-centered act, for it eludes both scrutiny and scholarly definition. We must take it on trust, as an act of faith—it is the awe-inspiring spark at the center of our very being. We must be appreciative of it, for we have a duty of gratitude and care toward others, the world, and ourselves to use it wisely.[4]

Let us now consider the practical relevance of this recognition, which embraces our capacity for reason and imagination and combines objective reality with our interpretation of it as subjects.

The Design Problem: Despite brief trysts with post- or late-modern sensibilities, much contemporary design retains strong modernist credentials, which it seems reluctant or unable to shake. A telltale characteristic of this approach is its focus on "problem-solving." For example, at the end of the twentieth century, after studying various best practices, Nigel Cross concluded that one of the most influential views of design is as a "rational problem-solving" activity and that design research is a purposive endeavor grounded in the identification of a problem.[5] Twenty years later, in a discussion of design thinking, we read, "Through observation, synthesis, alternatives, critical thinking, feedback, visual representation, creativity, problem-solving, and value creation, entrepreneurs can use design thinking to identify unique venture opportunities."[6] This statement reveals the dominance of rationalism and problem-solving in so-called design thinking, a term that simultaneously misconstrues and diminishes the meaning of design. It leads to approaches that involve much group work and lots of Post-it notes, diagrams, and schematics but preclude imaginative ways of *thinking-and-doing* and true creativity. It also reveals that the real purpose of all this problem-solving often has little to do with bringing any real benefit to people's lives and is actually much more about creating opportunities for financial gain. Problem-solving in design has come to be seen as an important driver of innovation and competitive edge for corporations and key to continual financial growth.

Significantly, too, in this milieu, innovation has come to be understood primarily not just in terms of technology but also in a highly selective, predominantly Western notion of it. *Technology* and *innovation* are words applied to machines, digital devices, gadgets, and industrially produced durable goods, but not to pottery, textiles, or traditional forms of architecture or agriculture. These are also technologies, and they, too, move with the times.

Through these dominant conventions, design and the highly contestable notion of design thinking have become caught up in a world that prides itself on its inventiveness and originality but excludes all those rich and varied creative practices that industrial-era corporate capitalism and the postcolonial European powers have chosen to discount and ignore.[7] The result is an impoverished and highly damaging version of design. Mainstream consultancies and in-house design departments help perpetuate a system of unrestrained production and consumption that is motivated primarily by the pursuit of profit. It is a system characterized by excess, waste, and a host of destructive ramifications for society and the world.

When we regard design as problem-solving, what should be an essentially constructive, creative, and imaginative activity takes on a negative, deficiency-oriented posture. Moreover, if we are constantly looking for problems, we will invariably find them. Such an outlook prevents us from viewing the world in a more affirmative light, where we see the good, the harmony, and that which is to be celebrated, conserved, and cautiously built upon. This more positive understanding is actually far closer to the root meanings of *innovation*, *invention*, and *originality* than the largely disposable novelty that these terms have come to represent in contemporary society. The word *innovation* derives from the Latin *innovāre*, meaning to "restore," "alter," or "make new." Similarly, the root of *invention* is *inventionem*, from the stem *invenīre*, meaning to "come upon," "discover," or "find out." And *originality* stems from *orīginālis*, meaning "that from which something originates or derives its existence."[8] Hence, these three terms, so lauded in modern business, higher education, and design as being all about "the new," once meant restoring and renewing *that which we already have*, discovering *what presently exists*, and building ideas on *that which already is*. Such understandings imply and entail a responsibility to history and the contributions of our predecessors. Innovation, invention, and originality mean not ignoring or breaking with the past but discovering and valuing our foundations, which we ought to learn from and wisely augment. Divorced from these foundations, neither factual propositions nor gut instinct offer the basis for a system of values that can guide our activities.[9] Thus, to ensure our design endeavors are judicious, inclusive, and appreciative, we must value and learn from the past as well as consider our present circumstances by being open to a range of contemporary voices. This will provide us with a well-informed perspective to creatively explore what is possible (figure 7.1)

An attitude of appreciation and respect is in keeping with time-proven ways of living meaningfully, sustainably, and in symbiotic relationships with the natural world. As Indigenous author and scientist Robin Wall Kimmerer writes of her people's traditional land: "It was everything: identity, the connection to our ancestors, the home of our non-human kinfolk, our pharmacy, our library, the source of all that sustained us. Our lands were where our responsibility to the world was enacted, sacred ground. It belonged to itself; it was a gift, not a commodity."[10]

Appreciative Inquiry: In keeping with an ethos of gratitude and obligation, the field of appreciative inquiry offers a way of looking at the world that transcends modernity's problem-focused perspective. Appreciative inquiry has its beginnings in the field of organizational development in the early 1980s and has since been more widely adopted. Instead of looking at situations primarily as problems to be solved, it takes an essentially positive stance toward people, interdependencies, and possibilities. It aims to identify, understand, and clarify favorable, life-enhancing aspects of situations, be they in organizations, communities, or broader society. It does this by looking for and recognizing individual and shared strengths, which become the basis for identifying opportunities and imagining preferred futures. The most interesting and engaging of these then become the basis for creative development. Thus, instead of focusing on problems, appreciative inquiry starts from a premise of hopeful possibility. Recognizing that the world and human communities are full of potential, it draws on relationships, ideas, and knowledge in order to enhance the current condition and develop fresh initiatives.[11]

Figure 7.1 *The Past, the Present, and the Possible*
learning from the past
hearing voices from the present
conjuring the possible

It may have its origins in organizational development, but its insights about the destructive nature of looking at the world as a series of problems obviously has resonances with design. Like organizations, the tangible products that designers develop—be they furniture, consumer electronics, digital devices, or buildings—are dependent on systems and services that, together, result in socially constructed realities. As such, the design approaches we employ to shape these realities are critical.

It is evident that the problem-solving methods that have long dominated the design field have often created just as many problems as they have ever solved.[12] These include not only the environmental consequences of overproduction, disposability, emissions, and waste but also the social consequences of a system deliberately concocted to stoke envy, division, and dissatisfaction.

One of the important features of appreciative inquiry is its framing of the question. The kinds of questions we ask are critical because how we create our realities is dependent on those areas we ask about. What we choose to examine determines what we discover, what we create, and what we move toward. Instead of asking problem-solving type questions, appreciative inquiry tells us that the questions we ask should be directed toward those conditions we wish to attain. If we ask, "How can we develop a more environmentally friendly product, such as a car or a clothes dryer?," we are framing the question in a way that implicitly subsumes a problem—that is, currently available models have a problem that needs to be fixed. By framing the question in this manner, the inevitable result will be a new design concept. Alternatively, we might ask, "How can we live in ways that are attuned to natural systems and facilitate environmental care?" Addressing this kind of question would result in very different understandings about our priorities, needs, and desires.[13]

By premising the inquiry on a positive, life-affirming question, we can then follow through with a number of further steps. From this point on, the process is similar to the regular design process. The key difference lies in the establishment of the premise, as well as the values and priorities one brings to the table. The aim is to explore positive opportunities and what-ifs and to move away from the problem-centered mindset. The former opens up our thinking, whereas the latter tends to narrow it down. The questions posed by appreciative inquiry, therefore, are more conducive to the creative process and the spontaneity and unpredictability of the human imagination. If the premise is thoughtfully developed, a rather different outcome will be forthcoming, one that is suffused by a sense of gratitude, love, moderation, renewal, and conservation.

Limitations and Criticisms: As with any approach, appreciative inquiry has its critics and its limitations. If it is to be usefully adapted to the field of design in a manner that is robust, we must bear these criticisms in mind. We must recognize that not everything about real-world situations is positive. Often, there will be genuine struggle, even hardship, and it would be naive to look at the world as if these did not exist. Besides, a meaningful life is forged not by having everything always being rosy and comfortable but by having to negotiate and overcome difficulties along the way. If we just look at the positive and make decisions in a rational manner about those things we think will be beneficial, not only might we be in error but we would not be facing up to the world as it truly is. It might nurture our sense of well-being, but focusing solely on the positive does not necessarily give our lives a sense of meaning, significance, and value. As Dostoyevsky said: "It's even somehow indecent to love only well-being. . . . Suffering is the sole root of consciousness."[14] Contrary to the messages of marketing and consumer culture, meaning is found neither in attaining a state of ease and comfort nor in endless pleasure-seeking but, as Victor Frankl has told us, in "striving and struggling for a worthwhile goal."[15]

Modernity's privileging of reason in its pursuit of certainty and progress, its devaluing of tradition, and the manner in which it has attempted to eliminate doubt and suffering has been both narrow-minded and demonstrably ineffective and misguided, but despite its many critics, we remain firmly in its thrall. Meaning in life is found not in abstract rationalizations and the accumulation of objective facts but through our experiences and interpretations of the world as subjects. There are countless examples of people tolerating enormous suffering, injustice, and misfortune and sustaining themselves through the attitudes they bring to the situations in which they find themselves. We can find this sustenance in our encounters with other people or in the healing beauty of nature, in religious faith, through our creative activities, through our memories, or through a sense of humor.[16] The attitudes we bring to the whole of what life offers—good and bad—help determine whether or not we are able to rise above our worldly fate and find a deeper sense of meaning, purpose, and responsibility in our lives. Even against physical and mental hardships, the inner or spiritual life can flourish.[17]

Hence, an exclusive focus on the positive fails to adequately acknowledge difficult issues, which may well be significant and should be taken seriously. Of course, a counterresponse to this is that the whole point of emphasizing the positive recognizes that there *are* inadequacies in the current situation and the aim is to move forward in a manner that strives to overcome them by developing a more balanced outlook and thus more holistic outcomes. This seems a somewhat weak and unsatisfactory defense. Appreciation should mean focusing on the positive aspects of current practices while *also* fully recognizing the complexities involved and making informed judgments so as to move forward in ways that are constructive and life-affirming. Throughout the process, we must keep in mind those things that are valued, and continually come back to them and reinforce them. When this happens, it becomes a process that builds on mutually reinforcing strengths to stimulate the imagination in directions that are creative and productive.[18]

Appreciative Design: Instead of simply adopting wholesale the appreciative inquiry approach, we can recognize its positive, life-enhancing qualities as well as its potential shortcomings. In addition, there is a need to reinterpret and modify it to better suit design's needs and contemporary responsibilities. This suggests an understanding of appreciative design that may be summarized as follows:

> *Appreciative design* is a creative approach that strives to value people and the natural environment at all stages in the development, use, and maintenance of goods, services, and other design outcomes.
>
> It strives to achieve codeveloped realities that are respectful of the past, that confront the challenges of the present, and that are self-generating, self-directing, collaborative, and cooperative, where individuals, communities, and the natural environment are mutual beneficiaries.

In this approach, people, nature, and other forms of life are all seen as stakeholders in the development of our ways of living. Achieving this means reengaging with community and place and restoring our knowledge of the natural environment, which has withered from generations of urban, predominantly interior living within artificially created surroundings cut off from the rain, sun, wind, and stars. Our societal atomization and detachment from, and therefore disregard for, nature is the result of a long, slow process. In modern times, we have become like Dostoyevsky's "educated man," *who has divorced himself from the soil and uprooted himself from his people.*[19]

To appreciate and value other people and nature, we have to refind, relearn, and reestablish meaningful bonds and mutually beneficial connections. Only then will we be capable of achieving more fruitful and respectful relationships, which will subsequently be reflected in our priorities and our actions. In this, we have much to learn from those whose traditions and ways of life have always been close to nature. For example, the Indigenous Environmental Network in the United States tells us: "Cultural survival depends on healthy land and a healthy, responsible relationship between humans and the land. . . . Ecological restoration is inseparable from cultural and spiritual restoration, and is inseparable from the spiritual responsibilities of care-giving and world-renewal."[20]

The Appreciative Design Process: In adapting appreciative inquiry to the field of design, we must recognize important differences in working processes and outcomes. While we may draw on many and varied sources and conversations during the purpose-setting and background-research phases, the creative process itself often benefits from being conducted alone, albeit with regular consultations for input and feedback to ensure everyone's voice is heard and their contributions taken into account. For many creative people, solitude and silence are essential conditions for invoking the kind of synthetical thinking commonly associated with the "right brain" (an admittedly imprecise but much-used shorthand to refer to more intuitive, holistic, creative ways of thinking).

In the field of organizational development, appreciative inquiry is typically carried out in large group forums and/or in small teams.[21] The atmosphere that ensues can actually be counterproductive to creative thinking. Talking, explaining, responding to interruptions, writing, and constructing diagrams within prespecified timelines are predominantly rationalistic, analytical, "left-brain" processes that are unconducive to the frame of mind required for creative practice. However, if there has been thorough and wide-ranging consultation and research conducted beforehand, this will have allowed for the accumulation of perspectives, ideas, thoughts, and possibilities that the designer can incorporate into the brief and bear in mind during the conceptualization and design development stages, which will focus on affirmative, inspiring, and, potentially, provocative propositions about how things might be.

Hence, even though designers may be working alone during certain creative stages, concepts and ideas are refined throughout the process by testing and evaluating, which includes consultations and discussions with the people involved in order to garner their input and feedback. Eventually, a design emerges that provides a clear and compelling picture of how things might be. We must also keep in mind that this should not be envisioned as a fixed "solution." Whatever its potential advantages, we should anticipate unforeseen inadequacies and ensure the design is mutable, lending itself to maintenance and future adaptations. We should not consider design outcomes to be complete and finished; if we do, we will fail to accommodate evolving needs and preferences and the inevitable effects of time. To avoid waste and also to create a lasting material culture that is meaningful, we should aim to develop outcomes that are inherently conditional—continuously and endlessly evolving.

With these considerations in mind, the following process steps combine aspects of appreciative inquiry with the conventional design process. These stages are typical and indicative but are not written in stone. They can be adapted to suit specific situations as required:

- **Purpose:** As with most design interventions, the aim is to generate a range of possibilities and through research, meeting with the people involved, and evaluation develop an optimal way forward. To do this effectively, the particularities and challenges of the specific context have to be considered. This can only be effectively achieved through research, discussion, and cooperation to understand the "best of what is and what has been."[22] Defining the exact purpose will likely take a number of iterations. Following an early research phase, a *provisional* statement of the purpose of the design undertaking can be made. Even though this will be further developed at a later stage, asking the appropriate design question early on is critical to the appreciative approach. From there on, the various stages, including the refinement of purpose, are similar to those of the usual design process. In formulating the question, it should obviously be one to which design can respond. It also needs to be framed in an appreciative way, so that any design proposals recognize and build on existing achievements, features, and positive qualities. For example: "In a specific context, how might design contribute to the development of a resilient local economy that respects the diversity of community beliefs, values, priorities, and traditions; adheres to the principles of sustainability; and helps develop and extend current successes, potentially beyond conventional sector boundaries or expectations?" Notably, no "problem" as such has been identified. Instead, the question recognizes those elements of an existing situation that are already working well and it seeks to build on them.

- **Context:** This stage looks into relevant examples and existing ideas. Design researchers have to read widely, talk with others, familiarize themselves with the field, and better understand the existing condition. Here, it is important to acknowledge that creative ideas do not appear out of nowhere. They develop from those things that have prefigured them. Acknowledging this—in terms of provenance, tradition, and legacy—is part of being appreciative and respectful. It recognizes that our endeavors rest on and develop out of the contributions of those who came before us. This challenges many contemporary notions of innovation, originality, and the notion of designer as sole creator; the contributions of others are essential and fundamental to the process, even though specific creative steps may be best done alone. It also challenges the whole sphere of intellectual property, which has become so critical in today's world of design and manufacturing. Traditional, more sustainable societies are typically less individualistic than modern, postindustrial societies. In their making practices, traditional societies recognize that their artifacts are products of the entire community, as well as of those previous generations who have passed down their skills and knowledge.[23] Designers may choose to work alone during certain stages of the process, but that does not mean their work is solely their own creation.

The research stage helps identify those factors that should be taken into account in creative responses to the design question. There is also a need for critique and scrutiny to ask both "Is the direction worthwhile? Does it warrant development?" and "Is it an area that is justifiable in terms of committing energy and resources, especially in a world that already produces too much?"

Hence, to refine and properly address the question identified at the purpose stage, extensive context-based research has to be conducted. This includes gaining an understanding of the knowledge, skills, and priorities of those involved, as well as the local culture and its resources. It involves identifying key, life-affirming qualities of the sector of interest, including place-specific environmental qualities and natural features and amenities. As the research continues, areas that might benefit from design can be identified. This stage can include local initiatives, as well as relevant examples from elsewhere. It involves meeting with local people, observing and perhaps conducting interviews and surveys, as well as desk-based research. The purpose of the design undertaking can then be further clarified. The aim is to identify the people and resources that can be drawn upon to achieve the overall goal. The outcome of this stage is a detailed design brief.

- **Conceptualization**: The next stage is creative ideation. Taking into account the factors identified in the context stage, conceptualization involves asking what could be and using design skills and the imagination to develop, visualize, and make manifest a range of ideas and directions. This involves generating inspiring concepts that begin to give expression to a number of markedly different possibilities or scenarios. Typically, this is achieved using quick, ephemeral means such as theme or mood boards, sketches, and study models. These conceptualizations might be in relation to a product, a process, experiences, interactions, or development strategies. Whatever the focus, they are delineated in visual formats that, while low in time investment and detail, nevertheless possess enough information to effectively communicate the ideas and key features. Here the designer is aiming to create a range of possibilities, each of which is distinctive in its synthesis and characterization. However, all the possibilities should be affirming and build on the attributes and optimal situations identified in the context stage. The visualizations should be able to convey how the concepts might look, feel, and function. To ensure the concepts are appreciative and respectful in nature, they should aim to integrate and build on the knowledge, skills, and priorities inherent to the existing condition, especially those aspects that are already working well. At the same time, this stage is an opportunity to creatively challenge conventions and expectations, to test boundaries and try out less orthodox ideas, new directions, and possibilities. It is an opportunity to explore "what might be," to be bold and hopeful, and to create concepts that are engaging, stimulating, and, perhaps, provocative.

- **Evaluation Phase I**: Through consultation and interrogation, the concepts are evaluated in terms of their ability to effectively address the design question, while considering factors such as their potential for future resilience and the possibility of disruptive events. Some iterative cycling between conceptualization and evaluation is normally appropriate to arrive at a set of constructive possibilities, one or more of which may be selected to go through to the next stage. This phase also allows for the purpose to be more precisely stated.

- **Design**: The design stage adds further definition by developing a limited number of options to a greater level of detail. Structure and specifics are progressed; mechanisms of functionality are worked through; and, where appropriate, aesthetic developments are advanced. If the outcome is to be a physical product, then ideas about materials, processes, and market will need to be considered. If the outcome is to be a service, then *who* will participate and *why*, what is their motivation, *what* is their role and contribution, *how* will they deliver that contribution, and do they need access to other people or resources to do so? An assessment will be needed of required skills, allegiances, materials, and so forth. Aspects of this will be consultative, facilitated by the designer or a community champion, with a range of participants, thereby helping ensure all those involved are able to contribute to the process.

- **Evaluation Phase II**: This stage is again consultative but by now the design proposals are becoming considerably more detailed. Consequently, they can be interrogated to a greater level of specificity to ensure that they are capable of fully addressing the purpose and that future resilience has been comprehensively addressed. Again, some iterative cycling may well be required to finalize requirements and further refine the purpose. This results in a preferred direction.

- **Design Outcome**: The design outcome is fully developed in all its details in terms of structure, resources, and aesthetics, and the roles and responsibilities of all those involved in the implementation phase are identified. Unlike many of today's designs, the outcome here is intended for sustained, adaptable use, rather than being disposable or having "designed in" premature obsolescence.

- **Implementation**: This may not be within the remit or direct responsibility of the designer, but as implementation progresses, further design services may well be needed to iron out unforeseen glitches and address inevitable changes that occur over time. Hence, designers should see their role as a continuing relationship to support ongoing development of paths forward.[24] In this way, appreciative design can offer leadership within a continual process of improvement and advancement.

Going Forward: At the beginning of the twentieth century, in the formative years of contemporary design, the early modernists insisted on breaking with the past. They may have had their differences in terms of philosophy or politics, but they agreed on one overriding principle, succinctly summed up by Ezra Pound as "Make it new!"[25] It was a fateful stance that set the scene for developments in design practice and education that are still with us. But the effects have been devastating, wreaking havoc on natural systems and contributing to the rise of individualism and societal atomization, with concomitant repercussions on community coherence, identity, and sense of belonging. Taking a more appreciative approach asks us to rediscover and build upon that which already is.

Our obsession with newness is not just destructive; we also ignore our traditions and deprive ourselves of our heritage. When we open ourselves to the past, we encounter a world of objects, practices, stories, myths, beliefs, and customs that are not only captivating but also anchored in culture, place, identity, and community (figure 7.2). Typically, too, they are inherently moderate and conservational, reflecting deeply ethical attitudes born of necessity and generations of situated knowledge, practice, and tradition. Moreover, these attitudes of sufficiency and respectfulness are entirely congruent with contemporary notions of sustainability. Unfortunately, too, in opening ourselves to the past, we also reveal a far less palatable side. Our past may have many wonderful examples of human creativity and charity, but it also has far too many instances of cruelty, prejudice, unconscionable bigotry, and social and environmental devastation.

However, all these things, both the good and the bad, are fundamental to who we are and where we come from. We must be prepared to learn from this, otherwise our contemporary activities and decisions will simply be repeating the same mistakes. As Santayana says, "Progress, far from consisting in change, depends on retentiveness. When change is absolute there remains no being to improve and no direction is set for possible improvement: and when experience is not retained . . . infancy is perpetual. Those who cannot remember the past are condemned to repeat it."[26] Instead of jettisoning the past, it is far more constructive to learn from it, to acknowledge the remarkable contributions as well as the many shortcomings of earlier generations, and to build on and out of this heritage by developing and renewing it to align with contemporary needs and sensibilities. The manner in which we do this requires careful thought and symbiotic integration of a wide variety of factors. This is what makes sustainability such a complex issue—it rests on achieving a delicate balance among a host of different elements. But while it may be difficult to achieve, there are many precedents for such ways of living throughout history. Traditionally, it was achieved through

Figure 7.2   *Objects of Place, Culture, and Identity*
top left: maté gourd and straw, Argentina
top right: carved inkstone, brush and ink, China
bottom left: traditional door lock, Nepal
bottom right: three-legged stool, Spain

accumulated contributions and collective wisdom built up over generations, which resulted in an effective and continuously evolving accordance between people and place—an accordance that was capable of sustaining people not just in terms of their physiological needs, but also culturally and spiritually.

Consequently, any interpretation of that elusive and much discussed term "sustainability" should not be conceived in purely instrumental, utilitarian terms—such as by analyzing the life cycle of products, ensuring circularity in materials use, or achieving net-zero carbon emissions. Important as these may be, we must go further and deeper. The most critical consideration in any understanding of sustainability must be its relationship to human meaning. People do not yearn to be "sustainable" in terms of their materials and energy use, and they do not yearn, primarily, to have many possessions, to lead a life of pleasure, or even to be happy. They yearn for their lives to have meaning. As Nietzsche put it, "If we possess our *why* of life we can put up with almost any *how*."[27] This search for meaning in one's life is the principal driving force in human beings.[28] For this reason, our interpretation of sustainability, and particularly *design for sustainability*, must include more profound understandings of what makes a meaningful life; in other words, we need a meaning-based interpretation of *design for sustainability*. And fundamental to such an understanding is *appreciation*—it involves appreciating what is positive about the current condition, including its material, cultural, and spiritual heritage, which we can constructively and thoughtfully build upon and take forward.

The elements we have to concurrently address and bring into a synthesized whole have to be meaningful in practical, social, and personal terms.[29] At the practical level, we have to furnish our physical needs while avoiding harm to the natural environment. Similarly, our actions have to be ethical and socially meaningful, allowing us to live in community with others. And they have to be personally meaningful and capable of providing us with a sense of purpose, hope, and spiritual fulfilment.[30] In addition, our design *thinking-and-doing* has to be considered in *a context*; meaningful ways of thinking and acting can never be generalized, they have to be formulated for a given situation—which again contests modernism's international style and today's globalization of product markets with their one-size-fits-all approach.

If our approaches are to be genuinely meaningful, we must understand the context in which we find ourselves and ensure our actions are appropriate to that particular situation.

Achieving these things through design requires a rather different set of priorities from those common in much contemporary practice. It means focusing not just on the end goal but also on the means of achieving it, and it requires us to commit to the *inner* goals of seeking excellence and striving for virtue for their own sake.

The term *praxis*, rather than *practice*, more accurately conveys this merging of *means* and *ends* into an inseparable whole; it suggests a way of working that simultaneously strives to embrace theory, human values, context, tradition, and practice. When all these factors are held simultaneously as the basis for intervention, appreciative design praxis can improve the current condition by sensitively aligning creative propositions with the physical-environmental conditions and the culture-dependent values, notions of virtue, traditions, and belief systems in the context for which we are designing.[31]

8 DESIGN CRITICISM

Criticism in the context of art and design is concerned with analysis and evaluation of creative works and judicious discernment of their contribution. It is an interpretive process that may involve reference to theoretical perspectives and historical precedents, and it strives to understand and contextualize the content, themes, merits, and deficiencies of a work or works. A *critique* is the resulting piece of writing, usually in the form of an article or essay, that articulates that criticism.

Unfortunately, the discipline of design does not have a well-established culture of criticism. The term *design critique* is more often used to refer to the oral or written reviews that take place during studio courses in design schools. When people do write about design, as Glenn Adamson, head of graduate studies at the Victoria & Albert Museum, has observed, it is usually, "so deeply entrenched within the design field, so closely tied to its professional goals, that the writing's ultimate effect would always be promotional rather than critical."[1] This contrasts with art criticism, which does have a lineage and conventions, even though it has become much diminished in recent times.[2] In the early twentieth century, art criticism was more prominent, and its critics were inclined to think on a larger scale, comparing works by different artists as well as the views of other critics. In this way, their discussions and judgments were contextualized within broader comparisons, rather than being confined to the particular exhibition or work at hand, which is often the case today, especially among critics whose work appears in the popular press.[3]

Design criticism is seldom taught in universities. There are some post-graduate degree schemes that use the term, but these are relatively rare and, even here, most of the teaching revolves around history, theory, and research methods. While design criticism involves these topics, it also requires consideration of different positions and perspectives and the development of critical judgments. It aims to understand, interpret, contextualize, and critique a work of design in terms of its significance to the time in which it was created, to the history and development of the discipline, and to broader societal concerns. It might include reference to aesthetics, design theory, design history, other works in the same genre, or the relationship of this particular work to other designs by the same person. It can also include considerations such as the originality and innovation of the product or process, the quality of production, and the relationship of these to broader issues, such as ethical, environmental, and economic factors. The view that design needs to develop a more broadly informed approach to design criticism is shared by others. Katherine Moline points out that while research has been growing in design history and contemporary practice, design criticism lacks weight and is usually limited to pragmatic and functional concerns, especially as they relate to the market.[4] The discipline of design needs substantive, broader-based design criticism because active critical engagement and reflection are essential if the discipline is to move forward in ways that are informed, thoughtful, and relevant to the times.[5] The writer, design historian, and curator Stephen Bayley is probably the best-known design critic in the United Kingdom, and he *does* contextualize and evaluate design within a wider vista.

In this present discussion, I will consider examples of recently created material culture and, in the process, demonstrate the need for design to become more reflective, self-critical, and discerning—both in professional practice and in academia. However, by *design criticism*, I am not meaning high-flown discussion that is so specialized and esoteric that it is neither accessible nor appealing to practitioners or a wider audience. Design affects everyone, so design critique is not something that should be confined to the rarefied atmosphere of the university.

The examples I draw upon here raise questions about surface over substance as well as fakery and fiction over authenticity and depth. Among them are notable differences that place some in a rather different category from others. They include a restaurant in China; an exhibition in Venice; a chain of American superstores; and, at a smaller scale, a clock, table lamp, and chair.

BOGUS BOHEMIA

A colleague in Changsha, in south-central China, invited me to give a talk at the university's design-research symposium. I was pleased to accept as I was already conducting research in other parts of China, and this was a good opportunity to learn more and meet new people with similar interests.

I arrived the day before the conference and was given a tour of the campus, which has a number of ancient buildings and a history dating back to 976 CE, and I learned something of the culture of this strikingly beautiful region. The final evening was given over to the conference dinner, and we had been promised a special treat. The venue was a place called Wenheyou Laochangsha Lobster Restaurant, or simply Wenheyou Market, the name at the entrance to the complex.

To all intents and purposes, Wenheyou Market is a large, highly stylized food court attached to a shopping mall. It occupies several floors, and in addition to restaurants and smaller food outlets, there are various retail stalls, a crayfish pond, barbershop, lottery-ticket seller, billiard hall, and bookstore. The market is newly built but seems old because it has a decrepit style that mimics a working-class urban district of 1970s China. It has "designed-in" tumbledown walls, broken cables, defunct air-conditioning units, poor housing, and hole-in-the-wall shops, all rendered in a carefully choreographed, dirty-looking, and well-worn aesthetic—a kind of large-scale shabby chic. There is even a period cable car regularly circuiting the top floor (figure 8.1).

During dinner, everyone was enthusiastically extolling the place. I seemed to be the only one in our party who was feeling perplexed and uncomfortable. None of it sat well with me because none of it was real— all was illusion and facade driven primarily by commercial intent. The whole concoction abuts and is part of a conventionally designed shopping mall, selling all the usual brands in all the usual layouts. Just this part

Figure 8.1 *Wenheyou Market*
Changsha, China

had been done up in what can only be described as an "urban-poverty theme park."

Yet despite its contrived aesthetic, its questionable moral qualities, and the fact that the whole thing is a pastiche, it recently won an international design prize—a "Best of the Best" Red Dot design award. The award statement says the mall aims "to allow the elderly to recall every detail of their childhood, while young people can experience and partake in the old lifestyle. . . . As a successful alternative to familiar and globally identical shopping malls, visitors can here experience the recreation of an authentic atmosphere—an experience that also invites them to connect emotionally to the past."[6] I was amazed at the design team's meticulous attention to minutiae in their attempts to recreate the past, in the architecture itself as well as the interior design of the restaurants and shops. It had all been accomplished with considerable expertise, a remarkable eye for detail, and impressive technical skill. And the mall is undoubtedly successful—it has proved to be especially popular among young middle-class urbanites and tourists. However, contrary to the award statement, it is anything but authentic.

During the flight home, I thought more about my experience at Wenheyou Market. The reason it troubled me was not just that the architecture was a conceit—a piece of nostalgic flimflam—it was also the fact that it had received an international design award and was being liberally praised by senior design academics. What did this say about the state of contemporary design? Whatever the answer, I felt it was probably not very complimentary!

The award statement claimed that visitors can "experience the recreation of an authentic atmosphere." This piece of designer doublespeak bears little scrutiny. Something can be either authentic or a re-creation, but it cannot be both. Moreover, while it may be a re-creation, it is more precisely a re-creation of whatever was in the designer's head. It is certainly not a re-creation of the past. Rather, it is a selective, idealized notion of the past—one that is supported by a host of modern conveniences, technologies, expectations, and standards. It is all surface and fakery, creating an emotional experience with none of the true implications, responsibilities, or deficiencies. There is no depth to engage with, no requirement for commitment and no *real* feelings. It is a simulacrum—having merely the appearance of the real thing but possessing neither its substance nor its authentic qualities.

It aims to conjure a time not so long ago that, supposedly, was filled with warm, deep communal relationships, and everyone led peaceful, harmonious lives. A time when one's daily needs could be satisfied by street vendors selling vegetables, eggs, fruit, and snacks, and one could get a haircut from an itinerant barber. A time when children could play safely among the narrow, winding streets, or *hutongs*. The Wenheyou complex is created against this background, and it skillfully paints a vivid picture. However, the fact that it is so visually convincing makes it all the more disconcerting; it misleads through plausibility. But unlike true art, the attention to detail and accuracy of the reproduction actually closes down the imagination rather than opening it up. Consequently, the mall's aesthetic is entirely specious, and it is this quality of deception and insincerity that makes it so morally questionable.

This kind of design can be understood as kitsch, that category of creative production, whether art or design, characterized as pretentious and of little value. Wenheyou Market falls into this category because it aims to touch its visitors by invoking superficial emotions, which are consciously elicited through aesthetic evocation.

Its nostalgic references are designed to promote a sentimental longing for a time now passed. It is kitsch because of this attempt "to have your emotions on the cheap . . . the easy avenue to a dignity destroyed by the very ease of reaching it."[7] It conjures a world of never-ending childhood, a world of fantasy aimed at adults, and, consequently, it represents an infantilization of adulthood. Through such means, adults in contemporary society suppress and constrain themselves by transforming reality's more unsettling and disturbing questions into pacifying, puerile answers.[8]

With their relatively recent rise in wealth, many people in China seem to be proving just as susceptible to the beguiling indulgences of kitsch as any Hollywood tycoon or European aristocrat. In China's development of commerce and tourism, there are new "ancient" castles built in traditional styles imported from different regions. The resulting mélange is blandly representative of some idealized notion of a past that never was. In Beijing, just south of Tiananmen Square, the creation of Qianmen Street involved displacing thousands of citizens and demolishing a centuries-old neighborhood. The area has been turned into an upscale shopping and tourist destination—all in a kind of 1930s style architecture that looks, feels, and *is* entirely phony.

Wenheyou Market may be the latest trendy place for young metropolitans, and it may be less obviously kitsch than Disney's Main Street, U.S.A., or Thomas Kinkade's cutesy cottages, but it is kitsch just the same—a bogus Bohemia bolted onto a shopping mall.[9] As its restaurant menu confirms, it is pretending to be a China of a different time, when grandmother still made wholesome, home-cooked dishes and the family sat around the kitchen table together watching old shows on a fuzzy black-and-white TV.

Theodor Adorno suggests that when architects become tired of conventional functional forms and try instead to give free rein to their fantasies, their work inevitably falls into kitsch: "Art is not more able than theory to concretize utopia, not even negatively."[10] Umberto Eco reinforces this by pointing out that history always defies imitation—history has to be made.[11] Eco was discussing the artificial edifices created by the wealthy in Florida and Southern California, but his words apply equally to many of the nouveau riche projects found in today's China. Wenheyou Market, in particular, seems to suggest a longing for a simpler, less-wealthy time and some nostalgic remorse for what has been swept aside during China's recent economic boom.

AN ERSATZ EXTRAVAGANZA

An experience that left me equally dissatisfied and with a similar feeling of being duped was an exhibition by British artist Damien Hirst, titled *Treasures from the Wreck of the Unbelievable*. It filled two very large galleries in Venice, the Palazzo Grassi and the Punta della Dogana. The pieces on show were made by hundreds of highly skilled craftspeople. They were supplemented by beautifully made films of the underwater recovery of these seemingly sunken treasures. High-definition screens in the entrance halls showed stunningly vibrant, underwater footage of the "lost artifacts" being carefully lifted from the ocean floor by scuba divers and brought to the waiting support vessel.

This was all part of the elaborate ruse, which was augmented by a backstory about an ancient collector whose ship, the *Unbelievable*, had foundered two thousand years ago. The lost treasures that made up its cargo, so the fiction went, had been recently discovered and were being exhibited for the first time. The catalogue plays along with this narrative, authoritatively reinforcing its credibility with contributions by underwater archaeologist Franck Goddio, historian Simon Schama, former director of the Louvre Henri Loyrette, and exhibition curator Elena Geuna.[12]

It all seemed rather immature and self-indulgent—an unoriginal, lazy idea not unlike the opening scenes of the 1957 movie *Boy on a Dolphin*, in which a Greek sponge diver, played by Sophia Loren, finds a two-thousand-year-old treasure. But Hirst's "treasures" were executed on a far grander scale—an ersatz extravaganza that went on and on and on through room after room of statues, weaponry, coins, and jewelry in bronze, marble, and gold. An exhibition of look-alike museum pieces with none of the history. Distributed throughout were also objects that were clearly meant as visual jokes—an "antique" sword bearing the name SeaWorld, three pink marble torsos stamped with Mattel, and coral-encrusted Disney characters (figure 8.2). Conceivably, and as we shall discuss, these pieces could be termed "preemptive kitsch," but their physical presence only emphasized the feeling of shallowness. It was all mildly entertaining, but even during the experience, it seemed spectacularly facile. As Jean-Jacques Rousseau said, fictions that have a moral end are called parables and fables, but the majority of stories possess no real instruction or moral value; their object is mere entertainment, and they are quite empty.[13] He also said that to present a fiction as if it were true is "a pointless joke . . . a foolish piece of childishness."[14]

In general, the critics were quick to praise Hirst's exhibition, which perhaps says more about how pervasive this kind of self-referential but essentially trivial affectation has become in the contemporary art world and how difficult it is to see the forest for the trees. For example, Jonathan Jones, the *Guardian*'s art critic, wrote: "It takes a kind of genius to push kitsch to the point where it becomes sublime . . . The kitsch doesn't so much grow on you as wrap you in its tentacles and drag you down into its underwater palace. . . .

Figure 8.2 *"Coral-Encrusted" Mickey*
Treasures from the Wreck of the Unbelievable, Venice, Italy

Throughout this exhibition, real historical information is offered about what are clearly fakes."[15] It may be "genius," but if it is, it is a genius for showmanship. This grandiose exposition of beautifully crafted frippery—created for Hirst's wealthy clients[16]—certainly does drag you, and art, down, but not in a good way. Jones suggests that it is "a subtle meditation on the practice of collecting, on museums and why we go to them."[17] When I visited, *subtlety* was not a word that came to mind.

As Roger Scruton has pointed out, this kind of work "triggers the quick response of the establishment critic, who knows that he will make no mistake by praising it."[18] Even so, things have reached a sorry state when art commentators accept such trivial indulgence without more serious appraisal.

One critic who saw through the hype and was prepared to say so was Alastair Sooke, who described it as

> a spectacular, bloated folly . . . an overblown, kitsch pastiche, characterised by lifeless surfaces, lurid emotions, and vile, excessive details . . . There's a lot of craftsmanship on display, but not much art . . . Ultimately, though, Treasures from the Wreck of the Unbelievable offers scale in lieu of ambition, and kitsch masquerading as high art. . . .
>
> Many of these trinkets, knick-knacks and baubles have been issued as multiples, replicated in different materials and on various scales, like products for the schlocky end of the art market.[19]

While these objects are classified in today's society as "art," they have much in common with contemporary design. This is not just because many of them are notionally practical—including implements, weapons, coins, jewelry, even a pair of golden doors—but also because their primary purpose is commercial. Instead of advancing artistic ideas and elevating the spirit, they have the opposite effect. These are "socio-positional" objects, which are peddled among circles that deem such work to be exclusive and therefore desirable. They serve much the same function as an antique or limited-edition car, watch, or necklace. In our fiercely materialistic, money-oriented society, the acquisition of such things ascribes to their owner a certain social status. The whole cynical endeavor is targeted at the wealthy's craving for visible distinctiveness through ostentation and opulence.

Such possessions of demarcation and division are evident not only in the relatively recent Euro-replicas and phony imitations of Los Angeles but also among the long-established royal families of Europe; we need only witness the gold carriage and shining horse guards brought out in London on special occasions to impress visiting heads of state. These crass manifestations of self-importance are modulated by time and tradition and dignified by familiarity and by the fact that they are much loved by royalists and tourists. The large houses of Britain's faded aristocracy, many of which are now run by the National Trust, are filled with similar spectacles. Here, too, the visitor is immersed in all the gaudy ornaments of conspicuous affluence, and here, too, there is no hesitation in embracing fakery. Interior walls are painted in trompe l'oeil pediments, pilasters, marbles, and murals.[20] And in Harewood House in Yorkshire, there are even finely crafted "wooden drapes" by Chippendale, "a celebrated feature of the room—are the pelmets, made of wood and beautifully carved to imitate a heavy material—the only 'curtains' the room was intended to have."[21] From a commercial perspective, kitsch can be very successful because it is so popular, not least because it demands nothing of us. Its clichéd tropes do not contest or disturb our established view of the world. Kitsch doesn't ask us to see or think about the world differently; it simply reinforces our existing perspectives and wraps us in a security blanket of manufactured banality. This is a poor reason to produce such work, especially when it fosters excessive consumption, as it so often does. Just because something is popular does not make it good. Popularity is no measure of quality, significance, or lasting contribution to the field. Kitsch is popular because it is so easy to digest. In the history of art, for example, no one has sold more works than has the late Thomas Kinkade, American painter of idyllic, sentimental scenes. In the late nineteenth century, the most renowned painter in Northern Europe was the Austrian Hans Makart. Like Kinkade, Makart, too, painted sentimental scenes. Today, he is all but forgotten, eclipsed by figures such as Paul Cézanne, whose work was the precursor to Cubism, and Vincent van Gogh, who was unappreciated at the time but is now considered one of Western art's most influential figures.[22]

Design is often deeply implicated in the creation of kitsch. It is, for instance, a major factor in the commercial success of the US hunting and fishing superstore Bass Pro, which has dozens of outlets across North America (figure 8.3).

These stores feature log-cabined fantasy landscapes, forest lakes, constructed mountain crags with "real" waterfalls and life-size herds of animals, and, in another area, authentic-looking stagings of down-home, fly-tying workbenches. They offer what one business writer, using more doublespeak, called "an authentic themed environment," and at the front of one store, "designers planted mature, 30-foot-tall live oak trees to give the appearance of history and permanence."[23] The stores, which may also feature a restaurant, shooting range, or bowling alley, are as much theme-park entertainment centers as they are retail outlets.

KITSCH WITH A WINK

The above examples of large-scale extravagance flout both moderation and discernment and are preeminent examples of kitsch. However, there are other examples at the smaller product scale that are also very popular and cheesily sentimental—religious kitsch, for instance, which is especially common at Catholic pilgrimage sites such as Lourdes, Rome, and Santiago de Compostela. Shops in these places are well stocked with plastic statuettes of Jesus, Mary, and miscellaneous saints as well as a plethora of crucifixes, wall plaques, rosaries, snow globes, and fridge magnets.

There are, however, other examples that come very close to being kitsch, that display many of its traits but do not fall so firmly into the kitsch camp. These include much design termed *postmodern* that began to appear from the late 1970s and is still prominent today. These designs differ from those of modernism in that they are more decorative and there is a wry humor in their forms and finishes and in the names given to the various pieces. There also tends to be an emphasis on surface.

One of these designs is based on the traditional Jagdstück cuckoo clock from the Black Forest region of Germany. This type of clock dates back to the seventeenth century and is an intricately carved wooden hunting lodge in miniature enclosing a mechanical clock. The CuCu clock designed by

Figure 8.3 *Interior of a Bass Pro Store*
the North American hunting and fishing retail chain

Pascal Tarabay references the original in a knowingly ironic manner. The elaborate ornamentation of the original is pared down to a simple profile rendered in laser-cut ply with finishes in walnut, birch, or oak. Behind this two-dimensional facade is a modern electric clock. It reminds us of the original but in a much simplified, more contemporary and humorous manner (figure 8.4).

The Bourgie table lamp designed by Ferruccio Laviani is made entirely from clear polycarbonate, with options in black or gold. It is created from three elaborately curlicued profiles arranged into a triform pedestal and topped by a lampshade of the same material. The overall design recalls the ornate baroque styles of the early eighteenth century.

A further example is Philippe Starck's Louis Ghost armchair in clear polycarbonate. This plain café or dining chair references the original Louis XVI version in both form and name.

All these designs are for mass-produced products, but they abandon the austere *form follows function* philosophy of modernism in order to include interpretations of historical ornamentation and form. While they, too, are nostalgic, it may be argued that they are saved from being kitsch through their use of contemporary materials and techniques and their conscious inclusion of irony and humor. This, however, does not necessarily mean they are examples of good design. We are not out of the woods yet. Arriving at an informed view involves some additional considerations.

This kind of design can be understood as preemptive kitsch. In contrast to true kitsch, which is done seriously, this is design that is deliberately executed in a kitschy way—kitsch in ironic quotation marks. It represents an embracing of kitsch, retaining its emphasis on facade but presented as parody, kitsch with a knowing wink.[24] This is design as plasticky, mass-produced one-liner—design as surface, as two-dimensional cutout. It represents an approach that is willfully superficial. Being created in shiny transparent polymer—as are the Bourgie lamp and Louis Ghost chair—the result simultaneously appears luxurious and tacky, glitzy and unrepairable, like a tuxedo and bow tie printed on the front of a T-shirt. It is design as nouveau-sophistiqué junk that attempts to separate itself from authentic kitsch but, in doing so, smacks simultaneously of cynicism and elitism.

Figure 8.4 *CuCu Clock*

designed by Pascal Tarabay

The problem with kitsch is that it effectively neutralizes the aesthetic phenomenon.[25] It encourages seeing without perceiving, and thinking without pondering. We are left only with fake appearances and superficial thoughts. When we yield to this, we end up seeing only that which is bearable to us and live in a world that already conforms to our preexisting views.[26]

In terms of design, while this kind of work can be seductive and is undoubtedly popular, it contributes nothing to the development of the genre; it has no depth or lasting relevance. It is design as replication, design as film set, where presentation eclipses substance.[27] It is the endless regurgitation of cliché, which is neither original nor interesting. More than this, it is morally corrosive and deeply irresponsible—first, because its production depends on synthetic materials and the use of energy resources that create a host of negative impacts, and, second, because the materials used are frequently neither maintainable nor repairable. When this kind of design is applied to consumer products, it results, effectively, in the mass production of disposable trash. For the associated professional bodies to acclaim such work suggests a discipline that is self-serving, limited in vision, and woefully out of touch.

Without critical discernment, mainstream design becomes increasingly meaningless for the simple reason that it fails to respond to the socioeconomic and environmental realties of the world in which it operates.

The continual production of trite permutations is driven not by the pursuit of either legitimate design inquiry or design excellence, but by commerce. It may be technically impressive, but fundamentally it is a sham. As such, it is worse than just bad design or bad art because it is more degenerative. It seeks to invoke superficial emotions that are consciously elicited through nostalgic references, fostering a sentimental longing for an idealized past. It offers us a comfortable and comforting view of the world, and because it is unchallenging, it persuades us to go along with its illusion. It gives us the world as we want it to be and, in so doing, encourages complacency and conceitedness. We allow ourselves to be led by self-interest and vanity, which, according to Kant, is incompatible with goodness and virtue.[28] Kitsch offers us only a facsimile of the good rather than the good itself. It has its form and appearance but none of its essential nature. As such it represents "the desecration of genuine value," and consequently its failing is not just aesthetic but also ethical.[29]

As theme-park fantasies, Wenheyou Market, *Treasures from the Wreck of the Unbelievable*, and Bass Pro, are glowing triumphs—they, along with the product examples discussed above, are popular, superficial, hedonistic, and commercially successful. But this kind of work stultifies culture by dampening the critical faculty. In doing so, it drains the vitality from the present. By accepting kitsch, we unthinkingly accept platitudes that idealize a time that never was. This contributes nothing to the living reality of today, but it does make us less accepting of it.

In essence, the type of design work that has been discussed here, with its "themed" experiences and its celebration of decadence, represents a return to the forms of social differentiation employed by the wealthier classes of earlier times. In eighteenth- and nineteenth-century Britain, when the rural and urban poor were living in overcrowded, squalid conditions, rich landowners and industrial magnates amused themselves by commissioning ornate craftworks—garish mantel clocks, bronze-work fountains, marble statues, facsimiles of Greek temples, and picturesque, purpose-built "ruins" or follies. Similar artifacts were reproduced in less-expensive materials for the middle classes, whose overpacked living rooms bore all the signs and symbols of social aspiration. It seems we are still encouraging and, indeed, applauding such extravagant absurdity.

We are living in a world of enormous socioeconomic disparities. Through globalization, favorable tax laws, and generous bonus schemes, corporate leaders and business executives ensure the profits of industry stay firmly in their own hands. In recent times, global integration has enabled transnational corporations to constantly avoid paying nationally administered taxes. We all suffer the consequences, in the form of cash-strapped public health, education, and social services, but it is the least-developed countries that usually bear the brunt of these economic injustices.[30] So when the richer echelons of society put their excess wealth into self-indulgent projects like some of the examples we have discussed here, they are effectively mocking the unconscionable levels of social inequity they have helped create and are displaying a brazen disregard for today's unprecedented environmental crisis.

Today, kitsch is everywhere, but, as designers, we have a responsibility to critique such inauthenticity and shallow imitation. The fact that Wenheyou Market was awarded a "Best of the Best" Red Dot design prize, chosen by an international panel of judges, seems especially egregious; it speaks volumes about the current state of design. Viewed within a wider context, it is difficult not to see the panel's decision as anything but a dereliction of responsibility—both to design and to a broader swathe of contemporary creative disciplines. The crafts, the fine arts, and marketing are often intimately involved in the production or promotion of such work, so they, too, become implicated.

DEEPER DESIGN

Design should certainly learn from and reference the past and build on earlier contributions to the discipline. Moreover, this does not have to be done in ways that are always novel and original; such contemporary preoccupations can themselves be criticized as being part of a system that constantly promotes newness and innovation in the name of progress and economic growth; a system that is clearly highly damaging and grossly unsustainable.

While the examples we have discussed here do reference the past, their approaches smack of flippancy rather than respect. Aesthetic qualities that resonate with the human spirit and create places and things that possess a sense of timelessness and rightness result not from glib, knowingly clever novelties, but from accretions, chance juxtapositions, and many thoughtful individual acts that accumulate over generations. This applies equally to cities, buildings, and individual artifacts—think of the provenance-revealing features of a building that has been repaired, added to, and repurposed over time, or the patina of a well-used wooden chair, kitchen table, or hand tool. These aesthetic qualities emerge from context and culture, and consequently such artifacts often have a unique and satisfying "fit" with place, an "at-homeness" that is a function of time, chance, tradition, and enduring use.[31] Notably, too, there is a complete absence of both facetiousness and banality.

As we shall see in forthcoming chapters, contemporary design can build on these traditions by ensuring that processes are capable of producing good work and contribute to place and community, and the resulting products are purposeful, warranted, environmentally responsible, and relevant to the present in terms of their aesthetic expression.

If design wants to be taken seriously, it has to become far more reflective and self-critical. If it is to rise to the challenges facing us today, it has to renounce the seemingly obsequious behaviors discussed here and be prepared to confront the serious issues. It also has to develop a substantive body of work in design criticism in order to establish a basis for design articulation and informed discernment, discussion, and debate.

9 TOWARD RESILIENCE

When products and systems are designed to be resilient, they are able to withstand changing conditions, unexpected events, and the inevitable stresses that arise over time. Resilience prevents things from breaking down and grinding to a halt; it enables things to last.

Unfortunately, our modern cult of efficiency means many of our systems have been cut to the bone, and this makes them inherently unstable—there's no slack that can take up the strain. Consequently, our current ways of living and working, and the economic system that drives them, are anything but resilient. Nurses, doctors, teachers, and managers in our essential services, from transport to welfare, are constantly told they have to be more efficient, more cost-effective. We have made efficiency an end in itself, a value in itself, irrespective of the consequences for people, public life, and public goods, and irrespective of other values, like the health and well-being of people, the education of our children, and a sense of stability and security in our lives. The language of efficiency has come to pervade all sectors of society and all aspects of modern life;[1] but it is a development that is self-defeating, for, as R. H. Tawney pointed out many years ago: "To convert efficiency from an instrument into a primary object is to destroy efficiency itself. For the condition of effective action in a complex civilization is cooperation. And the condition of cooperation is agreement, both as the ends to which effort should be applied, and the criteria by which its success is to be judged."[2] Private-sector leaders are just as enamored with efficiency as those involved in public-sector governance. Manufacturing and food-supply systems are so finely tuned to just-in-time production and delivery of components and produce that there is no leeway if interruptions or delays occur—no stocks are kept in reserve. The putative efficiencies of these globalized forms of production have led to a precarious reliance on cheap fuel for goods transportation; continual, undisrupted deliveries from elsewhere; and the withering of domestic capacity and know-how in many areas of production and supply. The result is that when events like the COVID-19 pandemic occur, nations find themselves in an extremely vulnerable position because, having ceded their capabilities to overseas concerns, they are unable to increase their own production. In this instance, countries all over the world experienced critical shortages in the supply of personal protective equipment (PPE), which put health workers and others at unnecessary risk.[3] In addition, there are major environmental impacts associated with continually shipping enormous quantities of food, raw materials, and products around the world.

For a more resilient society, we will have to consider replacing just-in-time forms of production with a more flexible, robust, and environmentally responsible system that is not only capable of accommodating unforeseen occurrences but also inherently more sustainable. Change and unexpected events are inevitable, no matter how effective we think we are at forecasting, but our current economic system and its associated cult of efficiency have led to a system of powerful, globalized, but precarious monocultures. Hence, we need to look at ourselves, challenge our assumptions and be open to new sensibilities that encourage quite different values from those in our present, highly consumptive but insecure ways of living.

Resistance to Change: Some areas of life are full of changes, and we embrace them and find them exciting—we look forward to the arrival of new products, new fashions, and new entertainments. Not only are these seen as fresh and stimulating, but their development and launch—often with much hoo-ha—are also important factors in driving the economy.

We are far more resistant to the kinds of change that would lead us away from this system of constant but relatively trivial novelty. We tend to be suspicious of substantial change—the kind of change that might involve different ways of living and working. Even the thought of it can be intimidating and disrupting. Few private- or public-sector leaders are confident enough to give their employees the freedom to explore new ways forward. In most large organizations, great emphasis is put on planning, key performance indicators, and measurement—to work in other ways seems too uncertain. We become comfortable in standardized routines—all of which conspire to bolster the status quo.[4] So, despite constant talk of innovation, we generally prefer to leave things as they are, which may be fine when things are going well—but evidence that things are not going well has been building for a long time. The signs of serious problems are there for all to see, but we still strive to doggedly preserve our current lifestyles, which are firmly based in consumption, waste, and growth. Two recent US administrations, from both sides of the house, have clearly demonstrated that, fundamentally, they favor maintaining the status quo. A recent Republican president dismissed concerns about climate change and global warming, saying: "I don't think science knows . . . It'll start getting cooler, you just watch."[5] And the US climate envoy for the Democratic Party displayed extraordinary, not to say foolhardy, confidence in the power of technology when he claimed that Americans will not have to alter their way of life, and 50 percent of current emissions can be cut using yet-to-be-invented technologies.[6] Similarly, in the United Kingdom, a recent study concluded that, despite its proclaimed commitment to combating climate change, "neither the government nor relevant regulators have taken adequate action to address global emissions financed and enabled by UK private financial institutions." Based on year-end disclosures, the study estimated the carbon emissions associated with this sector to be 805 million metric tons CO_2e (carbon dioxide equivalent). This figure, which is likely to be an underestimate, is nearly twice as much as the UK's domestically produced emissions and constitutes a significant contribution to climate change.[7]

Our determination to maintain the existing state of things means we fail to make the connections between our everyday activities and the larger issues. Effectively, it means we turn a blind eye to the rapid ice melt in the polar regions; the increased intensity of forest fires in the United States, Russia, and Australia; and the unprecedented storm surges and flooding in Europe and Asia. Since 1970, there has been a 68 percent decline in the population sizes of mammals, birds, reptiles, and fish—a statistic that should concern us all, not least because human life is dependent on biodiversity.[8]

While some in major leadership positions continue to publicly deny the scientific evidence of climate change, others are actively working to resist change. A number of large, international corporations are investing millions to lobby against policies aimed at curbing climate change and are confusing the debate through misleading propaganda. The London-based nonprofit InfluenceMap, which analyzes how companies impact climate-motivated policy, reports that in the three years immediately following the Paris Agreement, "the five largest publicly-traded oil and gas majors . . . invested over $1Bn of shareholder funds on misleading climate-related branding and lobbying."[9] Oil companies have also attempted to influence policymakers in areas such as vehicle emissions, in order to reduce standards and thus delay the adoption of electric vehicles.[10] And organizations like the Heartland Institute in Chicago and the Cato Institute in Washington, DC, which receive funding from a variety of corporate and individual donors, regularly publish documents that deny or cast doubt on the overwhelming evidence— supported by over 90 percent of published climate scientists—that global warming in modern times is real and, to a very large extent, due to human actions. The Heartland Institute's publications include a book attacking climate science, which has been distributed to public schools and colleges across the United States.[11]

Embracing Uncertainty: To continue on our present course is not going to solve anything—the environmental and social effects are too severe and are only going to get worse. Resisting change and turning a blind eye to the evidence hinders us from looking constructively and positively at viable alternatives and delays the start of effective action. Entrepreneur and academic Margaret Heffernan argues that "the greatest risk inherent in wilful blindness is that it is easy—and easiest of all to ignore is its cost," and it is just this that business leaders and politicians have been doing for far too long—they have ignored climate change, social division, gross inequality, and overpowerful corporations.[12]

We do not know what the future holds and so we can never be entirely sure about the exact way forward, but we do know that we have to change the way we live. And though we may not have a clear picture of what a different way of life might look like, it is not an intractable problem. The important thing is to take the issues seriously, to start the journey and learn and adapt as we go. Once we embrace the need for *change for the right reasons*, we can put in place processes that enable everybody's voice to be heard and a wide range of perspectives to be taken into account. This will be an essential part of the process because we cannot expect to develop new, more positive directions if we simply rely on the same knowledge and the same perspectives that brought us to our current state.

In moving our ideas forward and finding direction, it is important to recognize that modern simulation and forecasting techniques are very sophisticated and can be very helpful, but they are only useful in a very general way—for example, to better understand the cumulative effects of climate change. They cannot tell us precisely where a forest fire or a flood will occur. They can give us a good idea of general trends but are less capable when it comes to particulars. This, however, is no reason to delay change— our knowledge will *always* be incomplete because the specifics will always be both uncertain and ever changing; life is simply too complex to accurately predict individual events with any level of precision. But this must not prevent us from facing up to the reality of our current situation and the state of the world today. If we are prepared to take ownership of it, we can creatively and enthusiastically embrace positive and constructive change. Leaders of business and other organizations can show greater trust in their employees, encourage new ideas, and offer enough flexibility in the system, as well as time and resources, for people to explore new directions. It is far better to be prepared for and steer change than to maintain the status quo and then, sooner or later, reach a crisis, at which point room to maneuver becomes extremely limited. When governments and private- and public-sector organizations reach a crisis point, they usually feel they don't have time to develop and test a variety of scenarios. Instead, overwhelmed by the seeming complexity of the situation, they reduce their options and attempt to quickly build a single, perfect plan.[13] This is neither a creative nor an effective way of dealing with the situation, and, needless to say, it rarely works.

Positive Change and Creativity: The setting aside of vested interests, self-oriented thinking, and ego is a prerequisite for working toward the common good. This has been taught for millennia and is fundamental to all the world's major spiritual traditions.[14] In Christianity, for instance, the term *kenosis* refers to *self-emptying*—stilling our mental busyness and transcending our cravings and desires in order to open ourselves up to those intuitively apprehended values and the sense of higher purpose that are characteristic of our common humanity but, all too often, are suppressed or allowed to remain dormant:

> with no other light or guide
> than the one that burned in my heart
> . . . I abandoned and forgot myself
> . . . all things ceased; I went out from myself[15]

If we are to build community cohesion and care for the natural environment, it is in the intermediate realm—between the outer, sensory world and the inner, spiritual self—where creativity and virtue flourish. It is here that we can bring together the reality of existence with perennial human values and our own creative potential.

My home country of Wales is one example of a small nation that has been proactive in showing effective leadership for positive change. During the nineteenth and twentieth centuries, Wales had its natural resources plundered and its southern valleys ravaged by industrialization. Today, it has few resources and little economic power, but this does not prevent its people from being creative, collaborative, and flexible in the pursuit of the common good. Structured around the UN Sustainable Development Goals, Wales has adopted a program that centers on the well-being of future generations. The program provides the motivation, permission, and legal obligation to work toward long-term improvement across a wide range of sectors.[16] It aims to improve the country's

- resilience, which includes reversing the decline in biodiversity;
- equality, health, social cohesion and cultural vibrancy;
- global responsibilities; and

- prosperity, which strikingly is *not* limited to economic growth and gross domestic product (GDP) but instead recognizes that prosperity includes a healthy environment, a skilled and well-educated population, and decent work.

The program blends pragmatism with long-term vision and is led by a non-politician supported by a small team from various government departments. Research is commissioned, decision-making processes are reviewed, recommendations are assessed annually, and long-term thinking helps overcome entrenched assumptions. These pioneering approaches to positive change are now being adopted elsewhere, including countries as far afield as Canada and the United Arab Emirates.[17]

Toward a Resilient Economy: As is evident in the Welsh initiative, as well as other farsighted programs around the world, including Bhutan's Gross National Happiness Index,[18] a country's prosperity cannot be effectively measured by GDP, nor can it be based on economic growth at any price. National prosperity "is not just about material wealth—it is about every one of us having a good quality of life, and living in strong, safe communities."[19] Yet most governments and the media continue to cite GDP and economic growth as key indicators of how well a country is functioning.

Reform of our economic system is probably the single most pressing issue to be tackled if we are to bring about substantive and lasting change. Necessarily, such reform would affect virtually every walk of life, including design, as we shall explore in subsequent chapters. Despite this, and notwithstanding the fact that it is a key driver of entirely unsustainable ways of living, many seem to regard the current economic system as inevitable and immutable, and suggestions of reform are dismissed as unrealistic, even utopian.[20] On the other hand, philosopher André Gorz argues: "It is impossible to avoid climate catastrophe without a radical break with the economic logic and methods that have been taking us in that direction for 150 years. . . . Degrowth is therefore imperative for our survival. But it presupposes a different economy, a different lifestyle."[21]

Drawing on the work of Alasdair MacIntyre, we can, perhaps, best understand the idea of resilient, sustainable, and socially desirable ways of life as those that strive to embody traditional virtues, build and support community, and contribute to the common good. But our present economic and political systems tend to work against such a direction. Liberalism, Conservatism, and Marxism all suffer from the shortcomings of modernity and the individualism it engenders. Liberal politics rejects the idea of a specific or commonly agreed conception of the "good" on which community life might be based. Liberalism purports to adopt a neutral stance but, in practice, is committed to permissive, often divisive, legislation as well as the promotion of an institutional order that is hostile to the creation and support of the forms of community outlined above. Conservatism is equally harmful because of its commitment to individualism and the free market and its history of prohibitive legislation. Marxism embodies similarly modern and modernizing traits, and its many shortcomings whenever it has been put into practice are well known.[22]

For a variety of reasons, more localized economies with local decision-making can achieve greater accordance with the principles of sustainability. In the case of smaller-scale farming, for instance, nature "constrains the farmer so that he has to be practically wise."[23] And while virtues—such as integrity, justice, lack of envy, love of liberty, and perseverance—are necessary ingredients of a flourishing and happy community, it is these very ingredients that are effectively counteracted and destroyed by our present, globalized economic systems, and by modernity more generally, because everything—land, labor, even money itself—becomes commodified. People become partitioned into different segments, each a distinct entity with its own behaviors, norms, and expectations—work life, private life, leisure time, childhood, economically productive life, retirement. Each is treated separately and specifically targeted, according to income level, for consumption opportunities. This has the effect of disunifying individual lives and devaluing the idea of a complete person and the concept of a whole life. It also has the effect of separating people into individuals rather than seeing them as part of and contributing to a community.[24] As Margaret Thatcher said: "Who is society? There is no such thing. There are individual men and women."[25]

The French economist Thomas Piketty argues that our market economy, which is based on the private ownership of property, if left to its own devices, will inevitably threaten

> democratic societies and the values of social justice on which they are based. . . . Wealth accumulated in the past grows more rapidly than output and wages. . . . The entrepreneur inevitably tends to become a rentier [with income from property or investment], more and more dominant over those who own nothing but their labor. Once constituted, capital reproduces itself faster than output increases. The past devours the future.
>
> The consequences for the long-term dynamics of the wealth distribution are potentially terrifying.[26]

Despite this, much effort is put into depicting our current economic system as the only plausible way forward, even though there *are* cogent, more ethical, and far more sustainable alternatives.

A century ago, as pointed out at the start of this chapter, Tawney argued that in complex societies the condition of effective action is not competition but cooperation. And cooperation rests on agreement—agreement on the ends, the means, the standard of values by which the different objectives are to be ranked, and the criteria by which success is to be evaluated.[27] Similarly, in the 1970s, Schumacher held that the life, work, and happiness of societies depend on certain factors that are precious but vulnerable. These include cooperation, social cohesion, and mutual respect. He urged directions that sought nonviolence, harmonious cooperation with nature; and low-energy, elegant, and economical solutions rather than "the noisy, high-energy, brutal, wasteful, and clumsy solutions of our present-day sciences."[28] More recently, Herman Daly has proposed a steady-state rather than a growth-based economy.[29] Barack Obama has advocated a spirit of cooperation whereby people take part in both shared prosperity and shared sacrifice. Michael Sandel has called for a new politics of the common good.[30] Tim Jackson has argued for a revitalization of the idea of public goods; a renewal of public space, public institutions, and common purpose; and investment in shared goals, shared assets, and shared infrastructures.[31] And Thomas Piketty has recommended a progressive annual tax on capital that would help ensure a more equitable distribution of wealth.[32]

All these voices point toward more egalitarian, localized, community-building approaches in which people work in cooperative ways to achieve shared goals. Cooperative forms of business help ensure a more equitable and just distribution of power and wealth, with worker-managers and limited differentials between the highest- and lowest-paid employees. In turn, this helps create a more engaged workforce and a more unified approach to business management by breaking down the often debilitating "them and us" mentality. Such approaches are commensurate with the common good because they help nurture a culture of sharing, which can include goods, services, spaces, and systems, rather than individual acquisition of an endless array of material products. Our prioritization of the latter might have resulted in a burgeoning of choice and convenience, but the cost has been global heating, enormous levels of toxic waste, drastic declines in biodiversity, and the pollution of the planet (figures 9.1 and 9.2).

The possibilities offered by contemporary communications technologies can contribute to new kinds of localization, the development of local initiatives, the decentralization of power, and the democratization of the economy. They can also help mitigate the potential limitations of localization, such as insularity and parochialism, to achieve the kind of informed, outward-looking cosmopolitan localism mentioned in chapter 3. They also have an important role in the transition from material consumption to services and the effective organization of shared goods and shared prosperity. We have seen the potential of online sharing and knowledge exchange in the development of open-source operating systems, such as Linux, as well as all kinds of software applications. We have also seen the development of a wide variety of web-based services. At the international level, these include services that enable people to rent out spare rooms and spaces or swap houses for holidays. In response to the travel and group-gathering limitations that arose from the COVID-19 pandemic, international conferences were quickly reorganized as online events, as was teaching in schools and universities. During this period, too, professional meetings, media reporting, and working from home all became normalized. Smaller, local-scale initiatives can also be

Figure 9.1 *The March of "Progress" I–Shaving*

top: straight razor (resharpen), wooden-handled brush, soap

bottom left: safety razor (disposable steel blade), plastic-handled brush, soap

bottom right: disposable razor (plastics, metal), disposable foam can (metal, plastic)

Figure 9.2 *The March of "Progress" II–Writing*

top left: swan-feather quill with oak-gall ink

top right: refillable fountain pen with commercially produced synthetic ink

bottom left: fountain pen with plastic disposable cartridges

bottom right: disposable ballpoint pen

facilitated with such technologies, including community groups, volunteer initiatives, and events; grocery and local-produce delivery services; and car and bicycle sharing.

Additionally, there is an important role for governments in developing international agreements that ensure large corporations contribute their proper share of taxes in the countries where they operate, and that their employment practices are fair, with workers receiving decent wages and reasonable benefits. And, as mentioned above, governments can implement progressive taxes on capital so that prosperity can be more equitably distributed among all levels of society. Such measures would help ensure sufficient revenues for public services and infrastructure, and local providers and retailers would not be unfairly undercut by multinationals profiting from outdated tax schemes and exploitative labor practices in poorer countries.

The transition from an economy that relies on consumerism and is characterized by gross socioeconomic injustices to one that is more inclusive, equitable, diversified, and resilient is both feasible and much needed. Effective political leadership can work to transform and redistribute economic activity by facilitating and supporting the revitalization of local economies. Regional and local governments can prioritize the procurement of local products and services and encourage other organizations to do the same. And they can support new, community-based work patterns enabled by digital communications technologies. A reinvigoration of local economies would help overcome many of the ills associated with overconsumption, societal atomization, and the centralization of power and economic activity.

In contrast to England's government, which encouraged people to return to the office as soon as possible after the initial COVID-19 lockdown, ministers in the Welsh government recognized that even when restrictions imposed during the pandemic were lifted, about 30 percent of people could continue to work from home and were able and happy to do so over the long term. Enabling people to work remotely, they argued, not only helps limit the spread of disease but also reduces the need for commuting and the use of private cars, thereby alleviating road congestion and air pollution. It also offers people more choice and flexibility in the way they work and can improve both productivity and work-life balance. It can also boost community-based economic activity and help engender local renewal. To support this kind of transformation, there is a need to ensure effective broadband and other forms of communication as well as the development of networks of remote-working hubs that would be within walking or cycling distance from home. Such initiatives would offer work options beyond just home or office. Local hubs and third spaces could be for those working in the private, public, and third sectors. They would suit those unable to work effectively from home or who prefer greater separation between work and home environments. They would also offer opportunities for knowledge exchange, new partnerships, and new initiatives among national and local governments and among different sectors. These kinds of government-backed schemes encourage people to live, work, shop, and learn within their own communities.[33]

Along similar lines, the municipal government in the former industrial city of Preston in northwest England is supporting initiatives that help revitalize the local economy. Preston's hospital, university, police headquarters, and council have been encouraged to purchase goods and services locally in order to support local businesses and ensure profits are kept within the community; local spending by these organizations is now four times higher than it was a decade ago. Local government representatives in Preston have looked to the success of the Evergreen Cooperative Initiative in Cleveland, Ohio, and Mondragon's worker cooperatives in northwest Spain. R. D. Wolff describes the latter as "a stunningly successful alternative to the capitalist organization of production" in which co-op members, amounting to around 80 to 85 percent of all workers in an enterprise, collectively own and manage the business.[34] Both Evergreen and Mondragon are founded on principles of social responsibility, participation, and economic equity. Preston is adopting a similar ethos to create new opportunities for local enterprises, with a refurbished covered market, new artists' studios in former council offices, and local government support for business start-ups. It also encourages businesses and other organizations to behave more ethically, by ensuring a living wage and a diverse workforce. In the longer term, it is aiming to make cooperatives a mainstream form of business in the city, accounting for 30 to 40 percent of the economy.[35]

It is notable, but perhaps not surprising, that these initiatives in democracy and the development of an economy that works for everyone are not coming from central government. They are emerging, instead, from places that have suffered enormously from years of postindustrial decline, deprivation, and centrally imposed austerity. Crucially, they are based in local self-reliance; cooperation; long-term thinking; and people striving to do the right thing for their communities, for the natural environment, and for future generations. They serve as reminders of the importance of working together for the common good and are meaningful demonstrations of a viable economic alternative. As such, they are beacons of hope in a world where positive examples are sorely needed.

10 TEN WAYS TO CREATE MORE WASTE

1. Wrap all the food we buy in plastic.
2. Design things to be disposable.
3. Make repair more expensive than replacement.
4. Promote novelty and fashion.
5. Base the economy on consumption.
6. Prioritize unrestricted growth.
7. Praise innovation.
8. Advertise everywhere.
9. Make shopping exciting and fun.
10. Obstruct discernment through endless entertainment.

11 ANOTHER KIND OF PROGRESS

Human advancement was made possible because in agrarian societies throughout history a highly privileged class of people lived lives of leisure. This sector of society, so the story goes, had the time to devote itself to creative pursuits, contemplation, and study, and, as a result, ideas in philosophy, science, and the arts flourished. The elite few maintained their position by force, fear, and heavy taxes on the majority, who were subjected to exploitation, hand-to-mouth existence, and, in many cases, enslavement.[1]

When accounts of this kind are put forth as the necessary price of progress, they sail pretty close to the wind, seeming to excuse the gross inequities and injustices. Moreover, they rest on very particular, largely Western ideas of what constitutes "progress," and carry the attendant implication that other, less techno-scientific societies are somehow backward. While this kind of exploitation may have arisen in early agrarian societies, industrial and postindustrial societies also create highly privileged elites. Today, the richest 1 percent are wealthier than all the rest of the world's population, and over the last thirty years, while income growth for the bottom 50 percent has stagnated, the income growth of this privileged 1 percent has ballooned by around 300 percent. Much of the world's wealth is now owned by just eight men,[2] which allows them to pursue all kinds of vanity projects—be it new kinds of technologies, superyachts, space rockets, or charitable works in areas *they* feel are important. This notion of "progress" rests on large numbers of people working long hours for low wages, a highly exploitative gig economy with few or no worker benefits, the phenomenon of the "working poor," the rise of foodbanks in the world's wealthiest nations, and millions of people around the globe living in abject poverty.

However, there are many examples of highly sophisticated peoples, communities, and civilizations whose development has never been contingent on the existence of a privileged few. They have their own stories, works of art, technologies, and philosophical outlooks and have developed ways of living and understandings that unlike the "advanced" cultures of the West have enabled people to tread lightly on the earth and live in relative harmony with each other for centuries. The difference seems to be that they are not *our* cultures, languages, stories, artworks, and technologies and so have often remained invisible to us or else been dismissed as "primitive" and of no consequence.

One key difference between these societies and our own is that contemporary Western society tends to focus on the future, new possibilities, and what is coming next but pays little regard to its own history. In contrast, traditional societies internalize the historical process and make it "the moving power of their development."[3] The transmission and continual renewal of traditional forms of knowledge caters for people's practical needs by providing for food security, health care, warmth, clothing, shelter, and strategies for responding to changes, including changes in the environment. And it does all this in ways that are interwoven with symbolism and metaphor, permeated by mythologies and beliefs, and embodied by the repetitions of ritual. Consequently, in providing for people's practical needs, life becomes suffused with meaning and significance. Also, while much traditional or Indigenous knowledge is shared among men and women, there are also areas of knowledge that are gendered according to differing and complementary roles.[4] These ways of living are complex and sophisticated, and they have enabled people to live in harmony with the natural environment and in relative peace with one another. In many ways, therefore, they can be regarded as far more "advanced" than our highly technological, artificial societies in which consumption and greed are out of control and we are rapidly destroying the very systems needed for the sustainment of life.

Today, all kinds of interest groups are paying attention to vernacular and Indigenous knowledge and expertise in which place-based wisdom and practices have developed over generations. These cumulative bodies of knowledge are contained not in books but in oral histories, myths, songs, artworks, rituals, and beliefs (figure 11.1). They have been continually handed down and, in the process, have been adapted and refined in response to changing understandings and circumstances. In this way, over many centuries, they have been able to remain current and relevant to people's lives.

Designers and environmentalists have been studying vernacular material and built cultures emerging from these kinds of traditional knowledge—in the wealthier Western countries as well as in countries where such "nonmodern" ways of life are more common. A repeated theme associated with such practices is the spiritual resonance one feels in natural places, the sanctity of the land, and a recognition of the holistic, interrelatedness of natural systems.[5] By examining and learning from such cultures, designers and others are beginning to question the assumptions, conventions, and dogmas we have built around our characterizations of what is and what is not technology, innovation, and progress. Through these studies, we are at last recognizing that our long-enculturated understandings are products of Enlightenment humanism, colonialism, and racism combined with a disregard for other cultures and their contributions and innovations. We are also learning that unlike Western notions of industry-dependent progress, these context-specific practices and technologies work not *against* but *with* nature.[6]

Similarly, scientists are learning about traditional knowledge to better understand climate in general and especially global climate change.[7] Among the different peoples and traditions is an enormous diversity of deep local knowledge tied to ancestral lands and the natural ecologies present in them. As one might expect, people in their various locales, and with their unique knowledge and intimate relationship to the land, are acutely aware of any effects caused by climate change and the impacts these are having on the local environment, wildlife, habitats, and so on.[8]

In addition, environmental scientists are studying ethnobotany to better understand how plants provide for people's needs—supplying natural materials for tools, shelter, transportation, and clothing, as well as insect repellents, cleaning materials, and perfumes.[9] They are also recognizing that

Figure 11.1 *Aboriginal Sand Drawing*
Australia

traditional ecological knowledge contains vital principles and practices that include the interrelationships and connections among all elements of the natural environment, ecological indicators, methods for the sustainable harvesting of resources, modes of knowledge acquisition and transfer, respectful attitudes and philosophies, a deep knowledge of the land, and a recognition of the spirituality of nature. Knowledge of all these things as an interrelated and interdependent whole has enabled many Indigenous groups to live sustainably within their environments for thousands of years.[10]

In Australia, author Bruce Pascoe has researched his people's precolonial ways of life. He shows that, contrary to the received history put forward by the colonizers, Aboriginal peoples had created highly sophisticated modes of sustainable farming, harvesting, irrigation, and food preservation and storage, as well as a pan-continental system of governance that fostered both peace and prosperity: "The songlines of Aboriginal and Torres Strait Islander people connected clans from one side of the country to another. The cultural, economic, genetic and artistic conduits of the songlines brought goods, art, news, ideas, technology and marriage partners to centres of exchange."[11]

If we are prepared to listen, and before they become lost forever, these kinds of knowledge can inform our understandings of "progress" and our contemporary approaches to sustainability. We have much to learn from these traditional wisdoms, which not only embody holistic, interrelated systems of thought, belief, philosophy, and practice but also cultivate sensitive, responsive, and respectful relationships within their particular contexts and conditions.

PART II   PRECEDENTS

12 RESILIENT ARTIFACTS AND ACTIVITIES

All responsible designers are duty bound to reflect on the nature and implications of their decisions. When designs are transformed into material things, their production and use can have significant and lasting repercussions. Eliminating negative effects becomes especially important when products are manufactured in tens of thousands or even millions of units, packaged, distributed globally, and, often far too quickly, discarded and replaced.

Some argue that we *need* all our contemporary products to live the kinds of lives today's society demands. They also argue that we *need* our food to be packaged in single-use plastics to ensure freshness, extend shelf life, and maintain consumer choice, especially when so much of it is imported from thousands of miles away. Any suggestion of systemic change is quickly thwarted by this kind of shortsighted pragmatism. If we want to maintain our current way of life, then of course all those things that support it will need to be kept in place, but arguing for such a position is a recipe for inaction and disaster. It also reflects a failure of the imagination and a lack of faith in our ability to develop new ways of living that are better. And a large part of this will be down to envisioning ideas of society and economy that are neither dependent on nor addicted to uninhibited consumerism.

In the chapters that follow, I will consider other forms of material culture, which emerge from a very different ethos. In a variety of ways, these can be understood as resilient, and, as such, they help orient us toward a postconsumerist society. They cover a wide range of categories but are united by the fact that they challenge our present culture of unrestrained consumption and growth. Their impact on the environment is minimal, and they are meaningful on a number of levels—in terms of purpose, symbolism, history, and modes of creation and use.

We will begin by considering issues that apply to them all before looking at each in turn. Hence, through real-world case studies, we will learn about the nature and meaning of material productions that are better attuned to the perennial needs of people and planet. We will also gain insights about the attitudes, values, and responsibilities necessary for a more principled under-standing of design—one that is capable of contributing to the development of resilient ways of living.

A good starting point has to be the contestation of some of the accul-turated norms and expectations that have brought us to our current, unsustainable state. These include the design conventions inherent to our growth-oriented economic system, the most important driver of which is the insatiable pursuit of originality and innovation—long regarded as the goose that lays the golden egg of corporate profits. As Nicola Gardini says: "What matters now, or seems to matter, is . . . technology, spontaneity, the easy, the ephemeral, the new at any cost and in every instance. Few are those who believe—and none, unfortunately, among the political or economic elite—that newness and renewal depend on engaging with those very things that seem obsolete or old."[1] If design is to address resilience in a serious manner, this preoccupation with novelty and "cutting-edge" products has to be challenged. The costs of this obsession are many, not least the loss of continuity, cultural meaning, and identity. Here, we will look at design in terms of environmental impacts, resilience, and aesthetics.

ENVIRONMENTAL EFFECTS

Traditionally, things for everyday use were made by hand or with the aid of simple mechanical devices. For the most part, components would have been created from locally available, natural materials. Their making, their use, and, when no longer needed, their repurposing would have had few long-term impacts on the natural environment. Little if anything was thrown away; to do so would have been regarded as wasteful and unappreciative, and therefore ethically unacceptable.

As recently as the mid-twentieth century, people spent a much higher proportion of their income on food, which meant less was available for nonessential items. The industrialization of farming together with rising levels of prosperity have led to increased spending on things associated with negative environmental impacts. We now have ready access to an ever-expanding range of consumer products, including a plethora of electronic devices and low-value, disposable, and/or unrepairable products.[2] Many of these are intentionally designed to have very short useful lives, and they quickly end up in landfill. In addition, the proliferation of single-use plastic packaging in which many of these products are sold is entirely irresponsible.

At one time, all this would have been seen as reckless, even immoral, reflecting attitudes of restraint that were undoubtedly linked to economic necessity and perhaps also to the more pervasive presence of religion and traditional teachings, both of which tend to encourage moderation. Over the course of just a few decades, however, through incremental accumulation spurred on by relentless marketing, these kinds of products have become normalized and socially acceptable.

RESILIENCE

The word *resilience* has a number of meanings, but the one that applies in this context refers to something that is robust, adaptable, and long-lasting. To design a material artifact that is resilient, four main principles have to be adhered to:

1) *Durability of the concept*: Is its purpose well-founded and likely to have lasting value in society?
2) *Durability and effectiveness of the product's utility*: Is it dependent on technological means that are rapidly evolving, stable, or in decline?
3) *Durability of the physical thing*: Is it made from good-quality materials, is it well put together, and can it be maintained and repaired?
4) *Durability of the design*: Will its form, finish, and styling wear well and have enduring aesthetic appeal?

A product will fall into disuse if the first condition is met but the second and third are not. And if only the first three are met, it will quickly become unappealing and again fall into disuse.

By relearning more traditional ways of doing things at a more local level, we can refind and reexperience the pleasures of using and handling artifacts made from natural materials and the particular aesthetic encounters they offer. In creating postconsumerist artifacts, and bearing in mind the four principles of resilience above, we can also consider the following:

- *Tradition*: Ideas and concepts rarely appear out of nowhere; they build on the things that went before. Continuity and continual refinement are more relevant to resilience than endless novelty.
- *Designing*: From ideation to product definition, we should ask: Is the artifact being designed in a manner that is appropriate and moderate in its features, styling, construction, and materials? Is it likely to endure?
- *Materials*: We can consider sources, constituents, qualities, and modes of production, and greater attention has to be paid to the potential impacts of use:
  - *Natural materials* such as stone, wood, bone, and fiber can often be effective alternatives to plastics and composites and, if sourced responsibly, are generally far better for the environment.
  - *Reused materials* that we may usually think of as trash can be incorporated into new designs.
- *Making*: We can also consider the human skills and knowledge that go into the processes of making, the care taken, and the precision shown. Are there opportunities to learn new skills or refine existing skills while simultaneously providing useful, fulfilling work?
- *Using*: We must always bear in mind the experiences our decisions will offer during use. Are they meaningful experiences? Is the aesthetic experience rewarding?
- *Maintaining*: Can we easily repair and maintain the materials or replace a component if one is lost or beyond repair? Are the materials or components familiar, available, and affordable?

- *Disposing*: Nothing lasts forever and eventually the artifact will no longer be wanted. What happens to it then? Will it be benign, or will it create harm?

When things are designed to be resilient, they are able to cope with normal wear and tear and can be readily repaired and upgraded to suit changing circumstances. If we allow it, our material culture can acquire a history that gives depth and meaning to the environments in which we spend our lives.

Our consideration of the fundamental raison d'être of an artifact and its lasting relevance will benefit from paying attention to traditional knowledge and ways of doing that have evolved over generations. We can learn much from those who have gone before us about enduring ideas and the efficacy and wisdom of conservation, continuity, and stewardship—all of which are consistent with sustainability. Attendance to traditional practices is also relevant to the ways in which artifacts are made, their ability to be cared for, and their resilience. And while we can never know what the future holds, especially when it comes to anticipating new technologies, the detrimental costs of disposal and replacement can be ameliorated by designing for longevity.

In recent times, designers have been deeply implicated in the creation of short-lived products. Functional obsolescence progresses quite slowly, especially when the product is based on a mature technology. But to drive sales, designers constantly develop new styles and often trivial features for otherwise largely unchanged products. Updated models, new devices, and all kinds of disposable objects endlessly appear on the market (figure 12.1). For many years, the "new" has been constantly promoted as better to "create obsolescence-in-the-mind."[3]

Unrestrained innovation—in education, economics, politics, research, and business—is a fundamental contributor to unsustainability. This will be the case even when newer products are supposedly "greener." First, they make existing products obsolete, and, second, their production requires more resources and energy, impacts more habitats, and produces more emissions. They also help perpetuate a culture of novelty and consumption. Traditional forms of material culture contrast strikingly with these contemporary preoccupations. They are apt to be moderate and simple because they have

Figure 12.1 *Disposable and Short-Lived Products*
new devices, new styles, and all kinds of disposable objects endlessly appear on the market

benefited from being perfected over time and are, therefore, well-suited to their purpose.

AESTHETICS

The aesthetic experience of long-lasting, well-used artifacts made from natural materials can be far superior to that of short-lived equivalents. We can appreciate their polished, timeworn surfaces; their muted colors; and the tactile qualities of wood, leather, linen, and wool. Such things are rewarding because there is a sense of harmony between outer and inner experiences. The inevitable effects of use—the scuffs, scars, and burnished patinas—mean that, over time, they acquire a poignant kind of beauty. And when we reuse materials, we not only save them from the waste stream and give them new life but we also require fewer virgin materials. This, too, contributes to an aesthetic experience that speaks of moderation, discernment, and caring. Through such means, our material productions gain a deeper sense of significance and value because these visible signs of age are the traces of past lives—the expressions of cultural legacy and our common human story.

By comparison, there is a paucity to many contemporary products that are aesthetically flawless, beguiling, and all too temporary. They are manufactured from materials and processes we feel alienated from, and they are creating a legacy of harm.

TRANSITION

There is growing evidence that the wealthier countries of the world are reaching the endpoint of a macroeconomic model based on consumerism. The transition to more resilient, postconsumerist ways of life will entail, among other things, new forms of work, reskilling, far greater individual and communal self-provisioning, retrofitting of infrastructure, use of low-carbon technologies, and the development of urban, suburban, and peri-urban forms of agriculture.[4] All this this can benefit from and, indeed, be enabled by the opportunities offered by digitally connected communities. Such a transition will require us to rethink our material expectations and learn to resee and reappreciate forms of material culture that may be old but, nevertheless, offer practical benefits and simple pleasures while simultaneously being gentle on the planet.

RESILIENT ARTIFACTS AND ACTIVITIES

In the following five chapters, I discuss a wide range of artifacts and activities that conform to ideas of resilience and sustainability that include:[5]

Practical meaning—utilitarian benefit that takes into account environmental impacts;

Social meaning—the potentially positive and/or negative effects of a design on other people or the larger society, in the design's creation, use, and disposal;

Personal meaning—the relevance of a design in relation to a person's inner development and spiritual well-being; and

Economic means—financial viability, which is a necessary element but should be regarded as a *means* to achieve the other three, rather than as an end in itself.

The forthcoming examples are also in accord with understandings of *progressive design praxis*, a values-based approach I introduced in my book *Design Realities: Creativity, Nature and the Human Spirit*, which respects and embraces traditional knowledge and practices that are culture- and location-specific and time-tested. It is defined as follows:

> *Progressive design praxis* is a form of design practice that aims to change the situation for the better by striving to interpret, understand and apply the ethical values and notions of virtue found in the philosophical and spiritual traditions of one's culture.[6]

The artifacts and activities I will discuss are very diverse, but each is representative of one or more of the elements shown in figure 12.2. Many of them are traditional solutions based on ideas that have stood the test of time and have evolved to achieve a finely tuned fit within their context of use. They are moderate and of low impact but are, nevertheless, effective. Such

PRACTICAL	SOCIAL	PERSONAL	ECONOMIC
effective	environmental	moderate enriching	affordable

traditional knowledge	advances continuity, stability, and culture of permanence	locally available materials
local practices and skills		natural materials
context-appropriate	minimal or no waste	clean, renewable resources
expressive of cultural identity	individual and/or shared use	low-impact making and use
particular to place	enduring use or meaning	skill building
holds practical, cultural, and/or spiritual meaning	local maintenance, repair, and upgrade	reuse, repurposing
relevant to individual and/or communal needs, activities, or beliefs	open-access design	environmentally responsible
	ad hoc and egalitarian design	practically, culturally, and/or environmentally restorative

Figure 12.2 *Pillars of Resilience for Artifacts and Activities*

well-honed designs have little need for innovation, originality, or novelty; indeed, instigating change can sometimes be counterproductive because it can disrupt ways that have achieved a harmonious and sustainable balance with the natural environment. Being of a modest nature and having been a part of human culture for so long, such artifacts can easily be taken for granted, and their quiet effectiveness and unobtrusive benefits can go unnoticed. Even so, we can learn much from them about accumulated wisdom, living less wastefully, and developing a more caring, conservational outlook.

The examples also raise issues about the relationship between design and humility and the merits of putting aside one's ego. An associated concern is the assumption that a creative idea is the product and indeed the property of a particular individual or enterprise. One consequence of this is that some artists and designers are raised up to the level of "star" status. The emergence of this individualistic notion of creativity and design goes hand in hand with the development of the modern sensibility, consumerism, and unsustainable expectations. It is also an understanding of creativity that is incompatible with more egalitarian approaches to design and their long-enduring contributions to the development of useful and beautiful material cultures. In contrast, traditional forms of creativity often involve numerous members of a community—past and present. The designs, products, and practices emerge from many minds and become refined and improved over time. They are considered productions and expressions of the community as a whole and tangible manifestations not just of cultural identity but also of a community's ethos and values.

Hence, if we are to advance less consumptive and more communal, resilient ways of living, we have to develop new understandings of creativity and design—understandings that will, necessarily, challenge many of our assumptions and design norms.

In addition to material productions, we also engage in a wide variety of activities and practices, and these, too, must be consistent with sustainability and resilience. Like artifacts, activities can be understood as resilient when they are able to be sustained over long periods by being continually adapted to suit changing conditions and needs. When particular activities have been present throughout human history, we can be sure they embody aspects that resonate at a deeper level and touch those things that are permanent within the human condition. These may be predominantly practical, sociocultural, or spiritual in nature, or they may span two or all three of these areas. Some are related to our basic physiological needs—the provision of food, warmth, shelter, and safety. They involve everyday tasks that require knowledge, skills, and expertise, much of which is acquired through practice and real-world application rather than from theory or speculation. These kinds of pragmatic activities deal with real-life situations, seek achievable results, and are conducted in ways that lead to useful outcomes.

Other activities concern human relationships, contributing to our sense of individual and collective identity and strengthening social bonds. Those that help build social relations may revolve around communal, recreational, or cultural events, festivals, fairs, and religious rituals. They all involve interactions with other people, and they benefit from attitudes that are genial, considerate, and welcoming, thereby allowing associations to flourish. Practices that are concerned more with individual identity may involve distinctive forms of aesthetic decoration, display of skills, or, if sexual attraction is the motivator, forms of dress and adornment that aim to enhance appearance.

Still other activities respond to intuitive apprehensions that concern life's bigger questions about why we are here and how we should live. These are related to people's sense of well-being and their inner or spiritual development. For some, this involves belief in an all-encompassing god; for others it may involve nontheistic notions of the numinous. Whatever the particular belief system, traditional teachings are united in the idea that inner growth depends on transcending one's own selfish or egocentric desires; recognizing a larger, more profound sense of reality; and developing a disposition of care toward others and the whole of creation.

In the chapters that follow, we will look at examples of artifacts and activities from all these categories in more detail.

13 RESILIENT HOME

Some regard home simply as the house where they currently reside, while others think of it as the place where they were born and raised. For still others, home is tied to their culture and its history and associations. Or it may be a combination of all these things. Thoreau summed it up well when he described home as "a place of warmth, or comfort, first of physical warmth, then the warmth of the affections."[1]

Whatever our understanding of home, we have to live somewhere, and the people and things we have around us and the society of which we are part, all influence how we live, our material expectations, and our behavioral norms. In this chapter, we will consider a variety of artifacts and practices related to the domestic environment, including common objects such as a chair, a table, a lamp, and ceramics; practices such as knitting and weaving; and the creation of practical ad hoc solutions. In one form or another, these have all been part of human culture for a very long time and their enduring usefulness and value are well established.

The particular examples considered here reflect principles that accord with the social and environmental concerns of sustainability. For the most part, they employ natural or reused materials, they are moderate in their conception and execution, and they are largely place-specific. These traits help foster diversity, regional forms of aesthetic expression, and relatively small-scale, distributed forms of enterprise and income generation, in line with the arguments presented in part I.

CHAIR

In the last century, the chair became something of an obsession and a rite of passage for designers. It seems to have begun with developments in mass production, which separated the design process from the making, but it is an interest that continues up to the present.

Why this fascination with the chair? Perhaps because it is seen as the quintessential object—it is created to fit the human body and combines function with aesthetic expression. Whatever the reason, designers love chairs—they even give them names, which isn't the case for many products—we don't talk of the Red and Blue bookshelf, the Barcelona hairdryer, or the Wassily chest of drawers.

It is an interest that now extends well beyond the design community. Furnishing a space with "designer" chairs becomes a statement of one's taste and design acumen. When this happens, however, their primary role shifts from one of utility to that of sign—that is, a sociopositional marker.

What tends to get lost in this is the simple wooden chair—unpretentious, basic, functional, exceptionally useful, and surprisingly uncommon, as the American artist George Brecht found out when he needed one for a work he called *A Chair with a History*: "I went out to buy a wooden chair in Nice—and that was quite a piece, because it turned out not so simple to get a simple wooden chair."[2]

Not so simple to get, but a must-have around the house. I have had one for years, I found it at a lawn sale when I was living in Canada. It was coated in a thick, glossy pink paint and was in a forlorn and much-neglected state. But I liked its shape as well as the serendipity that accompanies such finds, so I paid a dollar or two for it, and for a couple of years I used it in my makeshift workshop at one end of the garage. One warm summer's day, I spread newspapers out on the grass, stripped the glutinous pink gloss from it, and refinished it in water-based paints that were left over from an earlier project. Since then, and as we've relocated houses and countries, it's found a home variously as a kitchen chair, a bathroom chair, and a spare dining chair. It has also served as a bedside table and a step stool. Currently, it is the chair I use when having online meetings. It's become like a trusted and familiar friend—no airs and graces, just an easy, unaffected familiarity (figure 13.1).

Figure 13.1 *Chair*

a simple wooden chair bought at a lawn sale and refurbished

This simple wooden chair isn't part of the world of designer statements and look-at-me furniture. Nor is it part of the world of ornamental craftwork in which the pieces serve as vehicles for displaying the skills of the maker, often with little concern for moderation or uncomplicated utility.

Part of the appeal of the simple wooden chair is that it is free from disciplinary pigeonholing—design, craft, art, aesthetics, sustainability, resilience, economic viability, brand, and the like. Instead, all these things are present, integrated, and inseparable in a humble form that is anonymous, independent of both fashion and status, and consequently rather timeless.

The chair—a seat for one person with a rest for the back—is one of the oldest kinds of household furniture. The earliest evidence of its use comes from the civilizations of the eastern Mediterranean. Tomb paintings from the Fourth Dynasty of ancient Egypt, ca. 2649–2130 BCE, include chairs.[3] Even older evidence comes from the islands of the Cyclades in Greece, where a marble carving of a seated harpist dates from ca. 2800–2700 BCE. It depicts a basic side chair with four straight legs and a slightly sloping back, with tenon joints where the legs connect to the seat-rail.[4] In other words, it is an example of the simple wooden chair, not unlike the one I found at the lawn sale—unpretentious, useful, and surprisingly uncommon.

TABLE

In the Middle Ages, furniture was relatively scarce, so when wealthy landowners moved between residences, or when visitors came to stay, they would bring their furniture with them. Consequently, chairs, stools, tables, and beds were often designed to be folding or collapsible.[5] This helps explain the design of the trestle table, the oldest form of table in the Western world. It comprises a plain wooden board laid across two or more trestle frames or horses, which typically fold flat. It can be easily dismantled, not only for ease of transport but also for storage so that a room can be used for other purposes—a facility mentioned by Shakespeare:

Come, musicians, play.
A hall, a hall, give room! And foot it, girls.

Figure 13.2 *Hewn Trestle Table*
Studio Team, Sebastian Cox Ltd.
Greenwich, London
Photo: courtesy Sebastian Cox, with permission

More light, you knaves! and turn the tables up,
And quench the fire, the room is grown too hot.[6]

Early trestle tables were narrow because diners sat only on one side with their backs to the wall, allowing food and drink to be served from the front. Later, they became shorter and wider so people could sit facing each other.[7]

The trestle table is an excellent example of an enduring design that has been refined over the years to a point of essentiality. It is functionally effective, materials-efficient, and beautiful in its simple lines. It is also lightweight and can be easily dismantled. The example shown in figure 13.2 is by a contemporary designer-maker whose small furniture company adheres to sustainable principles. The wood is from sustainable sources in Britain, with the majority coming from within a hundred miles of the workshop. The top is ash, and the legs are hewn hazel, which are wedged into a solid ash cross brace. It is a design that is long-lasting and elegant and uses a minimum of entirely renewable materials.[8]

LAMP

Throughout the long history of human civilization, the most abiding form of artificial illumination has undoubtedly been the simple oil lamp. It was invented in prehistoric times, and, in various incarnations, it has been in continuous use ever since.

The ability to create a flame at will was discovered between one hundred thousand and fifty thousand years ago, after which simple lamps were devised to light dwelling places.[9] The earliest were made from shells or stones with cup-shaped depressions for animal fat or vegetable oil and a wick of dried moss, lichen, or juniper. Around 17,000 BCE, lamps like this allowed people to create beautiful wall paintings of animal life deep within the Lascaux caves in France.[10] In Denmark and northern Germany, pottery lamps that used blubber oil have been dated to ca. 5000 BCE.[11] And from ca. 1500 BCE, civilizations in the eastern Mediterranean were producing clay lamps that burned olive oil.[12]

As one might expect of an artifact of such antiquity, in addition to its utilitarian role, the oil lamp has acquired various symbolic meanings.

In Buddhism and Hinduism, it represents discipline, wisdom, and the contemplative life. In Western spirituality, it has similar connotations but is especially associated with the light of understanding, granted through divine grace.[13]

In the early modern period, as populations grew so did the demand for affordable lamp oil. In the eighteenth and first half of the nineteenth century, large quantities of fuel oil for domestic lighting were supplied by the American whale-oil industry. This industry, which peaked around the 1840s, devastated whale populations. They were only saved from extinction because inexpensive alternative fuels became available, including kerosene (or paraffin) and gas.[14]

A major development in lighting technology was the incandescent bulb. Englishman Joseph Swan produced the first viable electric bulb in early 1879. Later that year, a similar but more efficient version was demonstrated by the American Thomas Edison, who also developed electricity distribution. In the decades that followed, the incandescent bulb was lighting streets, public and commercial buildings, and homes. It became the standard form of domestic lighting in the twentieth century until, in the last few decades, alternatives began to compete with it. The 1980s saw the appearance of the "compact florescent lamp." Tungsten halogen lamps began to be widely used in the 1990s, and in recent years, low-energy, low-cost LED (light-emitting diode) lamps have become the preferred option.[15]

In many parts of the world, domestic lighting is now primarily based on electricity. Even so, over a billion people still rely on the simple clay oil lamp, especially in rural areas of Asia and Africa where electricity is either not available or too expensive.[16] Even where electric lighting is the norm, oil lamps are often chosen to illuminate a table or room because of their soft ambience. They are also a prominent feature of Diwali celebrations—the five-day Hindu festival of lights (figure 13.3).

In terms of resilience, the simple oil lamp outstrips all other contenders by many millennia. Gas lighting in the domestic setting was in use for a few decades but was quickly replaced by incandescent bulbs. These lasted a little over a century until more energy-efficient and affordable electric lamps became available. But in one form or another, the simple oil lamp has been in

Figure 13.3 *Oil Lamp*

a modern clay version for use in Diwali celebrations

continuous use for some seventy thousand years. As such, it is a preeminent example of a resilient design.

However, just because something has proved its resilience does not mean we should automatically accept it as the most desirable option. In this case, its longevity is due to the lack of viable, affordable alternatives. The oil lamp provides only a dim light, it can be expensive to use, and open flames in enclosed environments are hazardous. Nowadays, better options are available. While LED lamps have yet to prove their long-term resilience, they offer a brighter light and one that is clean, safe, and affordable. Furthermore, low-voltage LEDs can be combined with microgeneration systems, such as photovoltaics and advanced batteries, to create off-grid lighting. These developments have already brought electric lighting to tens of millions whose only previous option was fuel-based lighting, and elsewhere the widespread use of LEDs is reducing the burden on grid-based systems.[17] This combination of environmental and social factors is entirely compatible with sustainable principles and means that this technological development holds significant potential for the future.

POT

The earliest examples of pottery found in the Sultanate of Oman date from the third millennium BCE.[18] For many centuries, Bahlā has been the country's main pottery producer because of the presence of good-quality clays. Beautifully simple pots from the Bahlā kilns have been found by archaeologists at Late Islamic (sixteenth–twentieth century) sites throughout the Arabian Gulf and countries bordering the western Indian Ocean.[19]

When I visited Bahlā forty years ago, the pots were being made on very basic but highly effective foot-operated tournettes, or slow wheels (figure 13.4). Using this method—the origins of which date back to ca. 4500 BCE[20]—an experienced potter could make fifty jars in a day. They were fired in large dome-shaped mud-brick kilns fueled with brushwood and were large enough to accommodate dozens of pieces. Skills were handed down over the generations, and some potteries had been in the same family for centuries. The pots were used in cooking and as containers for water and foodstuffs.

Figure 13.4 *Highly skilled Bahlā Potter at Work*
Bahlā, Sultanate of Oman, 1983

There were also water cups, *laban* (yogurt) jars, *halwa* bowls, incense burners, and roof guttering. A common sight in the villages of the Jebel Akhdar mountains used to be a large, round-bottomed pot hanging in a window. These unglazed pots contained water, which would permeate through the porous ceramic to the outer surface, evaporate on the breeze, and cool the water inside. Containers for food were glazed on the inside using locally available minerals.[21]

Today, a government-established training and production center teaches the craft to young people while producing goods for the tourist market. These interventions are needed to help perpetuate this ancient tradition because mass-produced products are now available for everyday use and are far less expensive.[22] Pottery-making in Bahlā now employs modern electric-powered and gas-fueled kilns, where temperatures can be more accurately regulated and the quality of production can be raised.[23] Traditional potters, however, tend to use these modern kilns for test firings and experiments with glazes. The results are then put into production using the more labor-intensive, traditional kilns, which are more economical because of their higher capacity.[24]

The traditions of pottery-making in Bahlā are sustainable, socially responsible, and highly resilient. For centuries they have provided creative, skills-based employment; drawn on locally available materials for the kiln construction and the pottery-making; used renewable fuel woods; and made use of economical, manual techniques. The production supplied local needs as well as those of the wider region and offered plastic- and waste-free ways of storing, cooking, and serving food, as well as an ancient method for cooling water.

PLATE

The distinctive blue and white pottery known as delftware has been made in the Netherlands for over four hundred years. Its production began as a response to the popular but expensive Chinese blue and white tableware that was being brought to Europe by the British and Dutch East India Companies in the seventeenth century. The locally made products were more affordable and of similar appearance. Unlike the Chinese porcelain imports,

Figure 13.5 *New Delft Plate*
designed by Jacob de Baan
Royal Delft, the Netherlands

delftware was earthenware, but it looked so similar that it was marketed as Dutch or Delft "porcelain."' Today, it is described as tin-glazed earthenware and known as faience, after Faenza, in northern Italy, where this type of glazing originated, or simply as delftware.[25]

The traditional blue and white surface patterns include elaborate depictions of Chinese or Dutch scenes, ornamental flower arrangements, and geometric borders. The best-quality delftware is expensive because the process requires highly skilled craftspeople. Stencils are used to pick out the patterns on the biscuit-baked vessels; the designs are then carefully painted by hand—accuracy is paramount because the process is unforgiving, the liquid color being absorbed deep into the porous clay.

The traditional ornamental designs are not to everyone's taste, and their high cost makes them rather too expensive for everyday use. To better address modern needs, the Royal Delft pottery recently started producing its New Delft collection, created by Dutch designer Jacob de Baan.[26] These pieces have a contemporary aesthetic—the forms are simple and have a clean white minimalist appearance—but they also bear the marks of tradition and the company's long history. The pattern of a faint, stippled circle with dark blue markings is a faithful reproduction of the symbols found on traditional delftware but which normally go unseen. These are the makers' marks found on the underside of plates and vases, the stippled circle being indicative of the unglazed rim around the base. Instead of being hand-painted, these patterns are applied using a transfer process, which allows the pieces to remain affordable (figure 13.5). This contemporary design is strikingly modern but encompasses the traditions and long history of delftware. As such, it is a design that respects the heritage and legacy of pottery making in the Netherlands while also updating and transforming it into an attractive and—in the way it is produced—affordable product suited to the modern market.

BAG

Oak swill basket-making is a traditional craft of the South Lakes region of Cumbria in northwest England. The baskets are made from long narrow

Figure 13.6 *L'al Yak Bag*
small oak swill basket with leather lid and straps
Lorna Singleton, Cumbria

lathes of oak, woven over a loop, or "bool," of hazel, which forms the top rim of the finished basket.

The oak is locally grown in coppiced woodlands—a pruning technique in which the trees are cut back close to the ground, resulting in shrub-like growth that produces multiple straight stems rather than typical oak trees with large single trunks. These fast-growing stems are periodically cut, stripped of their bark, and softened by boiling overnight. They are then split or riven into thin flexible lathes. Prior to weaving, the lathes are dressed and soaked to make them more flexible. The waste bark is not discarded but is sent to a tannery in Devon, which uses it in the ancient craft of oak-bark tanning (see also chapter 3).

The traditional oak swill is a large utilitarian basket that at one time was used for collecting root crops; carrying laundry, logs, or animal feed; or even as a baby's cradle.[27] The more diminutive L'al Yak, or "Little Oak," bag shown in figure 13.6 is a modern adaptation for a contemporary market. It is the work of Lorna Singleton, one of the few oak swill basket-makers still practicing. Based on the traditional angler's creel, it is of a finer weave than the conventional utility basket and is finished with a lid and carrying straps of natural, oak-tanned leather. The result is a highly durable bag that is capable of aging well—both the oak swill and the leather will acquire patinas that change over time.[28]

The L'al Yak bag is an excellent example of how traditional crafts can remain relevant by adapting to new circumstances—indeed, if they fail to do so, they tend to disappear. We can be sure that any practice that has endured for so many years will have reinvented itself many times to meet the changing needs of successive generations.

HOMESPUN

Both a practice and a product, *homespun* refers to the making of yarn, cloth, and clothing within the home or community using locally available raw materials and relatively simple, inexpensive equipment. Materials will differ according to place and climate but typically include wool, flax, and cotton. Homespun, however, is more than this. It has an extraordinarily long history;

it is readily adaptable to changing needs; and it encapsulates ideas of independence, creativity, and skill building. In recent times, it has even been used as a political instrument and a national symbol. In a variety of ways, it embodies the environmental and social attributes of sustainability and the benefits of more equitably distributed production and wealth.

In the ancient Near East, evidence of cultivated plant fibers, especially flax, together with early forms of knitting and loom weaving, date back to the ninth millennium BCE.[29] In southern Mesopotamia during the late fifth and the fourth millennia BCE, new techniques were developed for producing woolen cloth, including spinning using a distaff and spindle whorl; weaving on a vertical, weighted loom; and felting. By the second half of the third millennium BCE, wool workshops in this region were producing fabrics and clothing in quantity.[30]

In early twentieth-century India, homespun, or khadi, came to represent the movement for independence from British imperial rule, and it remains an enduring symbol of Indian identity.[31] Mahatma Gandhi promoted the making and use of homespun within the Swadeshi movement, which emphasized Indigenous goods and using the resources of one's own locale as a path to self-reliance and socioeconomic justice. But by the 1920s, he had relaxed his insistence that only hand-produced goods should be included, suggesting that industrially produced cloth could also be part of the movement.[32] However, he also warned against industrial production becoming too large because this means raw materials have to be imported from elsewhere, production then exceeds regional needs and is geared to export, and profits become the main concern of the producers.[33]

For many years in the United Kingdom, domestically produced wool had little or no value and no market; in fact, sheep farmers had to pay to have fleeces safely disposed of. Recently, new businesses have arisen that focus on domestically produced wools and yarns, and now some farmers are being paid for their fleeces. New products have been developed including tweed bags; natural wool mattresses; and interior fabrics for curtains, cushions, and upholstered furniture.[34] There are also retail outlets specializing in domestic wools and even an annual wool festival, which attracts people from around the world.[35]

Figure 13.7 *Homespun*
loom-woven linen and hand-knitted Herdwick wool

Homespun is an exceptionally resilient applied art that still holds an important place in today's society (figure 13.7). It is characterized by affordability; the use of local, renewable resources; and technologies that are small-scale and relatively simple to make and maintain.

WASHING LINE

In its most rudimentary form, the washing line is simply a length of sturdy cord, each end of which is tied to a firm support. It is basic, effective, and affordable and offers a low-energy method for drying clothes that is pollution-free, noise-free, and long-lasting (figure 13.8). The washing line works just as well in a cool, windy climate as in a hot climate, and clothes dried this way tend to be fresh and largely free of creases.

Despite its numerous attributes and the ever-worsening climate crisis, the washing line has actually been made illegal in some parts of the United States. In Fairfax County, Virginia, hanging washing outside is regarded as unsightly, and having a permanent clothesline is a punishable offence. Fairfax County is not alone. Rules laid down by community associations and landlords prevent tens of millions of Americans from drying their clothes outside. Reasons include unsightliness, danger of strangulation, and a lowering of property values. However, good sense does seem to be prevailing. In the last few years, nineteen states have passed "right to dry" laws that override local bans, allowing people to choose this more environmentally responsible option.[36]

AD HOCISM

Ad hoc design employs any suitable materials that come to hand to improvise an effective solution. It is a creative activity characterized by spontaneity and expediency.

Ad hoc solutions have been part of human culture for a very long time. In fact, the oldest artifact in the British Museum is an example. Created nearly two million years ago, it is a stone chopping tool with a distinctive edge shaped by skillfully placed blows.[37]

Figure 13.8 *Washing Line*
Ventimiglia, Italy

Modern design has made frequent forays into ad hocism, often as antidotes to established, corporate design conventions. The results have been mixed. While the designs may have been successful in terms of their being lauded in design circles, their loyalty to true ad hocism is less convincing. The Italian design movement of the 1960s—variously called Radical Design, Anti-Design, or Counter-Design—attempted to challenge the dominant rationalistic approach to design and its role in promoting consumerism.[38] Today, however, many of the movement's productions seem as much a part of the problem of consumerism as anything they sought to displace.

In 1972, combining the two parts of the term, Charles Jencks and Nathan Silver published *Adhocism*, in which they set out a case for the use of improvisation in design. They recognized ad hocism for its qualities of speed and economy and its use of readily available materials to solve problems quickly and efficiently. In the book's 2013 edition, Jencks adds that it prospers like most hybrids on the edge of respectability. *Adhocism* is filled with examples, most of which have not been created by trained designers but have been observed within the built environment. They include makeshift protest signs; temporary solutions on building sites; improvised toys, musical instruments, and housing structures; and hacked-together engineering prototypes. However, like the productions of the Radical Design movement, the examples generated by designers tend to be too considered to be truly ad hoc. In the case of Jencks's own *Madonna of the Future*, a retail-store mannequin holds a copy of Henry Miller's novel of the same name, and an electric heater replaces the mannequin's head. Unlike true ad hocism, however, which is about utility, Jencks tells us that the purpose of this piece is to question stereotypes. His inclusion of Ron Arad's 1983 *Distressed Concrete Record Player and Speakers* is equally problematic. While it *is* utilitarian and challenges the pristine newness of mass production, it lacks the informal pragmatism of genuine ad hocism.[39]

In the 1990s, Droog Design in the Netherlands showcased a variety of seemingly ad hoc objects, including a bench made from a log with three cast-bronze seatbacks and a large chest made from a bundle of haphazardly strapped together secondhand drawers, each encased in its own purpose-built box. Such designs have a clever wit and lightness about them but, again, are too consciously *designed* to be true ad hoc. And contrary to the one-off nature of ad hocism, many of these designs have been put into production—they command high prices and are aimed at the more exclusive end of the market. As such, and like their earlier Italian counterparts, they tend to fit into and support the world of consumerism and fashion.[40]

Real ad hocism is an unplanned, practical response to a perceived need and yields functional solutions that are "good enough" in terms of their utility, as in figure 13.9. For trained designers, this level of rawness is difficult if not impossible to achieve—they cannot *unlearn* their training and experience. The very act of *consciously* trying to create ad hoc designs prevents them from being able to do so.

Examples of true ad hoc design, free of societal airs and expectations, can be commonly observed in the built environment. Jane Fulton Suri of the IDEO design studio does just this in her book of photographs *Thoughtless Acts? Observations on Intuitive Design.* She includes hundreds of examples, including informal constructions, such as a reflective bird-scarer for a vegetable garden made from old CDs strung together; a door propped open with a hammer; and sheet music held on its stand with clothes pegs.[41] More complex ad hoc constructions—often driven by poverty, hardship, scarcity, and need—have also been documented, some of which seem inherently unsafe. Artifacts from Cuba include stove lighters made from copper coils that spark when plugged into mains electricity, a razor created from a blade and a pencil, a range of lamps and cooking devices made from tin cans and jars, and a soft-drink dispenser from a plastic bucket fitted with a tap.[42] Similarly, Russian artifacts include a porch mat made from upturned beer-bottle tops nailed to a board, a TV antenna from bicycle wheels attached to a pole, and a snow shovel created from a breadboard and a length of metal pipe.[43] These kinds of artifacts may be ingenious, but too often they arise from impoverishment and a need to survive in woefully difficult conditions.

Perhaps the best example of ad hoc design comes from Australia. *The Saw Doctor's Wagon* was created by Harold Wright over a period of thirty-four years in an entirely ad hoc manner. It was fitted out with a vast array of grinding wheels, belts, and files to sharpen all kinds of household and farm tools (figure 13.10). It served as a traveling workshop but was also the Wright

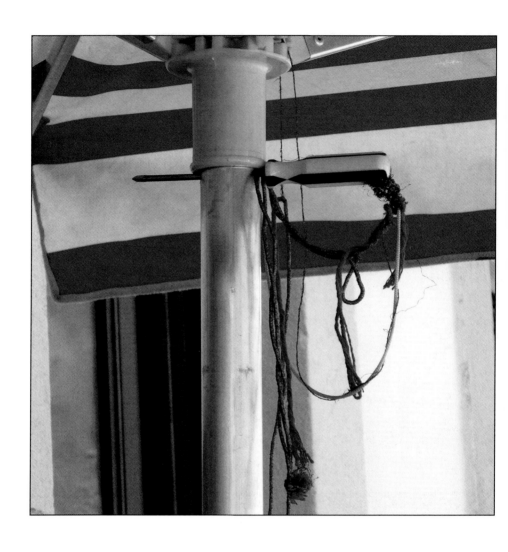

Figure 13.9 *Ad hoc Peg for Café Awning*
Turin, Italy

Figure 13.10 *Accrued Ad hoc Solutions–The Saw Doctor's Wagon* (detail)
created by Harold Wright between 1935 and 1969
National Museum of Australia, Canberra

family's home, accommodating two adults, a child, and three dogs; there was even a chicken coop. Originally horse-drawn, it was later enlarged and modified to be pulled by an agricultural tractor. In this ad hoc extravaganza, the Wrights roamed the farms, villages, and towns of northwest Victoria and New South Wales between 1935 and 1969.[44] Today, it is preserved in the National Museum of Australia.

One can appreciate ad hoc design when one comes across it and admire its unvarnished resourcefulness. But despite numerous attempts by designers over the years to engage in it, genuine ad hocism resists appropriation and remains defiantly free-spirited and true to its egalitarian roots. Such solutions have an immediacy and energy that are uninhibited by notions of good taste—characteristics that are critically important to creativity. As Picasso told us: "Ah, good taste! What a dreadful thing! Taste is the enemy of creativeness."[45]

With a history of some two million years, we can confidently say that ad hocism is humanity's most authentic and enduring example of resilient design.

Compared to the many technological innovations, appliances, and novelties found in modern homes, the examples we have looked at in this chapter are conceptually and technologically rather basic. Generally, they are also well made from good-quality materials and are long-lasting, culturally relevant, and environmentally responsible. They neither use nor come packaged in disposable plastics, and they create little in the way of adverse effects or waste. In their aesthetics and their use of local materials and production, they demonstrate that the attributes and qualities associated with resilience are actually not so difficult to achieve. Doing so today, however, raises particular challenges and requires a very different outlook and new priorities.

The need for fundamental changes across all spheres of modern life is both desirable for human well-being and urgent for planetary care. Given the impacts on people, their homes, and natural places, and the worrying increases in temperatures and environmental emergencies, to continue on our present course would be foolish in the extreme.

In tackling these issues at the individual level, our consumption habits matter. Contrary to the remorseless mantras of marketing, many of us living in the wealthier countries will have to consume far less in terms of products and services. And we will need to challenge our deeply embedded ideas of success—big houses, the latest model of car, second homes, and exotic holidays. Such ostentatious displays of prestige, which help drive unlimited consumption, need to be consigned to the past. New technologies, such as electric cars, wind- and solar-power generation, and greater efficiencies of appliances and other goods may help in the short term, but these kinds of solutions will not solve the problems we are facing. Indeed, in many ways they are contributing to them because their implementation demands further materials and energy resources for their manufacture and distribution. They also tend to couch us in a false sense of security.

In coming years, we will need to develop alternative ways of living that consume far less. This will mean smaller homes with less "stuff" and lower energy consumption, and those things we do have will need to be well made, durable, and repairable. Other important aspects of living well while consuming less will be cooperation, sharing, and community-based practices, some of which we will look at in the next chapter.

14 RESILIENT FOOD

The influential food writer Elizabeth David, who has been credited with introducing the provincial cuisines of France and Italy to Britain, once found a tattered old cookery book in a French market. She said of its contents: "The dishes described are not spectacular, rich or highly flavoured, the materials are modest ingredients you would expect to find in a country garden, a small farm, or in the market of a quiet provincial town. But it is not rustic or peasant cooking, the directions for the blending of different vegetables in a soup, the quantity of wine in a stew, or the seasoning of the source for a chicken reflect great care and regard for the harmony of the finished dish."[1] Modest, locally grown—these are the kinds of ingredients people have eaten for centuries. In this chapter, we will look at a variety of artifacts and activities that, in broad terms, are concerned with sustainable ways of acquiring ingredients for cooking—from community-based fruit and vegetable growing to traditional forms of fishing. The examples include environmentally responsible, socially equitable horticulture and water management; simple tools used in the harvesting and preparation of foods; and locally appropriate techniques that help protect and sustain fish stocks.

COMMUNITY AGRICULTURE

In modern times, food production has become industrialized and globalized. Alongside this, however, there has also been a significant increase in small-scale initiatives where people grow food in their own area for local

consumption. Ranging from individually run allotments to larger cooperatives and farmers' markets, this kind of civic agriculture offers an alternative
to industrially produced foods. It also helps build community while contributing to the local economy.[2]

Those who participate in these endeavors are often very aware of the
environmental effects of industrialized farming and are seeking to do things
differently—employing, for example, no-dig techniques to avoid disrupting
the soil, and on-site water collection and purification using natural bacteria.
Growing a diverse range of produce and using organic methods are becoming more common and, being local, food miles are drastically reduced, as is
the need for packaging and refrigerated shipping.

Arguments that we need the efficiencies of the intensive forms of agriculture provided by the big-agro conglomerates to feed the world simply do
not bear scrutiny. Acre for acre, small-scale, low-tech agriculture can be up
to ten times more productive than the monocultures produced by intensive
industrial farming techniques. Small-scale agriculture also produces greater
food diversity, with a large range of vitamins, nutrients, and minerals. And
unlike industrialized processes, which cause soil compaction, loss of organic
carbon, and low nitrogen levels, allotments and small urban farms produce
soil of a far higher quality.[3] Allotments and urban farms also host a greater
diversity of insect life than any other urban habitats, including domestic
gardens, city parks, and nature reserves. In addition, community agriculture provides opportunities for physical exercise that are productive;[4] and
time spent in nature is good for health and well-being.[5] Small-scale urban
farms also offer opportunities for children to learn, and, for small children
especially, their engagement in such natural environments can benefit their
immune systems.[6]

In the town where I live, an agricultural cooperative is run by volunteers
on a six-acre site that is held in trust for the community (figure 14.1). Fruit
and vegetables are grown using the latest methods in sustainable horticulture. Catchment ponds have been created and an irrigation system installed
to prevent flooding during periods of heavy rain. There is also a nature trail
for children. Any excess food is sold at local markets to help cover some of
the costs.[7] In another part of town, a community orchard has apple, pear,

Figure 14.1 *Claver Hill Community Farm*
Lancaster, United Kingdom

cherry, and plum trees and various kinds of nuts and berries. In the autumn, anyone can come along and pick the fruit directly from the trees.[8]

IRRIGATION BY FOOT

The notion of "irrigating by foot" may strike the reader as an odd turn of phrase. The word *irrigate* is thought to derive from the Latin *rigare*, meaning "to water" or "to wash," or possibly from *regere*, meaning "to direct" or "to lead," in the sense of leading water onto the fields. However, neither of these possible origins sheds light on the relationship of irrigation to the foot. "The land you are entering to take over is not like the land of Egypt, from which you have come, where you planted your seed and irrigated it by foot as in a vegetable garden."[9] Modern references that use the term cite examples from parts of the world where people operate some kind of foot pump to raise water from a river or pond to the fields—but the passage quoted above (written ca. seventh century BCE[10]) is referring to a much older practice that can still be found today in regions skirting the Mediterranean.

Irrigation is the process of supplying land with water via a series of channels.[11] This is aptly illustrated in figure 14.2, which shows shallow irrigation channels in an olive farm near Fontvieille in southern France. A similar system has been used in the Sierra Nevada of Spain since the Muslims introduced it in the ninth century CE. They built over 1,800 miles of channels, many of which are still in use, bringing water from high in the mountains down to the crops, grasslands, and forests at lower altitudes. The process makes good use of water resources because it slows down the hydrological cycle. It is being studied today to explore how it might be used to protect the region from the effects of climate change—an initiative that, it is hoped, will improve the resilience of the region's biodiversity.[12]

I first came across this system in the Middle East. It was being used in the villages along the Batinah coast, to the southeast of Dubai. Channels brought water from the mountains, and farmers were allocated a certain amount of time, measured out in *athars* (thirty-minute units), to water their parcels of land.[13] It was here I learned "irrigation by foot" meant that the foot—or more precisely the heel—was used to create small mud and stone

Figure 14.2 *Irrigation by Foot*
Olive Farm, Fontvieille, France

dams, just an inch or two high, to direct water along the shallow channels among the palm groves.

LOCAL PRODUCE

As a young boy, I would accompany my mother on Saturday mornings when she went into town to do the weekly shop. Starting at one end of the high street, we'd stop at the greengrocer; the butcher, with its hanging carcasses, massive chopping block, cleavers, and knives; and the baker, with all kinds of breads and cakes and warm, mouth-watering smells. But the most memorable was the fishmonger, whose storefront opened onto the street with whole fish lying in ice on a sloping slab, their beady eyes seeming to accuse. The owner wore a white coat with sleeves rolled up and black rubber boots. The stall was always wet and cold, with the floor covered in bits of bloody fish and constantly being hosed down. It was a hub of bawling busyness and buckets.

Most of the food was locally produced and available according to the season, and the shopping was full of life and color. I can still recall the banter and advice of the shopkeepers about what was just in and how best to prepare it—experiences made up of face-to-face exchanges, familiarity, and a sense of community and mutual trust. Nowadays, similar experiences can be had at farmers' markets. The produce changes over the course of the year, the food is fresh, and the shoppers are supporting local growers and small businesses (figure 14.3). Local food also has an authenticity that embodies both appreciation and moderation—the fruit and vegetables are not all of uniform size and shape; they come as nature intended. And eating local foods in season adds a sense of richness to the experience. By comparison, the supermarket may be more convenient but in other ways is a poor substitute.

Rediscovering local foods and preparing dishes from basic ingredients can be something of an epiphany. When I have been too long at the laptop, I go down to the kitchen, where I find the quiet, repetitive experience of chopping vegetables not just a relief from the screen but also meditative and curiously rewarding. In our small garden, we recently planted apple trees and fruit bushes, and grew potatoes, onions, and tomatoes in pots. A deer ate our only apple before it was ripe, but harvesting handfuls of blackcurrants

Figure 14.3 *Locally Grown Produce*
Northwest England

and blueberries was a small affirmation of our horticultural prowess. And if one doesn't have a garden, as we have seen, volunteer-run community-based alternatives are often available.

In the United States, similar rediscoveries are occurring. Chef Sean Sherman has been studying the traditional foods of his people, the Oglala Lakota. He recounts that when he was growing up in the 1970s, he hunted game birds and sometimes antelope and deer, dug for wild turnips, and gathered chokecherries. But he realized he had little knowledge of the foods of his culture, and this started him on a journey of discovery. Overturning clichéd notions about Native American food, he is reviving the traditional recipes and finding delight in using original ingredients.[14]

Local produce, Indigenous food, real food—these are not just better for us and the natural environment, they also reconnect us with the seasons, place, and our own culture. When we handle raw ingredients, we are handling the products of nature, and when we create and share meals made from these foods, we participate in the very essence of life itself.

SICKLE

The sickle is emblematic of the annual harvest and the cycle of planting and raising grain. It is a short-handled tool with a curved, serrated blade that is used for cutting and gathering barley, wheat, and other cereal crops.

Sickle blades from as early as ca. 18,000 BCE have been found near the Sea of Galilee and in Jordan;[15] and in the same region, there is evidence of sickles being used within settled agricultural communities from Neolithic times, ca. 10000–4500 BCE.[16] The use of this implement is indicative of the transition from nomadic, hunter-gatherer lifestyles to settled, agrarian society and the development of human civilization. The French philosopher Simone de Beauvoir writes of this transition: "Man learns his power. . . . This world of tools could be embraced within clear concepts: rational thought, logic, and mathematics could now appear. The whole concept of the universe is overthrown. The religion of woman was bound to the reign of agriculture, the reign of irreducible duration, of contingency, of chance, of waiting, of mystery; the reign of *Homo faber* is the reign of time manageable as space, of necessary consequences, of the project, of action, of reason."[17] The ancient origins and important function of the sickle mean that it has long featured in belief systems and stories. In Greco-Roman mythology, it is the symbol of Ceres (Demeter), the goddess of agriculture and fertility, and was one of the tools dedicated to the gods at the completion of the harvest.[18] In the allegory of Cupid and Psyche, as Psyche searches for her husband, she enters a mountaintop temple and sees "heaps of corn, some in loose ears and some in sheaves, with mingled ears of barley. Scattered about lay sickles and rakes, and all the instruments of the harvest, without order, as if thrown carelessly out of the weary reapers' hands in the sultry hours of the day."[19] The sickle is also the symbol of Cronos (Saturn), the god of agriculture, who, from ancient times, has been conflated with Chronos, the personification of time. Consequently, the sickle has been associated with temporal progress, death, hope of renewal, and rebirth. Harvest and death become symbolically linked—as the sickle is swung, the ripened grain is condemned to death, thence being used for either food or seed-corn.

The sickle is also frequently mentioned in the Bible; and in Celtic Druid ritual, a golden sickle is used to harvest the mistletoe, a symbol of immortality.[20] "The mistletoe, however, is but rarely found upon the robur [oak]; and when found, is gathered with rites replete with religious awe. . . . Clad in a white robe the priest ascends the tree, and cuts the mistletoe with a golden sickle, which is received by others in a white cloak."[21] From the early 1920s until its dissolution in 1991, the hammer-and-sickle insignia was adopted as the symbol of the Communist regime of the USSR. The hammer stood for industrial workers, the sickle for rural peasants, and together they symbolized physical labor and proletariat solidarity.

In the lands surrounding the Mediterranean, the sickle remained an essential farm implement and the dominant tool for reaping cereal crops until the late nineteenth century.[22] Being readily available, eminently affordable, and easy to master, it is still used in many parts of the world—for harvesting wheat in the Indian subcontinent, Africa, and South America; and for harvesting rice in many parts of Asia.

The earliest sickles were made from wood with inset flints to create the cutting edge, but for thousands of years, they have been made from

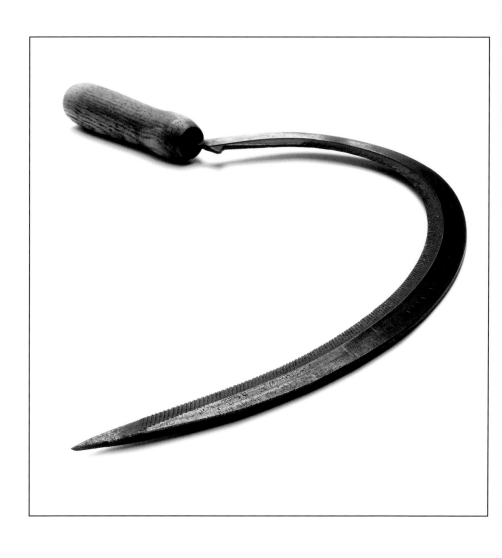

Figure 14.4 *Sickle*

its appearance in human history is indicative of the transition to agrarian society

bronze, iron, or steel using hand-forging techniques. The modern sickle is not much changed from its ancient predecessors—its serrated blade is manufactured from hardened steel and fitted with a turned hardwood handle (figure 14.4).

MORTAR AND PESTLE

The two-part mortar and pestle is a simple tool used for grinding seeds, spices, and herbs for cooking. It is also used in the preparation of medicines and for making powders for cosmetics and fine-art paints. The mortar is a receptacle made from a hard material such as stone, ceramic, or a hardwood. It has a cup-shaped cavity, which holds the substances to be crushed. The pestle, which does the pulverizing, is a club-like implement of a similarly hard material.

These are among the oldest tools known to archaeologists. Late Stone Age sites reveal that thirty thousand years ago, bowl-shaped grinding stones were used to extract starch from wild cereal grains and to prepare ocher, possibly for use in ritual or for decorative purposes.[23] A similar tool is the saddle quern, which has a relatively large, flat "bed" stone with a smaller round stone used to do the grinding. The mortar and pestle is mentioned in the book of Proverbs, which is among the oldest collections of Hebrew wisdom writings, compiled ca. 700 BCE: "Though you grind a fool in a mortar, grinding him like grain with a pestle, you will not remove his folly from him."[24] Like other artifacts that have a long history, the mortar and pestle is regularly featured in folklore. In a number of cultures, symbolism related to the obvious sexual connotations of the two parts can be traced to early times, where the grinding of grain serves as a metaphor for sexual intercourse: "If my heart has been enticed by a woman, or if I have lurked at my neighbour's door, then may my wife grind another man's grain."[25] In the traditional tales of Russia, Ukraine, and Belarus, Baba Yaga is a recurring character. She lives deep in the forest, which she protects as a Mother Earth figure. She is regarded as both a dangerous witch and a maternal benefactress;[26] and when she leaves the forest, she travels in a mortar and uses a pestle to steer: "Soon a dreadful noise came from the forest. The Tree

Cracked, the dry leaves rustled. Baba Yaga rode out of the forest; she was riding in a mortar, driving with a pestle, sweeping her tracks away with a broom."[27] Symbolically, the female-gendered mortar and male-gendered pestle represent Baba Yaga's all-embracing nature, not unlike the yinyang of Chinese tradition. The combination of traits represented by this common kitchen tool make her, like the Indian goddess Kali, an awesome figure who is able to mediate the boundary of death, allowing human beings to return "reborn" with newfound wisdom.[28]

In North America, traditional uses of this tool are documented in nineteenth-century reports for the Bureau of American Ethnology.[29] The following excerpt, about the Omaha people of Nebraska, precisely describes its use and materials: "The lower end [of the mortar] was sharpened to a point, which was thrust into the ground when needed for use. After putting corn in a mortar of this description, the woman grasped the wooden pestle in the middle, with the larger end upward; the smaller end, which was about an inch in diameter, was put into the mortar. The operation of pounding corn among the Omaha was called 'he.' The mortar (uhe) and pestle (wehe) were both made commonly of elm, although sometimes they were fashioned of white oak."[30]

In the United Kingdom, thick-walled ceramic versions of the mortar and pestle have been manufactured since the eighteenth century in Stoke-on-Trent, the center of British pottery production. In 1779, the firm of Wedgwood & Bentley introduced mortars made from a hard, vitreous (i.e., silica-based) stoneware that was impervious and resistant to wear, along with pestles of the same material that were fitted with wooden handles.[31] They were advertised as being, "For the Purpose of Chemical Experiments, the Uses of Apothecaries, and the Kitchen."[32] Similar versions are still in in production. Figure 14.5 shows a natural-stone mortar and pestle, a saddle quern, and a modern, stoneware mortar and pestle made in Stoke-on-Trent.

The sheer length of time the mortar and pestle has been in use, across highly diverse societies, demonstrates its enduring usefulness and resilience as a basic but essential tool. Its accumulated symbolic meanings also endow it with cultural and even spiritual significance.

Figure 14.5 *Mortar and Pestle*

mortar and pestle and saddle quern of natural stones, and a modern stoneware mortar with beechwood-handled pestle

KNIFE

The eighteenth and nineteenth centuries saw major technological and social changes and the emergence of industrialized society. Before this, and in some sectors long after, British manufacturing consisted of a multitude of small, family-operated enterprises that were essentially craft-based. Knowledge and skills were passed down from one generation to the next. Through marriage and community networks, these firms were capable of producing a wide array of high-quality goods that were distinctively and proudly products of place. For the manufacture of knives, cutlery, and bladed products of all kinds, this place was Sheffield, which over the centuries was home to thousands of small producers—self-employed master crafters known locally as little mesters.[33]

The first known reference to a knife maker residing in Sheffield appears in the city's tax records of 1297, which mention the name Robertus le Coteler, or Robert the Cutler. In 1340, a Sheffield knife was listed among King Edward III's possessions.[34] And in "The Reeve's Tale," written around 1400, Geoffrey Chaucer mentions, "A Sheffeld thwitel,"[35] a "thwitel," or whittle, being a short dagger.

Sheffield became a center for knife-making for many of the same reasons that led to Tintern being a center for wire-making, as discussed in chapter 3. The necessary raw materials of iron ore, coal, and timber for charcoal were locally available, and an abundance of water power was provided by the rivers Loxley, Rivelin, Porter, Sheaf, and Don. In addition, the local sandstone was suitable for making the grinding wheels needed for blade sharpening.[36]

> This town of Sheffield is very populous and large, the streets narrow, and the houses dark and black, occasioned by the continued smoke of the forges, which are always at work: Here they make all sorts of cutlery-ware, but especially that of edged-tools, knives, razors, axes, &c. and nails; and here the only mill of the sort, which was in use in England for some time was set up, (viz.) for turning their grindstones, though now 'tis grown more common.[37]

Most of the enterprises were located within the same square mile of the city; they were usually family run and had fewer than six people.[38] This concentration of interconnected knowledge, skills, suppliers, and outlets produced a robust local economy that benefited from a combination of cooperation, competition, regional identity, and international reputation. Division of labor was common, and the different families developed their own particular specialisms. Some produced horticultural knives; others made pocketknives, razors, palette knives, scissors, or surgical blades. Still others specialized in handles, engraving, or silver-plating—and, within these specialisms, tasks might be further divided—one person honing the blades, another polishing, and so on. And as is also the case today with the resurgence of working from home, the boundary between work life and home life was often blurred.[39]

This bustling milieu of interrelated activities forged not just steel but also a community spirit that was energized by strong social networks. It was an environment that helped spur innovation in processes and products, as well as the pursuit of excellence. The highly adaptable nature of the activities also meant that products were customizable, which allowed firms to be agile and responsive to people's needs. An important ingredient of this was good design, which transcended mere style and visual choice. Through incremental development and improvement over time, products attained an aesthetic refinement that simultaneously implied functional effectiveness, ergonomic comfort, and tradition.[40]

Products were exported all over the world, but particularly to America, and some were developed specifically for that market. For instance, the famous hunting and fighting knife named after the nineteenth-century frontiersman Jim Bowie, was mass produced in Sheffield.[41]

During World War II, production was diverted to support the war effort, after which knife-making once again flourished. In the 1950s, this manufacturing sector employed around fifteen thousand people. But by the last decade of the twentieth century, the number had dwindled to around one thousand employees among a dozen or so firms. Nevertheless, some seven hundred years after Robertus le Coteler, knives are still being made in Sheffield, and manufacturing is still carried out by small, family-run firms. They continue to produce a wide range of knives, including such distinct items as the Pusser's Dirk, also known as a Bos'n's Mate or Rigger's Knife, reflecting Britain's maritime history (figure 14.6).[42] In the mid-twentieth

Figure 14.6 *Pusser's Dirk*

Navy clasp knife made in Sheffield

century, this type of knife was standard issue in the Royal Navy. It has a sturdy folding blade, a marlinspike for splicing rope, and a loop for attaching it to a lanyard.[43]

HALIBUT HOOK

The halibut hook used by First Nations peoples of the Pacific Northwest exemplifies how an object—even a lowly fishing hook—can express much about traditional, holistic worldviews. This singular artifact combines functionality, carving skills, artistic expression, mythology, spirituality, ritual, cultural heritage, traditional ecological knowledge, sustainability, and evolving traditions (figure 14.7).[44]

Hooks are often about the length of a forearm, their specific dimensions being tailored to the size of the fish being sought. During the making process, the parts and angles are measured using the hands and fingers. Generally, hooks are sized to catch smaller male fish of about 20 to 100 pounds; these are tastier and more tender as well as easier and safer to handle in a small open boat than the larger females are, which can grow to well over 400 pounds. Targeting only males also helps sustain the stocks.[45]

The upper arm of the hook is usually made of yellow cedar, which is light and buoyant, while the lower arm is a heavier, denser wood like Pacific yew. The two are bound tightly together with twine of braided bull kelp, spruce root, or cedar bark.[46] The carvings generally feature the raven, otter, bear or other creatures that traverse land and air or land and water, and are believed to possess supernatural powers—controlling the weather or curing disease. Such carvings are shamanic references to the liminal space between the physical and spiritual worlds.[47] The barb inserted into the upper arm would once have been fashioned from the femur bone of a bear, but today a sharpened nail is more common. Prior to use, the hook is baited with octopus or herring. A cord from the lower arm is attached to a weight, which is lowered into the water from a boat while ritually "talking down the line" with a personalized prayer. A leader line, attached to the weight with a slipknot, runs to a surface float. The halibut feeds by sucking its

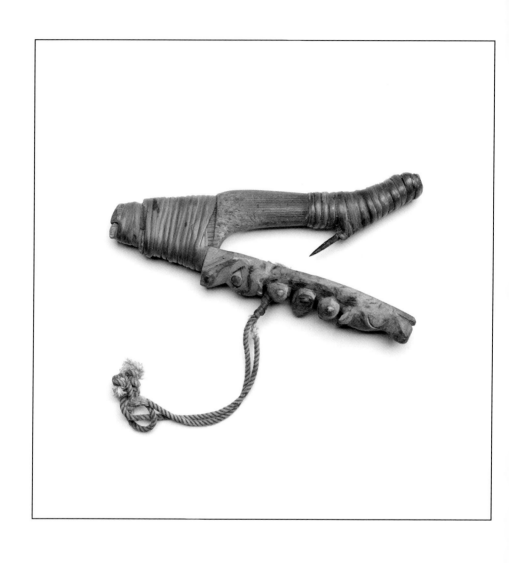

Figure 14.7 Halibut Hook
Kodiak Islands, Alaska (?), Cat. E200831
Department of Anthropology, Smithsonian Institution
Photo: courtesy Smithsonian Institution, with permission

prey whole into its mouth, so when the hook is found to be undesirable, it spits it out and, in that action, the barb takes hold. As the halibut struggles, the slipknot releases and pulls at the float, signaling that a fish has been hooked.[48]

As is so often the case, the availability of inexpensive, mass-produced alternatives has seen a decline in the use of these traditional hooks. However, they are still being made to teach young people about their heritage. Larger, more decorative versions are also being produced as art objects, as symbols of Pacific Northwest First Nations culture.[49]

FISHING HUTS WITH LIFT NETS

Traditional fishing huts with lift nets are a common sight along the estuaries and tidal rivers of the Marais in the Vendée region of France (figure 14.8). Dating from the nineteenth century, these diminutive structures are built on piles that are high enough to protect them from spring tides and sturdy enough to withstand storms blowing in from the Atlantic. They are constructed from wood, have corrugated metal roofs, and are connected to the land by a small footbridge, or *passerelle*. Typically, they are painted, or the treated timbers are allowed to fade to a natural patina.

Their large, square nets, or *carrelets*, are attached to a frame of acacia wood or metal. As their size makes them too unwieldy to be operated by hand, they are suspended from a simple crane—a pivoting mast fitted with a ratchet winch. The net is baited and lowered into the shallow waters. It is periodically raised with the hope of catching sole, mullet, eels, crabs, or prawns.

Today, these fishing huts cannot be owned by individuals but are rented from the state for a small annual fee. At one time they were regarded as something of an eyesore but are now cherished as an important part of France's heritage.[50] They are a creative response to very particular environmental conditions and are a highly distinctive feature of this region. They also represent a small-scale, locally appropriate, and entirely sustainable form of fishing.

Figure 14.8 *Fishing Huts with Lift Nets*
Marais, Vendée, France

JETTY

The small jetty shown in figure 14.9 is a contemporary example of an ad hoc artifact from the west coast of Turkey. Crudely assembled from odds and ends of timber, the result is a rough, entirely crooked, but locally made and reasonably serviceable tie-up for a small boat, and its worn and weather-beaten appearance testifies to its years of use.

For reasons not entirely clear to me, I have long been drawn to these kinds of material culture, which are unaffected by artifice and untouched by the mannerisms of urbane society and "designerly" ways. Perhaps it is a predisposition that was ingrained during a childhood in the industrial valleys of Wales, where privation meant a landscape peppered with sheds, lean-tos, pigeon coops, and gates—all cobbled together with whatever materials might be found or scrounged. A dilapidated goods wagon from the railways in the corner of a bleak moorland field was a familiar sight, repurposed as a makeshift shelter for a lonely Welsh pony. Fences encircling the fields would often be fashioned from a hodgepodge of corrugated sheets, wire netting, rusting angle-iron posts, and perhaps an old door or two.

Such artifacts can undoubtedly be ugly, but it is an ugliness borne out of necessity, purposefulness, and frugality. It is an ad hoc pragmatism innocent of artistry but also of affectation. Instead, it speaks of expediency and economy, and, compared to the extravagance and waste that are so commonplace today, a basic sense of prudence.

By definition, it is difficult to design in this way—for when we consciously bring design sensibilities to bear, spontaneity and extemporaneity tend to disappear. I have tried, but just as Ben Nicholson found when he attempted to paint more naively, in the mode of Alfred Wallace, it cannot really be done. Once we have learned too much, as it were, it is difficult if not impossible to refind such forthrightness. Nevertheless, this simple, crudely made jetty holds lessons for us in terms of sufficiency and humility.

Figure 14.9 *Jetty*
ad hoc construction from reused wood
Izmir, Turkey

BOAT SHED

There was a black barge, or some other kind of superannuated boat, not far off, high and dry on the ground, with an iron funnel sticking out of it for a chimney and smoking very cozily;

. . . If it had been Aladdin's palace, roc's egg and all, I suppose I could not have been more charmed with the romantic idea of living in it . . . It was a real boat which had no doubt been upon the water hundreds of times, and which had never been intended to be lived in, on dry land. That was the captivation of it to me. If it had ever been meant to be lived in, I might have thought it small, or inconvenient, or lonely; but never having been designed for any such use, it became a perfect abode.[51]

Until recent times, each year from October or November drift boats would slowly make their way down the east coast of Britain, from Scottish harbors to Great Yarmouth on the Norfolk coast. The fishermen who crewed them were following the herring shoals as they moved south. They would regularly call into the ports along the way to unload their catches. Traveling down by train, teams of "Herring Girls" would follow the boats to meet them at the quay, where they would gut and sort the fish by size and condition and pack them into baskets or barrels of salt, ready to be shipped. The guts were not wasted but were sold as fertilizer.[52] At one time, there were as many as thirty thousand herring boats working out of east-coast ports, and, at the industry's peak in 1907, some 2,500,000 barrels of herring were cured and exported to Germany, Eastern Europe, and Russia. After World War II, the herring industry, and the ways of life and traditions it supported, fell into steep decline.[53]

Lindisfarne, just off the Northumbrian coast, is most renowned for the *Lindisfarne Gospels,* created at its monastery in the eighth century. Visitors to the island can see the ruins of the old abbey and explore the castle, but they are also enchanted by several sheds sitting just behind the beach (figure 14.10). They are made from old, upturned herring boats. Once a common sight all down the east coast, these sheds are beautiful examples of reuse. They are cared for today by the National Trust.[54]

These long-used practices, tools, and other artifacts involved in the growing and harvesting of food reveal a number of important benefits and

Figure 14.10 *Boat Shed*
Lindisfarne (Holy Island)

characteristics. Localized growing and distribution not only reduce food miles, packaging, and waste, they also help build community and a sense of common purpose. Skills and methods are learned and expertise developed within a natural environment that is good for physical and mental health. We have also seen that many of the tools and techniques employed for harvesting and processing foods have acquired meanings and significance far beyond their basic utilitarian functions. These include historical and cultural associations and, in some cases, symbolic, mythological, or spiritual connotations. Developing a tradition of locally based cooking depends on the production and availability of local ingredients, which requires local farmers, small-scale fishing, dairy producers, butchers, market gardeners and fruit growers; without these, regional cooking will fall into the realm of folklore.[55]

In a variety of ways, these local approaches to food acquisition epitomize sustainability and resilience—they are distributed, adaptable, environmentally responsible, socially inclusive, and personally fulfilling, and they contribute to culture and to the local economy, understood as the effective management of resources rather than in purely financial terms.

15 RESILIENT CULTURE

While societies may have many things in common, their cultural practices often differ widely. These practices—expressed through traditions, customs, beliefs, and communal activities—contribute to our sense of identity and help define who we are and how we grow and develop as distinct peoples. This egalitarian understanding is one way of interpreting the notion of culture. Another interpretation, which is context-related but socially divisive, associates culture with cultivated society, where some people are seen as more cultivated than others. These two understandings are, of course, interrelated. In addition, some aspects of culture will be inherited through assimilation while others will be consciously learned, and both help forge our self-identity and inform our choices and pursuits, including what we do in our leisure time.[1]

The cultural practices discussed here span the performing arts, including music, song, dance, and theater, as well as the text-based arts of writing, correspondence, and story. We will also look at forms of adornment, which can have a variety of purposes and meanings. And finally, we consider walking in the countryside, which has long been not just a form of travel but also a peaceful, restorative, and sometimes contemplative leisure pursuit.

These practices transcend mere utility. They offer opportunities to ponder and express higher purpose and to consider life's meaning. Even a simple letter can be an opportunity to convey thoughts and ideas that may be difficult to say in any other way. And some of the world's most beautiful poetry and prose have resulted from slow, thoughtful walks in natural places. All these activities invoke the imagination and are quite different in intention and purpose from the practical activities considered in the previous two chapters.

MUSIC

Music making and musical instruments have been part of human civilization for thousands of years, featuring in religious rituals, cultural events, festivals, and entertainment. The earliest-known wind instruments are bone flutes from southern Germany, estimated to be some forty thousand years old.[2] The oldest surviving stringed instruments are two lyres found at Ur in Iraq, from ca. 2,600 BCE.[3] Also from this region come the first representations of musical notation, on cuneiform tablets.[4] These various examples demonstrate the enduring place of music in human culture.

Today, musical forms range from what has been termed "cultivated" music, which may be perceived as rather highbrow or esoteric, to more accessible vernacular forms, including folk music and contemporary popular music in which rhythm often eclipses melody and harmony. Such categorizations, however, are fluid, and there are many overlaps. Vaughan Williams held that "music has always spread from below upwards, the spontaneous song of the people comes first."[5] Williams, like French composer Joseph Canteloube, collected and drew on folk songs in his work—an approach that for much of the twentieth century was disregarded or even scoffed at, but today is greatly admired.[6]

Williams's recognition of the value and beauty of vernacular forms of creative expression was both egalitarian and entirely commensurate with notions of resilience and sustainability. These traits extend beyond the music itself to the instruments on which it is played. For example, the lute has its origins in Egypt, where it was primarily played by women. Over time, it was adopted in other regions of Africa and, in the process, was transformed into a larger instrument known as a *gunbrī*. Writing in 1928, H. G. Farmer called this instrument the acknowledged leader among the folk instruments of North Africa—an instrument of the people that was played by all and

Figure 15.1 *Traditional Vernacular Instruments*

from left to right: *gunībrī*, Morocco; *bansuri*, India; *ney*, Turkey; *kaval*, Turkey; *shakuhachi*, Japan

sundry right across the continent, from the beggar to the merchant and the fakir.[7] After their conquest of Morocco in the late seventh century, the Arabs developed the *gunbrī* into the more diminutive *gunībrī* (figure 15.1), which is still played by the Berbers of the Atlas Mountains.[8] This three-stringed lute has a hollow, poplar-wood body and a stretched animal hide soundboard.[9]

Wind instruments, due to their reliance on the human breath, have long been associated with spirituality. The Indian *bansuri*, a transverse flute made from a single length of bamboo, was played by Krishna and is associated with benevolence and divine love. The Turkish *ney*, an end-blown reed flute, has strong associations with Sufism. The first book of the *Masnavi* (*The Spiritual Verses*), by the Persian mystic Rumi, begins with the song of the reed flute—a metaphor for humanity's separation from God:[10]

> Listen to this reed as it is grieving;
> it tells the story of our separations.
> Since I was severed from the bed of reeds,
> in my cry men and women have lamented.[11]

The other Turkish instrument shown in figure 15.1 is the *kaval*, a shepherd's flute that is steeped in mythology. One story, from neighboring Bulgaria, tells of a young shepherd who was playing the *kaval* for his flock. The music attracted the attention of the Samodivi, the nymphs of the woods, mountains, and streams. One night he played at midnight, not realizing that, by playing at this hour, he would have to go with them forever. From then on, the place was known as Samodivi Hill.[12]

The Japanese *shakuhachi* spans a range of musical genres but also has spiritual associations. This heavy-walled, end-blown flute is made from the root end of the bamboo plant and has a bone insert that forms the blowing edge, or *utaguchi*. It is played as a form of meditative practice. Compositions known as *honkyoku*, or "original pieces," include spiritual compositions that suggest emptiness, an important concept in Zen Buddhism.[13]

All these instruments surpass simplistic, one-dimensional interpretations. They are complex, polysemous objects that, in their wide array of meanings, bring richness and depth to human culture.

DANCE

Dance has been a feature of human societies for millennia. The earliest evidence comes from India, where rock paintings at Mirzapur and Bhimbetka date to 20000–5000 BCE. Archaeological remains from Mohenjo-Daro and Harappa in Pakistan include bronze figurines, images, and seals that all bear witness to the significance of dance in ritual performance.[14]

Dance is an immersive activity that involves bodily movement, aesthetic expression, sensitivity, and feeling. It can be a form of entertainment, and it may be a part of cultural or religious ceremonies. In Sufism, the mystical branch of Islam, the hypnotic, whirling dance of the dervishes is a form of spiritual offering.[15] With one hand pointing to heaven and the other to earth, the dancers spin continuously, with their wide, circular skirts flaring outward (figure 15.2).

In many cultures, war dances preceded battles or celebrated victories. A stylized form of war dance is still performed by New Zealand's All Blacks rugby team at the start of a match. Based in Māori culture, the haka is a display of pride, strength, and unity, it is also motivational and intended to entertain the crowd while simultaneously intimidating and challenging the opposition.[16]

Dance may be described as traditional or contemporary, folk or professional, local or international, and it may be aesthetic or purposeful, patriarchal or feminist. But none of these classifications are very helpful because dance is never fixed and consequently it tends to defy categorization. Some forms of dance may possess specific cultural features and highlight distinctive traditions that embody aspects of regional, national, or ethnic identity, but these are in constant flux as they respond to changing circumstances and sensibilities.[17]

More clearly than most other art forms—and because of its essential "in the moment" ephemerality—dance tells us something important about the nature of tradition. It is capable of constantly responding, adapting, and evolving into something fresh and vital that is able to be a part of and contribute to the culture in which it exists. Consequently, it is inherently resilient. Here, however, change and innovation are not for their own

Figure 15.2 *Sufi dervishes*
Turkey

sake, nor is the past simply jettisoned in favor of the new. Rather, history and heritage are brought into and combined with the present to create something that speaks to people in ways that may contrast with, comment on, or be inspired by their contemporary circumstances. This process of bringing the past into the present and making it active and always new is true of, but perhaps less apparent in, all traditions—indeed, this is the very nature of the accumulated forms of knowledge and practice that constitute tradition.

Dance tells us something important about how to live. Seneca taught that "postponement is the greatest waste of life" because it deprives us of each day as it happens, it snatches the present from us by promising us something in the future. "The greatest hindrance to living is expectancy," he says and so urges us to live straightaway, now, in this present moment.[18] Unlike the products of design, architecture, painting and sculpture, which exist in space, or music and poetry, which exist in time, dance lives in both space and time. As Sachs points out, "The creator and the thing created, the artist and the work are still one and the same thing."[19] The combination of space, time, emotion, and choreographed movement—all concentrated into the very moment and act of performance—gives dance its intense sense of vitality. And in doing so, it touches the earth lightly. This imaginative, expressive, and sensitive discipline creates beauty and joy for their own sake while consuming nothing and leaving no trace.

THEATER

Theater is an art form that tells us stories about ourselves and attempts to make sense of our lives, and it does so in ways that change with the times and with evolving technical capabilities.

The origins of theater, like so many other artifacts and practices discussed in these pages, lie in ancient Greece. The first dramas were religious—where processions in costumes and masks were accompanied by the singing of hymns dedicated to Dionysus, the god of wine, fertility, and divine ecstasy. As early as the sixth century BCE, festivals and competitions featured music, singing, dance, and poetry, but the first person to recite poetry "in character" was Thespis in ca. 535 BCE. Regarded as the world's first actor, he gives us the term *thespian.* [20]

Greek theater was of two main types—*comedy*, which satirized those in power, mocking them for their foolishness and vanity; and *tragedy*, which told stories of love, loss, and pride and dealt with the relationships between people and the gods. Aristotle suggested that tragedy was capable of cleansing the heart by purging us of our concerns and worries and allowing us to realize that there can be nobility in suffering. He described it as "an imitation of an action that is serious, complete, and of a certain magnitude; in language embellished with each kind of artistic ornament, the several kinds being found in separate parts of the play; in the form of action, not of narrative; through pity and fear effecting the proper purgation of these emotions."[21] The oldest surviving play is *The Persians* by Aeschylus, first performed in 472 BCE. With writers like Aeschylus, Sophocles, and Euripides, the fifth century BCE is regarded as the golden age for Greek theater.[22] Many of these ancient dramas, such as *Oedipus Rex* and *Antigone*, both tragedies by Sophocles, are still read and performed today, which reveals much about the timelessness of their themes.

Comic plays appeared a little later, the major author being Aristophanes, ca. 446–386, who specialized in what today we would call political satire. His *Lysistrata* is an antiwar comedy that tells of one woman's mission to bring the Peloponnesian War to an end by convincing the women of Greece to abstain from sleeping with their husbands until they had negotiated peace.[23]

The influence of Greek culture also led to drama being embraced by Rome. Titus Maccius Plautus, ca. 254–184 BCE was among the first writers of literary Latin. His name is associated with 130 comedic plays, and his writings influenced many later playwrights, including Shakespeare and Molière.[24]

In Britain, theater evolved some 1,500 years after the first Greek dramas, but also had its origins in religion. It developed out of church services, which, in the mid-fourteenth century became cycles of *mystery plays*, based on biblical stories, and *miracle plays*, about the lives of the saints. Players traveled the country performing on "pageant wagons." The plays were hugely popular because, instead of being in ecclesiastical Latin, they were in the everyday language of ordinary people.

Figure 15.3 *Lancaster Grand Theatre*
Lancaster, United Kingdom

After the religious Reformation of the sixteenth century, theater became more secular, not least because the authorities prohibited religious dramas. The first purpose-built theater was constructed in 1576 for Leicester's Men, the company sponsored by the Earl of Leicester. Eighteen years later, a thirty-year-old William Shakespeare joined the Lord Chamberlain's Men, as actor and chief playwright. He wrote many of his best-known tragedies and comedies for this company, which also built the famous Globe Theatre in London. In the centuries that followed, courtly dramas known as *masques* became fashionable, which were often richly symbolic and featured music, dance, costumes, and elaborate stage machinery.

During the English Civil War, 1642–1651, theaters were closed and stayed shut for eighteen years. When they eventually reopened, they did so with extravagant *Restoration dramas*—blockbuster shows that featured spectacular effects. The nineteenth century saw a rise in *melodrama*, which focused on moralistic tales, and *pictorial drama* that concentrated on the historical accuracy of elaborate scenes. In the latter half of the century, theater also tackled serious social issues, including the prejudices associated with class and social mobility.[25]

During the twentieth century, theater maintained its interest in moral issues, with political plays by writers such as George Bernard Shaw and dramas about ordinary people that often challenged the conventions and privileges of power. After World War II, public interest in the arts grew and the Arts Council was created in Britain to provide support through government grants. For much of the century, theaters were censored, but unlicensed "club theatres" arose that performed experimental and more controversial works. These lasted until 1968, when the censorship laws were repealed, allowing more hard-hitting plays to be staged in mainstream theaters.[26] *The Romans in Britain* by Howard Brenton (1980) dealt with the abuse of power but also included scenes of sexual violence that shocked audiences. Sarah Kane's *Blasted* (1995) was described by one critic as a "Disgusting Feast of Filth," but it had a serious intent.[27] Perhaps of particular relevance in the context of this book, a play by Mark Ravenhill titled *Shopping and Fucking* (1996) addresses the primacy of consumerism in modern society. One reviewer said it "plunges you into a world of disposability, disconnection, and dysfunction, where relationships, to be trustable, have to be reduced to transactions."[28]

Theater's ability to adapt was demonstrated recently during the COVID-19 pandemic. Theaters were closed all over the world, and actors and production staff found themselves out of work; my local theater was among them (figure 15.3). But this trauma also led to new ideas and innovative formats. Productions were pared back and performances staged and filmed in imaginative new ways that enabled actors to stay safe and audiences to watch online. In the process, theater was made more accessible and equitable. For instance, the Old Vic in London staged an online production of Dickens's *A Christmas Carol* that was livestreamed to over 43,000 households in seventy-three countries. It was also streamed free of charge into 2,400 care homes, and over 3,000 school children watched it for free. This production also raised hundreds of thousands of pounds for a charity that provides food for those in need.[29]

And so, despite the shocking nature and controversies surrounding some modern productions, theater's core purpose remains much as it was when it first appeared in ancient Greece over two and a half millennia ago. It still entertains, while also examining and responding to prevailing social, ethical, and political mores and what it means to be human.

CHOIR

The history of choral singing in the West also has its origins in religion—in the monastic traditions of medieval Europe, where individual voices became a unified whole in Gregorian chant. After the sixteenth-century Reformation, choirs began singing more secular music and performing in nonreligious settings, such as theaters and community halls.[30]

Wales—the Land of Song—is famous for its choral singing, especially its male choirs, which emerged in the nineteenth century amid the smoke and grime of its industrial valleys. The choirs have their roots in hymn singing within the Protestant nonconformist chapels that sprang up in the valley towns, but they also owe a debt to European choruses, especially the French male choir, or orphéon. The cooperation and teamwork among manual

Figure 15.4 *Beaufort Male Choir*
Ebbw Vale, Wales
Photo: courtesy Beaufort Male Choir, with permission

workers in the mining and steel industries were well suited to the disciplined practices needed for this kind of collective singing.[31]

Over the last fifty years, the traditional industries have disappeared and many of the chapels have closed, but the towns and the people remain, and the choirs still flourish—in Wales and wherever Welsh people have emigrated; Welsh choirs exist all over the world, from Sydney to Boston.[32] Communal singing is also sustained through the national sport of rugby union, where the Welsh crowd is renowned for singing with gusto songs like "Cwm Rhondda" (Rhondda Valley), "Calon Lân" (Pure Heart), and the national anthem "Hen Wlad Fy Nhadau" (Land of My Fathers).

The age profile of today's choirs is older than it once was, and the repertoire has changed over the years, with works in English and Welsh and a wider range of classical music.[33] But, like other communal practices, the choirs still help overcome differences and foster common understandings, and, through song, they continue to weave a sense of common purpose, harmony, and joy (figure 15.4). And as Renaissance composer William Byrd wrote, "The exercise of singing is delightful to Nature, and good to preserve the health of man."[34]

ADORNMENT

Jewelry and cosmetics embellish and ornament the human body. They are commonly worn to enhance physical appearance and sexual attractiveness. They can be understood as forms of self-expression and social communication and as emblems of personal or cultural identity. Bodily adornments may also convey information about social class, achievement, ethnicity, belief, affiliation, or aspiration. These meanings are frequently interrelated and context dependent; something may have a particular significance in one context but an entirely different meaning in another. Beyond any decorative function, therefore, bodily adornments also have a symbolic role. A plain gold ring worn on the third finger of the left hand symbolizes the married state in many cultures. Objects may also be worn as symbols of good luck or to ward off the evil eye.

Bodily adornment has a very long history. Evidence of jewelry dates back to the Neanderthal period, 400,000 to 40,000 years ago.[35] In prehistoric times, materials included shells, bone, ivory, pearls, and corals as well as natural seeds, fibers, hide, and wood. In ancient Egypt, wigs were symbols of status but also had a more prosaic function—as a protection against insects and the heat of the sun. And false beards of plaited hair were worn by the pharaohs to signify status, masculinity, and divinity.[36] Figure 15.5 shows contemporary items of jewelry, including pieces made from recycled materials, as well as military medals, symbolizing service to one's country.

In addition to jewelry and other such items, the use of cosmetics also has a long history. Slate palettes for grinding and mixing powders and pastes have been found in Egypt dating from ca. 3300 BCE. Elaborate eye makeup was especially important in this ancient civilization. Ingredients used to produce kohl included soot, coal, charcoal, and galena. Greens were made from the copper ore malachite and reds from ocher; other ingredients included frankincense, almonds, and cinnabar. These were mixed with oil, fat, gum, or water to create a paste. Cosmetics were worn not only to beautify but also to shield the skin from the sun, for their reputed curative properties, and in religious rituals (figure 15.6).

Jewelry and cosmetics have not only very deep roots but also a wide range of decorative, functional, and symbolic meanings. Even so, a focus on outer appearance can conflict or compete with a person's own inner sense of identity. Bodily adornments are also bound up with cultural conventions and discourses on gender stereotypes and equality. Their use or nonuse may be simultaneously transformative, ideological, and paradoxical. In contemporary society, beauty has become commodified, with marketing images that elevate the importance of physical appearance and the critical gaze of others and self. As in the past, however, the wearing of jewelry and cosmetics enables people to negotiate and express their identity within the prevailing social context.[37]

Adornment and Resilience: Although the availability of inexpensive, mass-produced products has meant that handmade goods have become increasingly niche, jewelry-making is one area that may be more economically

Figure 15.5 *Articles of Adornment*
contemporary jewelry from new and reused materials
World War II medals

Figure 15.6 *Cosmetics and Makeup*
henna, indigo, and kohl

feasible than most as a small-scale enterprise. Only small quantities of materials are required, and the resulting artifacts are able to command relatively high prices. Jewelry can also be made at the local level with little need for specialized equipment. Many traditional materials are still used, including gold, silver, platinum, and natural gems, as well as less-expensive alternatives, such as stainless steel, brass, ceramics, and plastics. Even waste materials are being used to create imaginative, aesthetically pleasing pieces.

Jewelry is also capable of retaining its beauty and significance over time, often being passed down from one generation to the next. And it can be readily repaired, cleaned, and refurbished. As a consequence, jewelry is an especially resilient category of material culture. It is typically made from materials that are durable, and it has a multiplicity of meanings and interpretations.

While it may have many positive attributes, there are aspects of its making that can be environmentally and socially problematic. The precious metals and gemstones in much jewelry are usually obtained from mining operations, many of which are environmentally damaging. They may also involve exploitative, sometimes dangerous, labor practices. These high-value materials often come from the world's poorer regions, which is a recipe for corruption. Significant efforts have to be made to ensure materials are ethically sourced, but the complexity of supply chains make this difficult to achieve. We could also ask if such costly materials are really needed to produce attractive jewelry. Opting for locally sourced alternatives can increase transparency and reduce exploitation and transportation. Nonetheless, greater regulation and oversight are needed in the existing systems because millions of workers and their families depend on the artisanal mines that supply the jewelry industry. To this end, organizations like De Beers, IBM, and Hoover and Strong have been making some progress to better trace supplies, improve social conditions, and reduce impacts—but there is still a long way to go. Moreover, beyond the production issues, the processing of these materials can also be harmful. Gemstone cutting produces hazardous microscopic dust, and toxic chemicals and waste are common problems.[38]

With regard to cosmetics, two key issues need to be taken into account—their provenance and their providence. Compounds for makeup still employ many natural substances, such as beeswax, olive oil, and lanolin, as well as vegetable waxes produced from plants such as the candelilla shrub and carnauba palm. However, the fact that constituents may be natural does not necessarily mean they come from environmentally and socially responsible sources, and labeling can be confusing. Terms such as *natural* and *organic* can mean vegetable-based, organically farmed, or harvested from natural sources that may be farmed or wild. Cosmetics can also include inorganic substances and mineral salts, animal-based ingredients, and synthetic preservatives.[39] Although they may not be included in lists of ingredients, cosmetics such as foundations, mascaras, and lipsticks frequently contain additives to increase their durability and water resistance. Commonly used additives include a highly persistent and potentially toxic class of chemicals known as PFAS, or per- and polyfluoroalkyl substances. Ingredients may also include alcohols, methacrylates, and phosphate esters, all of which are known to be harmful. The production, use, and disposal of cosmetics that contain PFAS can damage ecosystems, and because these chemicals are directly applied to the skin, they can cause health problems.[40] Other problems associated with the cosmetics industry include animal exploitation, deforestation for palm oil production, and pollution from heavy-metal catalysts.

The cosmetics industry is now being forced to change its practices because of a combination of increased public awareness and regulation to ensure customer safety, legislation to prevent pollution, and declining availability of conventional constituents.

Excessive packaging, which is prevalent in this industry, also has to be addressed. Plastics, which are by far the most common form, are usually neither biodegradable nor refillable. In recent years, some efforts have been made to develop more environmentally responsible packaging from recycled glass, bamboo, wood fiber, paper, and cardboard. One company is even selling a significant proportion of its products without any packaging at all.[41]

Bodily adornment in the form of jewelry and cosmetics constitutes an ancient and continuous practice throughout human history. It transcends any particular time and culture, and it takes many different forms, which are related to people and context. In this sense, it can be understood as a highly resilient custom. However, as with so many other practices today, we have to make special efforts to ensure that contemporary forms of adornment, and the processes they employ, are also socially just, inclusive, and environmentally sustainable.

TATTOO

On glancing through the entries for *tattoo* in an academic library, one would be forgiven for thinking it is some kind of malign disorder related to infections, poisonings, medical complications, and abuse. Its cultural meanings, its indisputable popularity, and its exceptionally long history go largely unremarked.

The oldest examples of tattoos date back some 5,250 years. They were found on the mummified corpse of Ötzi the Iceman, discovered by hikers in the Italian Alps in 1991.[42] Tattoos were also common in ancient Egypt and Rome, until the practice was prohibited by Constantine after he converted to Christianity. The book of Genesis tells us that humankind was made in the likeness of God and should be honored and remain unblemished;[43] consequently, the practice has been long been disapproved of by all three Abrahamic religions—Judaism, Christianity, and Islam.[44]

Despite this, the many worldwide voyages and explorations that occurred in the eighteenth century stimulated new interest in tattoos. Captain James Cook is said to have introduced the word to Europe after his first voyage to Polynesia (1768–1771): "They have a custom of staining their bodies, nearly in the same manner as is practised in many other parts of the world, which they call Tattowing."[45] By the end of the nineteenth century, tattoos had become popular among the higher echelons of society, including such figures as Winston Churchill and Tsar Nicholas II.[46]

The connotations of the tattoo are many and very varied. In Nazi concentration camps, prisoners had a number tattooed on their arm, making it a mark associated with horror, inhumanity, and death. In contrast, among the First Nations peoples of the Pacific Northwest, the revival of ancestral tattooing is seen as a way of reawakening, reaffirming, and reasserting cultural identity and as part of a process of reindigenization, after years of cultural devastation caused by the ongoing impacts of colonialism.[47] Among Christians, and despite being officially frowned upon, a tattoo of a cross has been a

Figure 15.7 *RIP Mother* commemorative tattoo
David Curley, United Kingdom

nonmaterial souvenir for pilgrims to Jerusalem for generations, and remains so up to the present day.[48] And in contemporary Western cultures, decorative and dedicational motifs are popular forms of body art (figure 15.7).

WRITING

Writing has its origins in the city of Uruk in Mesopotamia, where, in the fourth millennium BCE, clay tablets were inscribed with protocuneiform texts.[49] The clay could be wetted for reuse or baked to create permanent records. The Greeks and Romans used wax tablets;[50] but whether clay or wax, writing was done using a reed stylus.[51] The Egyptians developed plant-based papyrus and writing with inks, made from various substances, such as soot, indigo, and iron sulphates.[52]

In Europe during the Middle Ages, parchments from untanned sheep-skin and goatskin and vellums from calfskin were used until, eventually, plant-based papers were developed. However, in China, methods were being explored for reproducing written documents. Wood-block printing was in use from at least the eighth century, and by the eleventh century, the process included movable characters. It wasn't until some four and a half centuries later that Gutenberg developed a similar system in Europe.[53]

The origins of the pencil are attributed to the county of Cumbria in northwest England, where, in 1564, a large deposit of graphite was discovered. The earliest pencils were simply pieces of graphite wrapped in string or sheepskin to make them easier to use.[54] The mass production of pencils was pioneered in Germany during the late 1600s, and in the late 1700s, French engineer Nicolas-Jacques Conté created leads using low-quality graphite mixed with wet clay and baked into narrow rods. A few years ago, *Forbes* ranked the simple lead pencil among the five most important tools of all time.[55]

The blackboard, which was to become such an indispensable feature of the classroom, was first mentioned in an English-German dictionary in 1739.[56] The earliest blackboards were simply large pieces of natural slate, with lumps of chalk for writing. Blackboards are still widely used in mathematics, the sciences, and the arts, despite the white board being introduced in the 1980s. While the white board prevents chalk dust, its disposable markers add to burgeoning levels of plastic waste.

Industrialization in the nineteenth century brought rapid innovations in writing technologies, but equally rapid product obsolescence. Natural quills were superseded by inexpensive steel nibs, produced in their millions by metal stamping.[57] The mechanical typewriter was developed, with the Remington of 1872 becoming the standard in the United States.[58] The years following World War II saw a profusion of cheap, single-use products, one of the most emblematic being the disposable ballpoint, the Bic Cristal, launched in 1950 and still in production. It is the world's best-selling pen—with well over 100 billion sold since its introduction—equivalent to 57 pens every second. It has been hailed by some as a modern design icon;[59] for others, it epitomizes our throwaway culture (figure 9.2d).

Personal computers entered the market in the late 1970s, and since their introduction, they have been in a continual state of improvement—becoming faster, more powerful, smaller, and increasingly indispensable. While desktop computers are still widely used, laptops have become the standard workhorse for many.

These developments have had significant impacts, benefiting people all over the world. They have increased levels of literacy and allowed greater accessibility to the world's literature and information of all kinds. They have transformed education and society and, as Francis Bacon (1551–1626) famously argued, "Knowledge itself is power."[60] These developments have also led the way to increased democracy and new opportunities for ordinary people, based on merit rather than wealth or birthright.

Transformational as these innovations have been, there has also been a heavy price to pay. The widespread availability of sophisticated technological devices for writing places an enormous burden on the earth's natural resources. The useful lives of most of these products are often disturbingly short, and their cumulative impacts are highly detrimental to the planet's ecosystems. For years, too, assembly workers have been exposed to harmful substances.[61] Billions of these products have been discarded, and thousands of other workers disassemble them, with severe impacts on their health, as well as on the air and water quality where these workers live.

Figure 15.8 *Fountain Pen and Notebook*
a more fluid, natural, and direct way of expressing thoughts

The social toll of all this accessibility to information can also be signifi-cant. In contrast to Bacon's view, the book of Ecclesiastes, written at a time of economic innovation but widespread insecurity, counsels us thus, "The more knowledge, the more grief."[62] And who can doubt it. Along with new opportunities and new horizons, there are aspects of these innovations that are anything but positive. News media inundate us with endless reports of human tragedy, and advertising is relentless in telling us that, no matter how much we already have, to be happy we need more.

Clearly, the age-old art of writing has come a long way. Relatively recent technologies have increased the quantity of production and the distribution of texts. But we should also acknowledge that some of the world's greatest and most resilient works were set down using the simplest of writing instru-ments. There is also a slowness of pace to traditional ways of writing that fosters deliberation about what is actually being written.

Throughout my own career, constant companions have been a simple notebook and a fountain pen (figure 15.8). While I use a laptop to write papers and books, my thoughts and ideas are first developed in my notebook. I find it a more fluid, natural, and direct way of thinking about and express-ing ideas. By comparison, the computer is rather too precise and too editable, hindering the free flow of thoughts and more intuitive forms of writing.

Perhaps more importantly in the context of this book, most of our rela-tively recent innovations in writing technologies fail miserably when it comes to resilience. By comparison, writing by hand using simple, natural materials is more adaptable, less harmful, and conducive to thoughtful practice. It is also more direct, more personal, eminently affordable, and socially inclusive.

CORRESPONDENCE

Rudimentary postal systems were first used by kings and pharaohs to dis-tribute orders. The clay tablets of earliest times were later replaced by light-weight papyrus scrolls, which allowed longer missives to be sent.[63] However, messages were not restricted to official business; more prosaic letters have also been discovered. In ca. 1750 BCE, an unhappy customer in Ur, Iraq, complains about being offered poor-quality goods;[64] and the earliest example of Latin handwriting by a woman is a birthday invitation: "On the third day before the Ides of September, sister, for the day of the celebration of my birthday, I give you a warm invitation to make sure that you come to us, to make the day more enjoyable for me by your arrival."[65] In Britain, a regular postal service was not established until the sixteenth century, during the reign of Henry VIII. Even then, it was for the exclusive use of the king and ran only between a limited number of "posts."[66] Subsequently it developed in reach and accessibility but also became increasingly complicated and expensive until, in the mid-1800s, the system was reformed. To ensure postal charges were both uniform and low, a method of prepayment was introduced that used adhesive stamps, the first of which was the Penny Black of 1840. This form of payment was adopted around the world;[67] and the era of affordable international correspondence for everyone was born.

The Power of Letters: Letters can have lasting significance and be cherished by successive generations. The most widely translated letters in history are those attributed to Paul of Tarsus. Their recipients were the nascent Christian communities in regions surrounding the Holy Land, but these were not private correspondence between two individuals; they were intended to be read aloud.[68] Their aim was to persuade people to adopt a particular course of action, and consequently they were written in a rhetorical style meant to challenge assumptions.

Other letters from ancient times that are still published and greatly valued for their historical significance include those of Pliny the Younger, ca. 61–113 CE. He wrote to the Roman emperor Trajan about how Christians should be tried and punished, as well as to the historian Tacitus, describing the eruption of Mount Vesuvius in 79 CE: "Its general appearance can be best expressed as being like an umbrella pine, for it rose to a great height on a sort of trunk and then split off into branches."[69] Pliny's description is admired for its objectivity, even though it was written twenty-five years after the event. The type of explosive volcanic activity he goes on to describe in some detail is still known as a "Plinian eruption."[70]

A more recent example, but also of historical significance, is the 1963 "Letter from a Birmingham Jail" by Martin Luther King Jr. written during the civil rights movement in the United States. Addressed to "My Dear Fellow Clergymen," he calls for ways to address the underlying causes of racial discrimination and outlines his views on nonviolent campaigning and the use of civil disobedience.[71]

Letters that may not be as renowned as these examples can, nevertheless, be very meaningful for those who write or receive them. Before computers became the norm in classrooms, cursive writing was an important skill, and pupils were expected to write letters home to demonstrate their prowess. In wartime, letters that allowed soldiers in the field or in prisoner-of-war camps to keep in touch with loved ones could be lifelines during dark times (figure 15.9). And contemporary historians are findings that research into the lives of ordinary people based on their letters and diaries reveals a very different picture from that given by official documents. This kind of research is providing new perspectives on relationships, love, and religious faith in former times.[72]

Correspondence and Technology: The first message sent over a telegraph line was on May 24, 1844, from Washington, DC, to Baltimore, a distance of forty miles; rather unpromisingly, it said, "What hath God wrought?" It was sent not as written text but in Morse code, which consists of a series of long and short signals—dots and dashes—that have to be translated into words. The advent of the telegraph and, early in the twentieth century, advances in wireless telegraphy meant messages could be quickly sent over great distances. However, Morse code was rather cumbersome and required trained operators to transmit messages character by character. Its use was generally restricted to short messages deemed important. It was certainly not conducive to more descriptive or intimate exchanges.

As technology continued to develop, the telegraph was replaced by the mechanical teleprinter and, in the 1980s, by the fax machine. These were usually restricted to work environments and so, again, did not lend themselves to correspondence of a personal nature.

Email was developed in the early 1970s and popularized in the late 1980s and 1990s. It quickly became the standard method of message exchange within and between organizations and, as computers entered the home, was increasingly adopted for personal use among family and friends.

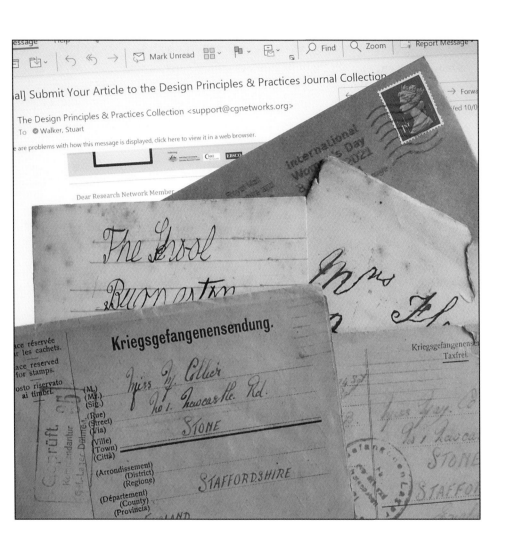

Figure 15.9 Correspondence
World War I prisoner-of-war letters, 1918
letter from a child to her mother, 1932
contemporary letter and email

The immense growth in smartphone use since the turn of the millennium has meant a return to short, concise text exchanges, using SMS (short message service) and mobile-messaging apps. These are used in business, for marketing and customer engagement, and for informal exchanges between friends, but they are unsuited to longer forms of descriptive correspondence.

The development, rapid take-up, and enormous popularity of a variety of technology-based forms of correspondence attest to the usefulness and convenience of virtually instantaneous communication. The ability to send not just text but also photos, videos, and larger documents as attachments, and to send these to one or a number of recipients simultaneously, adds to their usefulness in both work and private life.

As with writing technologies, when we consider these advances in correspondence, we also need to bear in mind their negative effects on natural systems and on people. We are becoming increasingly aware of their very substantial impacts, including the huge amounts of solid waste they create and the energy needs of data storage. Even so, the carbon footprint associated with posting a letter is actually much higher than that of an email or a text because of the paper production and distribution and the infrastructure needed for delivery. According to Mike Berners-Lee, a regular letter on virgin paper sent through the mail, which after reading ends up in landfill, has a carbon footprint fifteen to twenty times higher than that of an equivalent, moderate-length email, even if the latter is circulated among many recipients. And a text message's carbon footprint is far lower still.[73]

Despite the many advantages of technology-based correspondence, not least their speed and fingertip convenience, the traditional letter possesses important qualities than are not so easily retained when our ways of communicating are transmuted to the digital realm. The immediacy, ephemerality, and sheer profusion of emails and texts tend to encourage brevity and urgency rather than more reflective forms of writing. The fact that they have no physical substance also means that digital formats lack those very qualities that many people value. Novelist Kinran Manral writes: "There is a charm to letters and cards that emails and SMSes can't ever replicate, you cannot inhale them, drawing the fragrance of the place they have been mailed from, the feel of paper in your hand bearing the weight of the words contained within. You cannot rub your fingers over the paper and visualise the sender, seated at a table, writing . . . Smiley face icons cannot hope to replace words thought out carefully in order to put a smile on the other person's face, the sharpness or the laxity of the handwriting telling stories about the frame of mind of the writer."[74] Correspondence, whatever form it takes, is a way of communicating that most people can and do engage in. And although traditional letters have given way to newer forms, and the "artifact" has become virtual rather than physical, written correspondence remains a vitally important way of interacting with one another that has proven to be exceptionally flexible in form, quality, and substance, and remarkably resilient over thousands of years.

STORY

In his book *Six Memos for the Next Millennium*, Italo Calvino writes: "I would say that the moment an object appears in a narrative, it is charged with a special force and becomes like the pole of a magnetic field, a knot in the network of invisible relationships. The symbolism of an object may be more or less explicit, but it is always there. We might even say that in a narrative any object is always magic."[75]

Nails

I had recently suffered from the sickness that frequently plagues these shores in the dark days of winter. It had affected me badly, and I had been bedridden for several weeks. Now, in early spring, I was convalescing and had embarked upon a coastal walk to rebuild my strength.

It must have been the fourth evening of my venture when I found myself on a lonely part of the coast, with few signs of habitation. The landscape was flat and featureless and the shoreline mile upon mile of marshes, with muddy channels and still pools reflecting lowering clouds. These wetlands were home to all kinds of waterfowl, but they struck me as a cold, inhospitable place, particularly as the afternoon was already drawing into evening and I was still in need of a tavern or hostelry where I might put up for the night.

I tramped on, eventually coming to a low track through the marshes. On somewhat higher ground in the distance, I could pick out a few houses. The track wound its way towards them, here and there crossing a crude bridge that spanned one of the tidal channels, for I could see now that I was at the edge of an estuary, with the houses forming a row on the end of a jutting peninsula. When I finally reached them, it was almost dark. I knocked at the first house I came to, though I saw no light inside. I waited, and knocked again. In a little while, an old man opened the door a crack. He stooped low, and in the remaining dusk I saw he wore a waistcoat over a capacious white shirt. He asked, somewhat nervously it seemed to me, *"Who's there? What is it?"* I supposed I had unnerved him by coming to his door at such an hour and put his manner down to this. I replied, as cheerfully as I could muster,

"I am looking for a place to stay for the night—is there a guesthouse or anything of the kind hereabouts?"

"You'd best inquire at the inn—down at the end o' the terrace."

He nodded in the direction he meant me to go and, with that, closed the door.

I walked on with houses to my right and water lapping in the darkness down a-ways to my left. As the path bore round, the wind picked up but I saw welcoming lights just ahead with a swaying sign out in front proclaiming *The Ship*. It was a solid, stone-built establishment, with large bay windows. Shallow steps led up to a heavy oak door, which I unlatched, entered, and quickly closed again, to stay the wind.

I turned to see a long barroom, with well-worn tables and chairs, and two high settles either side of a roaring fire. It was a cheery sight, but no other soul was in the place that I could see. I called out, *"Hullo there,"* and soon a man appeared whom I took to be the landlord. He was large, ruddy-faced and balding, with substantial grey mutton-chop whiskers, and he greeted me with,

"Good ev'nin, Sir, what is your pleasure?"

"I'm hoping you have a room for the night, and a meal for a weary traveller?"

"Ay, them I can do for ye, Sir. A shilling and sixpence for your supper, and four shillings for board and breakfast. Now, sit'e down by fireside and I'll bring ye an ale."

I was flushed from the walking and felt in need of company, so instead of doing his bidding, I took one of the stools at the bar, and as he drew the beer, I asked what this place was.

"This here is the old port of the city upriver a way—afore the sandbank moved and silted up this side o' channel. Don't see many folks 'ere now'days, not since ships stopped. They all t'other side now, Glasson way, new sea doors they got there an' a pool, so no waitin f'tide to unload, or so I's told. All used to be 'ere. Sugar, rum, 'bacco, cotton, even lumber for Gillows fact'ry in' city. One time, unloaded 'ere at front of inn, come from all over—three masters from Virginia, Barbados and Jamaica. But s'all finished from 'ere now, them days is long gone."

The door banged open, and, turning, I saw the old man who had answered my knock earlier. The innkeeper looked up and called,

"Eve'n Mr. Watson, Sir, we got a guest with us tonight."

"He'd be the fellow I sent you who came to my door not an hour ago—frighted me half to death, I can tell you, rapping out of nowhere, and me can't see a candle in front of me."

As he came in, I could see the newcomer felt his way with a white cane.

Turning to me, the innkeeper whispered softly,

"You should ask old Mr. Wats'n 'bout place, he knows better than any how it were, he being a educat'd gentleman like."

The old man came up and sat next to me at the bar, and I offered him a drink.

"That's kind of you, Sir, I'll take a Black Barrel" at which, the innkeeper poured him a generous measure of Indies rum and, as he put it in front of him, said, "I'll be getting on with yors' food," and he disappeared from whence he'd come.

Mr. Watson and I sat with our drinks and soon fell into an easy conversation. He spoke softly, in a thoughtful, studious way but I felt there was an air of sadness in his manner. For many years, he told me, he'd been headmaster of the boys' school in the city of Lanchester, a few miles up-river, but was retired some time, since his eyesight had failed, and he'd come to live in the church cottage at the end of what they called here *The Terrace*. He apologized for the rather brusque reception he'd given me earlier, but explained that he wasn't used to callers in this place,

"It's a lonely enough spot alright, but I've learned to find my way around. I walk the headland with my cane and listen to the sea and the birds. The landlord is a kindly fellow—he looks after my meals for me. And on Sundays, when the tides allow passage across the causeway, my niece comes over to read to me."

The landlord reappeared with a loaded tray,

"I'll sit ye at fireplace—that'll be a'right for ye both?"

And without waiting for a reply, he placed a table between the two high-backed settles and laid it with cutlery and napkins.

"If ye'd both seat y'selves down, I'll get thee y'suppers."

As we took our places at the fireside, our meals were set before us—simple but wholesome fare—roast pork, potatoes, boiled cabbage, half a fresh loaf on a board with a hunk of mature cheese, and a glass of claret for each of us.

"I'm not much in kitch'n, so I trust this'll be to your liking Sir, Mr. Watson here is used to my cooking well enough."

And with that, he left us.

"The landlord says you know something of the history of these parts, Mr. Watson, I'd be grateful to know more."

And as we ate our supper, he told me the unhappy story of this forgotten place . . .

"When I was a young lad, well over sixty or more years ago, this was a thriving port but it dealt in a despicable trade. Just outside of where you are sitting now, it was one of the busiest slaver ports in all of England—e'en my own brother, to my everlasting shame. He ran ships

from here, carrying cargoes of calico and pots and such, down the west coast of Africa, trading for slaves and taking them to the plantations in the Americas. Then back here again to Lanchester with sugar and cotton and all kinds of exotic stuffs. He became a rich man, but it cost many a poor African's life—men, women and childer—treated them all like cotton bales, bought and sold and packed just as tight on those vermin-ridden vessels. One died here you know, in this very inn. He was a captain's boy who thought he'd been left here, forgotten by his master. Fell into despair and not many days passed before he died; lost the will to live, so they said. They buried him on t'other side, down the lane next to the inn.

That was all many a year ago, but they left no marker on his grave. So before my eyes were gone, I looked about and I found the spot myself and had a little plaque fashioned in bronze to remember him by.

Strange thing was, the captain shewed he had a conscience by the end. Seems he was fond of the boy, and when he harkened of his death, he anchored his ship off over the way when the tide was up, and never ventured to sea again—gave it all up, and a good thing, too. His ship sat there many a winter, pilfered bit by bit and the rest rotting into the mud. Its bones are there still so they tell me, at low tide sticking up like the ribs of some leviathan, which I suppose it was in a way. And all strewed about its beams and planking, the rusting spikes and nails that latched down the chains of all those poor souls.

I've talked enough of things that're a might too painful to recall, and I'll be on my way, I wish you a good night, Sir."

And with that, he took his leave, seeming to find his way easily enough with his cane tapping the flags before him.

The following morning, after a hearty breakfast, I made my way down the lane that Mr. Watson had mentioned. Under a clear sky, with a touch of warmth to the sun, the path took me past a brewhouse attached to *The Ship* and some farm cottages, and thence between fields edged with thorn. Primroses and bluebells brightened the way but their innocence seemed somehow incongruous with the history of this place. As I walked, the lane closed tighter between untrimmed hedges, which clawed and pulled at my clothes. The wind picked up and I came to the end of the path with the sea far ahead, beyond the marshes. Over to my left, in the middle of the channel, stood a light, its once-white paint blasted and worn, and its beacon rusted black. And in a corner of the field next to the path, I found the grave with its small bronze plate. I could read only the final words, which I took down in my notebook as best as I could make out,

> . . . still he sleeps—till the awakening sounds Of the Archangel's Trump new life impart Then the great judge his approbation founds Not on Man's color but his worth of heart.[76]

It was an isolated place to be interred, and desperately sad, continents away from his people, and spurned by his captors. It put me in a reflective mood, and I sat down beside him and looked out to sea. I lost track of time, and when I came to myself, the sun was already high.

I retraced my steps back to the inn and walked past the houses and onto the marsh, where, just as Mr. Watson had described, I saw ribs sticking from the mud, and amongst the blown grasses and rotting boards, I found dozens of old corroded nails (figure 15.10).

FOOTPATH

British Ordnance Survey maps show all public rights-of-way in the country, approximately 220,000 kilometers of them. Some are cycle paths, others are bridleways, but the majority are footpaths, including fifteen long-distance walks designated as National Trails.[77]

Many of the footpaths are very ancient—the Ridgway Trail between Avebury in Wiltshire and Goring in Oxfordshire is at least five thousand years old and is still in use.[78] Public footpaths are protected by law and maintained by local councils and volunteer groups organized by bodies such as the National Trust. There are also "permissive" footpaths that cross private land.[79] All these paths are indicated by a variety of objects—including

Figure 15.10 *Old Corroded Nails*

found amidst the boards of a hulk among blown grasses and mud

Lancashire coast, England

metal or wooden fingerposts on the sides of roads and small round discs on fenceposts, with a yellow arrow for a public footpath or a blue arrow for a bridleway.

Public footpaths and rights-of-way can be understood as functional artifacts that serve the common good (figure 15.11). They pass along riverbanks, over mountains, and through woodlands and farmers' fields, sometimes even through people's gardens. On route, walkers will regularly come to walls and fences, which they are able to traverse using another type of functional artifact for the common good—the stile, which we will discuss next.

STILE

The stile is a ubiquitous feature of rural Britain. It is generally a construction of steps that allows walkers to pass over fences and walls, while barring the way to sheep and cows. The designs of stiles vary and are often related to place. Some are made of wood, while others are built into stone walls. The most common type is the simple "step stile" in which two wooden steps and a tall wooden "steadying" pole enable someone to easily climb over a fence (figure 15.12). Others include the "ladder stile," a wooden stepladder that straddles a drystone wall; "stone steps" that project from either side of a wall; and the "squeeze stile," also found in drystone walls and consisting of a narrow gap flanked by flat vertical stones that taper toward the base. As the poet John Clare wrote, "Green lanes that shut out burning skies / And old crooked stiles to rest upon."[80]

The stile is a good example of design for resilience. It has been an element of rural life for centuries—one early reference dates from 1564, but the stile is probably far older.[81] It is constructed from natural materials and is simple to make and maintain, and the stone versions are especially long-lasting. Its design and materials are adapted to locale, and it fits unobtrusively into the landscape. And like the footpaths they serve, stiles are designed for public use and are freely available to all who are physically able.

The cultural practices we have looked at in this chapter are important to individuals, communities, and society as a whole, even though they are extra to people's practical concerns and everyday work.

Figure 15.11 *Footpath*
Jervaulx Abbey, Yorkshire, United Kingdom

Figure 15.12 _Stile_
Forest of Bowland, Lancashire, United Kingdom

Music is a vital ingredient of cultures everywhere, with regionally distinctive songs and musical compositions played on instruments traditionally made from locally available materials. As we have discussed, music spans folk dances and festivals, religious rituals and even meditative practices. In addition, dance and theater represent ways of enacting our own stories—they tell us about ourselves and help us make sense of our lives. As such, they contribute to and help build our sense of self-identity and our understanding of what it means to be human.

We have also seen that communal practices like singing together in choirs can forge common bonds, break down differences, and, through common purpose, create harmony and joy. And we have looked at self-expression and social communication in the form of bodily adornments—ancient practices that convey ideas about personal or cultural identity and our sense of belonging to a particular group.

Writing practices are another ancient way of expressing and recording ideas about who we are and what we believe. The same goes for letter writing, which may be public or personal. Some letters may be powerful expressions of belief and calls to action, others heartfelt expressions of friendship, consolation, or love.

And finally, we have seen that some cultural practices and their related artifacts are associated with the common good. Many of these have been eliminated over the centuries, including village greens and tracts of land that were once regarded as "the commons." But in Britain the footpaths and stiles remain and are used by thousands of people every year up and down the country.

16 RESILIENT PLAY

Play was defined in the mid-twentieth century by Johan Huizinga as "a voluntary activity or occupation executed within certain fixed limits of time and place, according to rules freely accepted but absolutely binding, having its aim in itself and accompanied by a feeling of tension, joy and the consciousness that it is 'different' from 'ordinary life.'"[1] He also pointed out that play is not confined to humankind because animals also play, and consequently play actually *precedes* notions of culture and human civilization, which add nothing to its essential idea.

More recently, Stuart Brown has described play in similar terms but suggests that rules don't have to be fixed and that sometimes play may not have rules at all. Based on his analysis, the essential properties of play can be summarized as follows:

- *Apparently purposeless*—it is engaged in for its own sake, not for some other reason, which is perhaps why in today's busy, results-oriented world it is often regarded as a waste of time;
- *Voluntary*—play is neither obligatory nor a duty;
- *Inherently attractive*—play is joyful and makes us feel good, which parallels Huizinga's conclusion that an essential characteristic of play is its fun element;[2]
- *Freedom from time*—when we become immersed in play activities we are fully 'in the present moment' and tend to lose track of time;
- *Diminished consciousness of self*—we stop thinking about ourselves, our usual preoccupations, and even that we are thinking at all. When we are fully engaged in imaginative play, we experience a different sense of self.

- *Improvisational potential*—we allow ourselves to embrace chance and serendipitous occurrences, and we tend to respond to these in a flexible, open-minded manner. We also allow elements into play that may seem irrelevant from a rational perspective, and this can jog thoughts, strategies, and ways of being that are new and outside "normal" or expected forms of behavior.
- *Continual desire*—spurred on by the fun and the sheer pleasure we feel when immersed in play, we want to keep it going.[3]

Play and Creativity: In design education, we often talk of the process of designing as being like play and that to develop creative ideas, we have to play with lots of different concepts and materials, move them around and fit them together. In studio teaching, we encourage our students to play and explore through sketching, creating collages, and engaging with physical materials. This is hardly surprising because many of the characteristics inherent to play are also essential to creativity—both draw on the human imagination and mix what we know with what we conjure in our minds. Many commercial companies are aware that play is an essential ingredient of creativity and innovation;[4] but whether engaged in within education or business, play is nonrational—it is neither logical nor systematic.[5]

Play is preconscious, preverbal,[6] and involves intuitive ways of thinking associated with the right hemisphere of the brain. These kinds of thought processes are also vital ingredients of creativity because they give us the "ability to make more and wider-ranging connections between things and to think more flexibly" than the more logical, time-conscious ways of thinking associated with the left hemisphere.[7] To be a good designer, one has to play. As we engage in play within the context of design, we experience tensions and frustrations but also feelings of joy when our ideas gel and things "work." And as in play, when we engage in a creative activity such as drawing, we also tend to lose track of time.[8] The setting is also an important factor—we have to be in a place where we feel comfortable and free to explore and try different things without the pressure to produce tangible or measurable results within a fixed period. However, we also know that when we are designing, we can only engage in these playful ways of thinking-and-doing at particular stages within the whole process, after which we have to move the work forward.

Play may be fundamental to creativity, but it is also at odds with many ideas about creativity that are prevalent today. Play is not engaged in for some *other* purpose, for some external requirement or at someone else's bidding. As Huizinga points out, human civilization with its necessities, wants, and everyday preoccupations, does not add one jot to play. Play and true creativity are *for their own sake*, which is why creativity cannot be produced at will or to a strict timetable. We can provide the right kind of conditions, we can set aside time, and we can allow the process to evolve, but we cannot guarantee a creative outcome.

Play may be for its own sake, but it also has an important function. It provides us with opportunities to challenge ourselves mentally, physically, and emotionally, and it helps develop social bonds, physical well-being, and emotional resilience. It is a vital element in the development and refinement of self-esteem, problem-solving, and cooperation, and it can also build empathy, be used to express emotions, and is essential for learning about the world. When children play, they often role-play, adopting different identities and perspectives and exploring relative power dynamics through make-believe. Children's play also absorbs and frequently reflects developments occurring in wider society. For a long time, educators have argued that instead of just concentrating on formal teaching, we should also be encouraging learning through play and child-led interactions with the world. Notably, too, in 1989 the UN Convention on the Rights of the Child declared that play was a basic human need.[9]

Play, including role-play, can also help designers break out of customary ways of thinking and allow different perspectives to be considered. In turn, this facilitates mutual learning and cooperation, and it can yield new ideas about how different views and needs can be integrated into an imaginative, multidimensional way forward.

The Decline of Play in Modern Times: Declarations like the UN Convention on the Rights of the Child tend to be instigated when there is a perception that something is under threat. Sadly, many of the elements of play that characterized former times have been in decline since the nineteenth century. As the social functions of sports have grown in scope and importance in the modern era, play has moved away from being an occasional, enjoyable amusement. With increasing organization, systematization, and regulation, along with rankings and divisions according to quality and a demonstrable ability to win, many traditional play qualities have been lost. This is especially the case with the professionalization of sports, but amateur sports have also been affected, and they, too, move further and further away from the sphere of true play and become something else entirely. They evolve into something that is neither fish nor fowl—they are no longer play, but neither are they work. Well-publicized, overhyped sports contests tend to destroy play as an activity that helps build culture: "However important it may be for the players or spectators, it remains sterile. The old play-factor has undergone almost complete atrophy."[10]

TOYS

When children play, they know perfectly well that they *are* playing. Play may be a nonrational activity, but it still has a function and therefore a meaning, which suggests that it has an inherent quality that is nonmaterialistic in nature.[11] Even so, children's play can be facilitated by toys, which are objects for amusement rather than practical purpose. The best toys are those that enable all kinds of imaginative activities and can change their purpose on a whim, as chance takes the child's thoughts from one idea to the next, like a butterfly flitting from blossom to blossom. This being the case, we must consider the role the imagination is allowed to have in the elaborate, franchised toys offered in today's market. In addition, those who object to the narrow stereotypes represented in many commercially produced toys argue for far greater diversity and broader societal representation.

The children's toys sector is where capitalism's methods are perhaps at their most nefarious. The marketing industry's use of sophisticated psychological techniques to promote cheap, often instantly breakable, plastic tat to children lays bare the moral vacuum and deep spiritual malaise at the heart of our corporate system. As David C. Korten explains: "Advertising aimed explicitly at children in the unregulated marketplace is one of the most pernicious, intentional, and well-funded assaults by corporate plutocrats on family values . . . Their efforts became truly sinister a few years ago when they learned that 'brand loyalty' begins to take shape as early as age two and that at age three, even before they are able to read, children are already making requests for specific brand-name products."[12] Over the last few decades in the United States, marketing that specifically targets children has ballooned from $100 million spent on television advertising in the early 1980s to over $15 billion across a wide variety of mediums by the early years of the twenty-first century.[13] This includes advertising via the mobile phone, which has become the constant companion of many children and teenagers. This relentless onslaught promotes excessive consumption, causes unnecessary environmental fallout, and can have deeply harmful effects on children's well-being, creating psychological and behavioral problems, such as low self-esteem and depression. It has also been linked to childhood eating disorders, obesity, family conflicts, and aggressive behavior.[14]

The marketing industries' use of the "nag factor" or "pester power" as a targeted strategy takes the manipulation of children to new lows by posing the question "How can money be extracted from young children who want to buy products but have no money of their own?"[15] The answer, of course, is to ensure the parents do the buying by encouraging the child to persistently nag and whine, which works especially well in busy situations such as supermarket checkouts. As George Orwell wrote, "There was hardly a soul in the firm who was not perfectly well aware that publicity—advertising—is the dirtiest ramp that capitalism has yet produced. In the red lead firm there had lingered certain notions of commercial honour and usefulness. But such things would have been laughed at in the New Albion. Most of the employees were . . . the type to whom nothing in the world is sacred, except money. They had their cynical code worked out. The public are swine; advertising is the rattling of a stick inside a swill-bucket."[16] In addition to these cynical corporate approaches toward play, our sometimes overly risk-averse attitudes can also limit children's freedom to explore, especially through physical play that may incorporate aspects that are mildly risky. Marjory Allen, who was a great advocate for the rights and welfare of children and a key figure in the introduction of adventure playgrounds said, "Better a broken bone than a broken spirit."[17]

A few years ago, *Wired* magazine drew up a list of what they considered to be the five best toys of all time.[18] Its selections were surprising, especially for such a technology-centered publication, but well chosen because they embody the very essence of play. All the "toys" on the list allow for unfettered, ever-changing child-led purposes. They also confound the best efforts of large toy manufacturers, their designers, and their powerful marketing divisions. Notably, too, all the selections create no additional environmental impacts and are preferable to most purpose-made toys because, even though they are not specifically created to be toys, they serve as conduits for the imagination. For these reasons they have a strong resonance with resilience, so it is worth taking another look at them here.

Stick

The first "toy" on *Wired* magazine's list is the stick (figure 16.1). Like the others on the list, it costs nothing, is readily available, and suits a wide range of ages. It is also well liked by children and has been played with for generations.[19]

The stick has multiple uses, which is a quality inherent to its "thingness." Unlike consciously designed toys, which are typically created with a specific idea in mind, the stick is "a 'loose part' with no designated role, and so it can be adapted to almost any" purpose.[20] Literally, "the rattling of a stick inside a swill-bucket"[21] can make a loud noise—but so can beating a rhythm on a box or dragging it along iron railings. Through the power of imagination, in the hands of a child, a stick can become a knight's sword, a wizard's staff, even a horse. It can be a wounded hero's crutch, a magic wand, a conductor's baton, a hunting rifle, and a very effective whacker for taking the heads off stinging nettles. It can be twirled in the air to lead a marching band and is a great thing to throw for a dog. It can also be a campfire poker, a fishing rod, or a useful accessory for reaching apples or conkers when the branch is a little too high. And when combined with other sticks or other "toys" on the list, further uses can be devised.

Sticks also have a long history of use in art and design. The Bestažovca cave in western Slovenia contains Neolithic ceiling drawings made using

Figure 16.1 *Stick*

a stick is not a stick when it becomes a knight's sword, a magic wand, or a marching baton

burnt sticks; the drawings have been dated to ca. 5000 BCE.[22] Later in life, the artist Henri Matisse (1869–1954) was photographed on many occasions using a two-meter-long stick tipped with charcoal or a brush—even using it to paint from his bed when in poor health. In his seventies, he used this technique to complete drawings for the Chapelle du Rosaire at Vence in the south of France[23]—partly because as it allowed him to create large works without having to climb a ladder, but also because it had other advantages. He was able to reduce the influence of his own style, remain at a distance from the work, and see the composition as a whole as it developed. Matisse said of his process, "I have always tried to conceal my efforts";[24] and by using a long stick, he was forced to relinquish a certain amount of control—the emphasis being on bolder strokes as it was not possible to work in fine detail.

Willow sticks have been used for centuries to make functional products such as woven baskets, hurdles, and fencing. Designers Johan Jeppesen and Jesper Su Rosenmeier used a different technique to create their STIK chair, constructed from a bundle of natural sticks, precisely cut and bound tightly together with cord.[25] I have also used sticks in my own practice to create lighting designs.[26]

There are even books devoted to the humble stick. *Not a Stick* by Antoinette Portis is a small, illustrated volume for young children that celebrates the power of the imagination.[27] *The Stick Book: Loads of Things You Can Make or Do with a Stick* by Fiona Danks and Jo Schofield is aimed at slightly older children and shows how to make everything from a campfire and spit for cooking fish to a sundial and a dreamcatcher.[28]

Box

The next "toy" on the list is an old cardboard box (figure 16.2).[29] Frequently discarded and available in all shapes and sizes, a cardboard box can be a place to keep special things and secret treasures, or larger versions might become a car, a house, or a shop. When I was a young boy, I remember painting the inside of an old shoe box, adding painted paper cutouts, and covering the top with stretched tracing paper to make an underwater diorama. A cardboard box can be shaped and painted to become a castle, with doors and windows, and figures added for playing out scenes of knightly adventures or fairy tales.

Figure 16.2 *An Old Cardboard Box*

a vessel for the imagination

Several boxes put together can result in a robot or spaceship, and a large open box combined with a stick can be a canoe and paddle, for river adventures through the Canadian forests or the South American jungle.

American artist Robert Rauschenberg used old cardboard boxes to create large wall sculptures, such as *Rosalie/Red Cheek/Temporary Letter/Stock (Cardboard)* (1971). He described cardboard as "a material of waste and softness. Something yielding" and regarded cardboard boxes as a material that would be available to him wherever he was in the world.[30] Cornish artist Alfred Wallis used rough-cut pieces of old boxes as his canvases and often left large areas unpainted, so that the cardboard itself became part of the painting. When questioned about this technique he said, "i Thought it not nessary To paint all around so i never Don it."[31]

Like the stick, the box has not been specifically designed to be a toy. Its use for imaginative play rescues it from the waste stream, at least for a while, and gives it a second life as . . . anything a child wants it to be.[32]

String

String is the third "toy" on the *Wired* list.[33] It comes in various lengths and types, and like the stick and the box, it is not designed for a specific purpose or intended to be a toy (figure 16.3), but its flexibility allows it to be used in a wide range of imaginative applications.

String can be used to make and fly a kite. It can be tied to a stick to create a bow and arrow, a diabolo, and a whip for a top, or a small child can use it to fish from a cardboard-box boat. The same elements can be combined to make a guitar or a single-string bass. And, of course, string can be used for tying things together, hanging things up, and pulling things along. In autumn, children can collect horse chestnuts and, by threading them with string, can play conkers. They can also practice all kinds of sailors' knots or make a plaited bracelet, a necklace, or a line of paper flags. With a loop of string, they can play cat's cradle, a pastime found in cultures all over the world, from the Inuit in the Arctic to the Māori of New Zealand.[34] A length of thick cord can be a skipping rope or, if one end is tied to a branch, a swing. String combined with two short sticks, a disc of card, and two buttons can make a fast-whirring button spinner or whirligig. Attesting to the creative

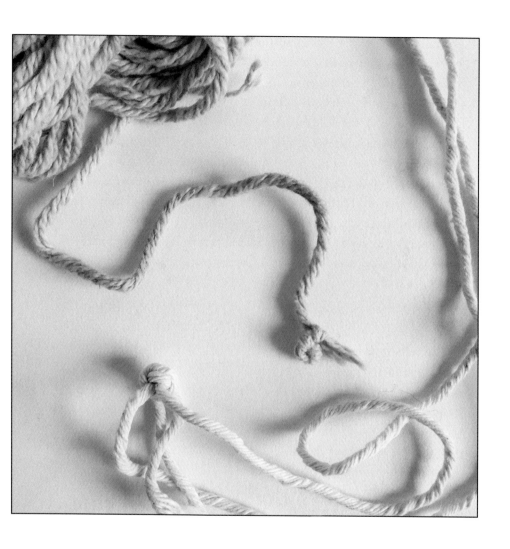

Figure 16.3 *String*
has all kinds of play possibilities

potential of play, the fast spin of the button spinner has also been adopted to create a low-cost medical centrifuge for use in places that lack electricity and/or the ability to buy expensive medical equipment; the "paperfuge" costs just a few pennies.[35]

String has inspired many artists over the years, including Barbara Hepworth, Henry Moore, and Antoine Pevsner.[36] Naum Gabo incorporated it into his sculptures, as in *Construction* (1936), and Marcel Duchamp created various works, including an installation titled *Sixteen Miles of String* (1942) and *3 Standard Stoppages* (1913–1914), in which meter-length pieces were dropped onto canvases.

String is a humble yet versatile material. Its possibilities are endless and a good length of it can stimulate a child's imaginative play.

Tube

Like the box, the fourth entry on the *Wired* list is another object whose primary use is to hold something else, such as toilet paper or cooking foil. Cardboard tubes come in various lengths, widths, and strengths—larger versions are used to package posters for mailing (figure 16.4), and long, thick-walled versions can be obtained from carpet suppliers.[37] Again, the cardboard tube is not specifically designed to be a toy. It can take on all kinds of imaginative roles and is a "must have" component in children's construction projects. For many years, the cardboard tube was a staple item in the many craft projects featured on the long-running BBC TV children's program *Blue Peter*.[38]

With paper, felt, glue, and paint, tubes can become puppets, robots, binoculars, or tunnels for toys trains. Combined with a box, they become the turrets of a castle. Long tubes can be sloping ramps for small cars or marbles, and changing the angle makes them run faster or slower. A small tube can be the basis of a kaleidoscope or a kazoo;[39] a larger one can be a digeridoo. For slightly older children, a large tube with two mirrors can become a periscope and, with lenses, a telescope or microscope. Cardboard tubes can also be a key part of a Rube Goldberg machine—a creation in which different components are deliberately arranged to carry out a simple task in a complicated way.[40]

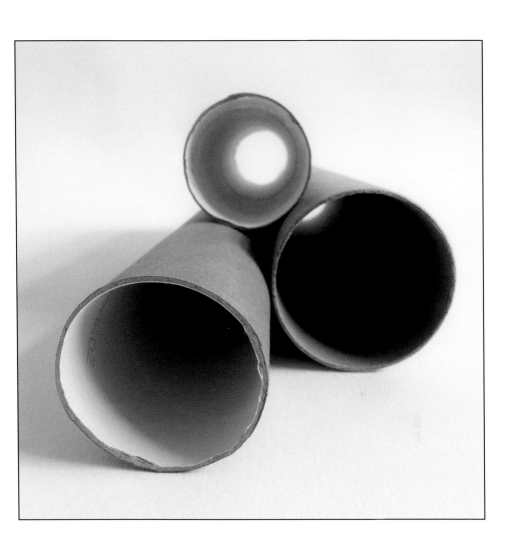

Figure 16.4 *Cardboard Tubes*

can be binoculars, a telescope, a periscope, or a marble ramp

Austrian designer and artist Manfred Kielnhofer has created functional, environmentally friendly furniture with cardboard tubes made from recycled paper, including an armchair and an elegant upright chair.[41]

Cardboard tubes offer all kinds of play opportunities, as well as activities that allow children to discover the world around them. Children can use them to produce sounds and learn about sound production; explore speed, acceleration, and gravity; and play with magnification and reflection. Constructing and making things for themselves opens up all kinds of creative avenues—few of which are provided by most off-the-shelf manufactured toys.

Dirt

The final item on the *Wired* list is not an object at all—it's simply dirt (figure 16.5).[42] This is something children are usually quite adept at finding for themselves. They spend a lot of time in it and bring much of it home on their hands and knees, spread around their faces and in their hair, and small children often eat it or at least explore how it tastes.

Dirt can be dug into and piled up. It can be a racetrack for cars, a building site for diggers, and, with a stick, a canvas for art.[43] And it's perfect for just playing in. Adding water creates mud, which can be even more fun than plain dirt because a child can make mud pies, a mud hole, and, that perennial favorite, a muddy mess.

The Boyle Family—a group of collaborative artists from London—have used earth extensively in their work, making exact reproductions from three-dimensional casts of sites randomly chosen around the world. In these artworks, they combine actual materials from the sites, such as stones, dirt, and twigs, with paint and resins to create one-off pieces that have a unique physical and visual presence.[44]

Playing in dirt also has advantages. Two experts in microbiome research (which studies the microorganisms in our body and environment and their interactions) have written a book on the benefits of dirt for a child's immune system.[45] They found that most exposures to dirt are positive. When a child's dummy or pacifier falls on the ground, a study of over three hundred thousand cases showed that children whose parents simply licked it and gave it

Figure 16.5 *Dirt*
can be dug, shaped, mixed with water, spread on hands and face, and tasted!

back to them developed fewer allergies; there were also fewer incidences of asthma and eczema, and the children's health was more robust.[46] The authors explain that the first three years of a child's life are very important in the development of the immune system, and this stage has the most lasting effect on health: "What they encounter in those early years serves as a critical inoculation for their well-being."[47]

GAMES

War, art, and religion have been constant features of human society throughout the ages. All three are concerned with a greater sense of purpose, and all three allow us to transcend the self and the ordinary routines and affairs of our lives.[48] It is perhaps understandable, therefore, that many of our most enduring forms of recreation and diversion, from indoor games to outdoor sports, involve the strategies of war and are, in effect, battles in miniature. Their skills, tactics, deceptions, and victories all proceed within agreed boundaries. As Sun Tzu said, "Ponder and deliberate before you make a move."[49]

Table and board games involving skill or chance or both were played throughout the Greek and Roman worlds. The poet Ovid, however, regarded such games as "dubious entertainments" that were not just superficial but also sinful because they waste our all-too-precious time.[50] Despite his criticisms, board games were very popular in Ovid's time and were played by everyone from ordinary soldiers to emperors.[51] Remains of game boards have been found carved on flat stones from Palestine to the north of England.

In Jerusalem, archaeologists discovered a massive stone pavement under the nineteenth-century Convent of the Sisters of Zion. Somewhat wishfully, it has been identified with the Stone Pavement referred to at the trial of Jesus. In fact, this pavement was built a century later, but conceivably it could be a reconstructed version of the one mentioned in the Gospel of John.[52] In places, it is inscribed with designs of various games played by Roman soldiers. One of these is a crown-shaped game board for "Basileus" or the "King's Game." Accounts by Latin authors indicate striking parallels between this game and the brutal mocking of Jesus, as told in the Gospels of Matthew and Mark.[53] It is similar to games found all over the Roman Empire and is, essentially, a form of Parcheesi or Ludo, in which dice are thrown and counters moved around a board.[54] A well-preserved Roman wooden game board dating from 375 CE was recently found in a grave in Poprad, Slovakia;[55] and others, etched on stone slabs, have been found in various places around the United Kingdom.

These games would have helped soldiers stave off boredom, and some, or ones derived from them, are still played today, which says much about their enduring appeal and their place in human culture. They may be pleasant pastimes, but they are also more than this. They embrace notions of conviviality and geniality and strengthen bonds of friendship. They are often the excuse rather than the reason for friends to spend an hour or two in each other's company. Playing such games may occupy the mind but not so much that we cannot think about other things, exchange friendly ribbing when an error is made, or engage in conversation.

Historically, all the elements of these games—the board, playing pieces, and dice—would have been made entirely from natural materials such as stone, wood, and bone. In contrast, the elements of most modern games are made from plastic. Many of the parts contain harmful materials that are easily broken, and the games come packaged in reams of single-use plastic wrap. When thrown away, they add to already burgeoning environmental problems.[56] However, this is only part of the story, the switch from natural materials has another effect. It alters and, it can be argued, degrades the aesthetic experience—the visual qualities, sounds, and textures. In the process, it erodes our knowledge and understanding of material things because it disconnects us from the natural origins of these games and from the world itself.

To address these concerns, we should bear in mind the four principles of resilience discussed in chapter 12, so as to reduce the negative impacts of games and toys and improve the physical experience of using them. There are many games of strategy and skill that have very lengthy pedigrees, and, traditionally, they would have been created from materials whose qualities were entirely consistent with *design for resilience*.

In the following sections, we will look at some games created from natural and reused elements. They have all been played in human societies around the world for centuries, and because they are locally made from readily available constituents, their fabrication requires no expensive tools or equipment and only the most basic of skills. Hence, they exemplify a form of design that is empowering. Importantly, too, they incorporate and are accepting of the imperfections and idiosyncrasies inherent to their materials.

Ludi Romani

Two Roman board games demonstrate the sheer longevity and continuing appeal of simple amusements in which two players pit their wits against each other. Unlike modern equivalents, however, these games would have been made entirely from natural materials (figure 16.6).

The original name of the first example has been lost to time, but E. T. Merrill has suggested calling it *Rota*, because the playing area is circular—like a wheel with spokes that divide it into eight equal sectors.[57] Game boards of this kind have been found at sites all over the Roman Empire. One example was found in Richborough, Kent;[58] another was etched into the roof of the temple at Kurna in Egypt. They have survived for over two thousand years because they were created on highly resilient materials. Boards were also made from wood and sometimes from precious materials like ivory and mother-of-pearl.[59] A similar game, but with a square playing area, is mentioned by Ovid, ca. 2 CE:

> There's a kind of game, the board squared-off by as many lines,
> with precise calculation, as the fleeting year has months:
> a smaller board presents three stones each on either side
> where the winner will have made his line up together.[60]

Like its original name, the precise rules are also unknown, but some have been proposed by modern authors—those suggested by Merrill are included as appendix 1.[61] The game is for two players, each of whom has three counters, distinguished by color, motif, or shape.

Rota is similar to Three Men's Morris or *Marelle*[62]—and to Tic-Tac-Toe or to Noughts and Crosses, versions of which are still widely played.

The second example is *Latrunculi* or, to give it its full name, *Ludus Latrunculorum*, which translates as the "game of mercenaries" or the "game

Figure 16.6 *Ludi Romani*

Rota and *Latrunculi*

inscribed stone boards, dyed fruit stones, and painted hazel counters of soldiers."[63] In 1876, a painting depicting two seated players with a *Latrunculi* board between them was discovered at Pompeii;[64] and a stone board was recently uncovered in a third-century building at Vindolanda Fort on Hadrian's Wall in Northumberland, one of sixteen such boards found at the site. *Latrunculi* was the most popular game in Roman Britain and was played among all sectors of society.[65] Boards and pieces have also been found in many other countries that were once under Roman rule.

The boards consist of orthogonal grids of lines of various dimension, but an eight-by-eight grid seems to have been the most common.[66] Again, the exact rules are not known, but we understand from Marcus Terentius Varro (127–116 BCE) that pieces were moved on the squares between the lines. Players could move pieces backward or forward;[67] and Ovid tells us that to capture an opponent's piece, one had to flank it on either side.[68] Ulrich Schädler has described it as perhaps "the most sophisticated game of strategy played by the Romans," but once the empire came to an end, its popularity waned.[69] In recent times, a number of authors have proposed rules of play based on clues found in contemporaneous writings; those that are the most cited are included as appendix 2.

Latrunculi is one of many strategy games played on boards divided into squares. These include draughts and chess, but the popular Chinese game of *Go* is probably the closest to the ancient Roman game. *Go* has similar rules and a comparable board that also has variations in grid size, and the game has many variants across different regions of Asia.

Nine Men's Morris
The fold stands empty in the drowned field,
And crows are fatted with the murrion flock;
The nine men's morris is fill'd up with mud,
And the quaint mazes in the wanton green
For lack of tread are undistinguishable
—William Shakespeare[70]

Nine Men's Morris, or Merels, is one of the oldest and most widely played board games in the world. A board from ca. 1,400 BCE was found in Egypt. Others have been discovered in County Wicklow, Ireland; at the Lindisfarne

Figure 16.7 *Nine Men's Morris*
game board inscribed on worm-eaten pine with black and white pebbles as counters

Priory on the Northumberland coast; in Gokstad in Norway; and cut into steps that ascend the mountain of Mihintale in Sri Lanka. Nine Men's Morris was especially popular in Europe in the fourteenth century and is illustrated in various Italian manuscripts of the time.[71] And when the *Mary Rose*, which sank in the Solent in 1545, was raised from the seafloor, a Nine Men's Morris board was found inscribed into the head of a barrel.[72]

It is evident from these various finds that although ornate, well-crafted versions of Nine Men's Morris boards have been used since medieval times, for most of the game's history, boards have been simply scratched on any convenient flat surface, from floor slabs to roofs tiles, and even scored into the ground, as Shakespeare indicates in the above quote. The rules are included as appendix 3.

The version shown in figure 16.7 is inscribed on an old, worm-eaten piece of pine found half rotted in a tumbledown stone barn. Its rescue from a former life and its well-worn appearance bring to mind the words of the great American environmentalist Aldo Leopold: "The autobiography of an old board is a kind of literature not yet taught on campuses."[73]

Draughts

Draughts, or checkers, which is thought to have its origins in Europe around the beginning of the twelfth century, is now played everywhere. Homemade sets like the one shown in figure 16.8 can be easily created from entirely reused materials—cardboard from an old box for the board and bottle tops for the playing pieces, the two sides being differentiated by simply inverting the bottle tops of one player. It is an ad hoc solution that is perfectly serviceable while also being unpretentious and costing nothing. Such sets can be made anywhere by anyone, and, in the process, what would otherwise be waste materials are given a second life. It is a simple way of providing enjoyment and conviviality for young and old.

I first came across sets like this when I was a teenager working in the steelworks that was the main industry of my hometown. Draughts was being played in the many cabins all over the plant where workers spent their lunch breaks. I have since seen similar sets in cafés and bars in Europe, Africa, and South America.

Figure 16.8 *Bottle-Top Draughts*
on a homemade board; sets like this are used all over the world

Over the years, the rules have changed. In the game's early form, the taking of an opponent's pieces was optional. Modern English draughts, in which players are compelled to take their opponents pieces, comes from rules developed in sixteenth-century France and the game of *Jeu Forcé*,[74] but there are still many variations in how the game can be played. For instance, in the Losing Game, players try to make their opponents capture their pieces, the winner being the first player to lose all of their pieces.[75]

Slate Game Board

Since Roman times, slate has been extensively quarried and used as a material for roofing, flooring, and paving.[76] For centuries, small rectangles of slate were used in schools and homes for children to practice spelling and arithmetic, as well as for general writing purposes. In his *Treatise on the Astrolabe* of 1391, Geoffrey Chaucer mentions writing on a slate on six separate occasions[77]—including the following: "And take alle the signes, degrees, and minutes, and secoundes, that thou findest in directe of alle the yeris, monethes, and dayes, and wryte hem in thy slate."[78]

By the late nineteenth century, there were some moves to phase out the use of slates in schools on health grounds—children shared slates and cleaned them using their licked fingers.[79] However, their use persisted well into the twentieth century, mainly because of their economy and durability.[80] In my own junior school in 1960s South Wales, my first writing implements were a small wood-framed slate, a stick of chalk, and a wiping cloth. Although slates are no longer used in schools, North Wales quarries still produce children's slates as well as larger versions as kitchen memo boards.

The durability and versatility of slate can also be put to good use in creating a multipurpose, endlessly adaptable game board. The example in figure 16.9 is made from an old roofing slate. With a piece of chalk, it can be marked up for draughts or chess, Nine Men's Morris, Parcheesi, or backgammon. It could also be used for Noughts and Crosses or for Hangman, or it could serve simply as a scoreboard. A damp cloth can wipe it clean, ready for a new game to be marked out, and all without waste or the need for separate boards for every different game.

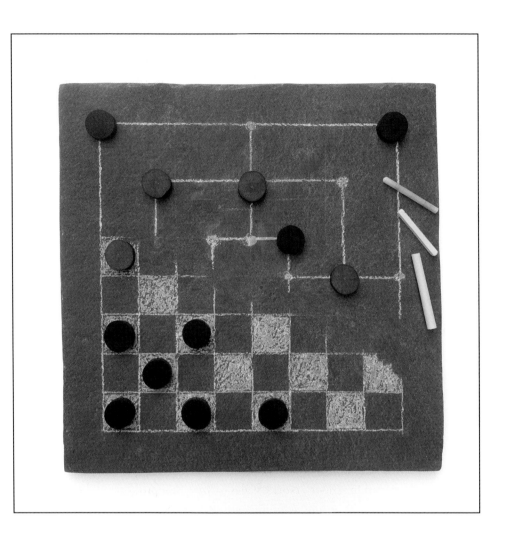

Figure 16.9 *Slate Game Board*
an old roofing slate, marked up with chalk counters cut from the branch and colored with water-based inks

Jacks

The throwing and catching game of Jacks is traditionally played with five sheep bones (figure 16.10). Also called fivestones, checkstones, or knucklebones, it is found in many cultures, from Europe and America to Russia, Japan, and Polynesia.[81] While today it is mainly played by children, historically it was played by adults, especially women.[82]

Jacks is a very old form of amusement, but its history is difficult to trace due to the fact that it can be played with ordinary stones, beans, nuts, or shells and so the pieces generally cannot be distinguished specifically as gaming pieces—unless they are modified or found in a particular context. Knucklebones, however, are something of an exception. Evidence from archaeology, ethnography, and iconography indicates that these bones, taken from the hock joints of sheep, were intentionally selected and carefully kept together. They have been found in groups at Neolithic sites across Europe and Asia, and their most likely use was as gaming pieces.[83]

Knucklebones was certainly played in ancient Greece, where it was called *pentelitha* or *astragaloi*. Sets have been discovered at a number of sites, and the game is frequently depicted in sculpture and painting being played by men, women, or children.[84] Homer mentions it in *The Iliad*, where the ghost of Patroclus recounts that when he was young, he had "the misfortune to commit homicide and kill Amphidamas' boy by accident in a childish quarrel over a game of knuckle-bones."[85] In his *Histories*, ca. 430 BCE, Herodotus suggests that the game originated in Lydia, in the westernmost part of present-day Turkey. The Lydians, he tells us, were suffering from a great famine, and as it lingered on, "they began to look for something to alleviate their misery. Various expedients were devised: for instance, the invention of dice, knucklebones, and ball-games. In fact, they claim to have invented all games of this sort except draughts."[86] Attesting to its popularity, playing pieces mimicking the shape and size of the original sheep bones have been found crafted from every type of material, including gold and glass.[87]

Folklorists have remarked on the similarity of knucklebones to divination by "throwing the bones," traditionally practiced by Zulu healers or shamans using the same type of hock-joint bones.[88]

Figure 16.10 *Jacks or Knucklebones*

an ancient throwing and catching game traditionally played with bones from the hock joints of sheep

In Lancashire, in northern England, a nineteenth-century song sung while playing jacks appears to link this name to the English Restoration.[89]

Jack's his own master, Jack's home agen.
He's well full o' siller[90] An' fond o' Nell Gwen
Here's one for his fayther, Whose head rolled in welter[91]
An' one for his brother, Who's douce fond o' Nell
There's two taps for Charley An' agen for Jack
There's three taps for Charley An' ne'er one for Jack
There's four taps for Charley An' nought left for Jack
But wait while he's merry An' douce fond o' Nell

The name Jack is probably referring to James (Jacobus, in Latin), son of Charles I, who was beheaded in 1649, and brother of Charles II. The reign of Charles II brought about the restoration of the monarchy following Cromwell's Commonwealth (1649–1660). Nell would be the actress Nell Gwyn, who was Charles's lover and mother of his children.[92]

Today, mass-produced versions of Jacks have star-shaped playing pieces made of die-cast metal or plastic, along with a rubber or plastic ball, which is bounced and caught, instead of tossing a designated "Jack" stone.

Jacks has an exceptionally long history, and in its earlier forms, the pieces were simply part of, and inseparable from, the natural environment and were entirely renewable and nondamaging. It is a game that has provided amusement for adults and children for generations, and through its sequences, rhythms, and rhymes, it has served as a retainer of references to sociocultural heritage. A brief overview of how to play is included as appendix 4.

Iyaga

In England, this game is known as "ring and pin" or "cup and ball," or by its French name, Bilboquet. Among the Inuit peoples of the Arctic, it is variously known as *Iyaga, Ayagak,* or *Ajaqaq.* The game is often played by children, but in the Arctic, it was endowed with spiritual significance and played in the winter or early spring as a rite to hasten the long-awaited return of the sun.[93] It was also played among the peoples of the Pacific Northwest. The Kwakiutl people called it *Dzagzegala,* where it was a gambling game and could sometimes involve considerable stakes.[94]

Figure 16.11 *Iyaga*
traditional Inuit ring-and-pin game
seal bone and sinew

Traditionally, the game is made from seal bone, specifically the humerus.[95] A small hole is drilled in the edge of the larger, hollow "ring" bone and a cord of plaited sinew attached, the other end being tied to the spike or "pin" bone (figure 16.11).

This simple game is played by tossing up the "ring" and trying to catch it on the "pin." The example illustrated has just one large hole in the "ring" bone. Other versions also have holes of various sizes drilled in the sides; it may even be the skull of a small animal.[96] Players can decide which end of the ring has to be speared, or if it has multiple holes, different scores may apply to different holes.[97]

Lest one may think that such a game is childish or a waste of time, Rousseau said of this pastime: "If ever I went back into society I should carry a cup-and-ball in my pocket, and play with it all day long to excuse myself from speaking when I had nothing to say. If everyone were to do the same men would become less malicious, and society would become safer and, I think, more agreeable. In fact, let wits laugh if they will, but I maintain that the only morality within the reach of the present century is the morality of the cup-and ball."[98]

SPORTS

Offering opportunities for physical exercise, recreation, cooperation, and competition, sports are also pleasurable and fun. Some of the oldest are quite simple—running, jumping, throwing—and they emerged from the needs of physical combat, where strength, agility, endurance, and swiftness of foot were essential. Speed and endurance were also important for carrying messages (see chapter 15). Many sports developed at a time when civilization had evolved to a point where people had leisure time and were no longer solely preoccupied with the necessities of survival. Terry Eagleton has likened sports to religion—both have traditions, assemblies, and champions, and both are outgrowths of communal forms of living.[99]

There are many different kinds of sports around the world, but space here allows for discussion of only one or two examples. Those I have selected are widely played, require little in the way of specialized equipment or facilities, and in one form or another have endured for millennia and thus have demonstrated their resilience.

Track and Field

Track-and-field events include running, jumping, and throwing certain kinds of objects, and there are many variations and combinations. Their origins lie in the ancient past. Distance running can be traced to Egypt ca. 2,000 BCE and included ceremonial runs by kings who wished to demonstrate their fitness for office. Runners and messengers were being used by the Hebrews ca. 1,100 BCE. And in Greek mythology, Atalanta is chiefly known for her speed in running races against suitors, who when defeated were put to death.[100]

Sports contests in ancient Greece developed both from warfare and from religious and funerary ceremonies; the Greek *athlos*, the root of the word *athletics*, means "combat" or "contest." And, of course, the origin of the Olympic Games—of which track and field are the high point—lies in ancient Greece. Beginning in 776 BCE at Olympia, they were part of Greek life for twelve centuries. Long-distance running was also an important part of military training in ancient Persia, Iraq, India, and China.[101]

Modern track-and-field sports evolved from rural games and folk and religious festivals. The rules were developed in the late nineteenth century and were first applied in amateur championships and competitions. Around this time, there were also attempts to revive the Olympic Games, and in 1896 the first modern Olympics were held in Athens. All competitors were male and strictly amateur, and the track-and-field events were the centerpiece.[102]

For over a century, amateur status was defined as "a person who competes solely for the love of the sport and for whom sport is a recreational activity. Also the person must not consider sport as a means to gain any material benefit."[103]

In later years, athletes who committed considerable time to their chosen sport began to be rewarded through university scholarships in the United States; token jobs in Eastern Europe; under-the-counter payments; and trust funds that enabled them to compete for prize money. These practices lasted until 2001, when the amateur stipulation was removed.[104]

Amateur-level track-and-field sports remain extremely popular and are open to everyone. Millions around the world participate simply for the love of doing so, and for most people, these sports remain an enjoyable form of exercise. Runners can use city streets and country lanes, and, in many countries, there is a five-kilometer Saturday morning "parkrun." This entirely free, volunteer-led, community event began in the United Kingdom in 2004, since when it has been embraced by twenty-two countries, with around 350,000 people taking part each week.[105] It is accessible and affordable—all that is needed is a pair of sports shoes, a T-shirt, and shorts.

Soccer

Many different games involve a ball, and one of these is the world's most-loved sport, the so-called "beautiful game." Soccer brings people and communities together, either to play or to watch. It is entertaining, unpredictable, exciting, and emotional.

Despite the commercialization of today's professional game, it remains essentially the simple sport it has long been—two teams on a field trying to kick a ball into a goal at either end of the playing area. It is played by children and adults in city parks, school playgrounds, and back alleys—virtually anywhere that has a suitable piece of flat ground. And volunteer-run, community-based soccer clubs are organized for all ages. The only equipment needed is a ball—goalposts can be anything from standard nets, often found in parks, to a couple of bags or jackets dropped on the ground a few yards apart (figure 16.12).

Antecedents of the modern game go back millennia. *Cuju*, or kickball, was being played by the military and upper classes in China around two thousand years ago, and similar games were played in Mesoamerica. However, the modern version evolved out of folk games and was developed in Britain. In *The Comedy of Errors* of 1594, Shakespeare wrote:

Am I so round with you as you with me,
That like a football you do spurn me thus?
You spurn me hence, and he will spurn me hither.
If I last in this service, you must case me in leather.[106]

Figure 16.12 *Amateur Soccer*

played in local parks all over the world

In Shakespeare's day, it was a far more dangerous affair, being played by neighboring towns and villages with unlimited numbers of players. It was more like "mob football"—the only sport that was more lethal was archery. It is little wonder that in *King Lear* someone is called a "base football player."[107]

The modern game was formalized in the nineteenth century by the upper classes of British society, especially in the "public schools" (which is how the country's fee-paying private schools are misleadingly referred to). The game was only later adopted by the working classes, and over the last century or so, it has witnessed a remarkable rise in popularity around the globe. This seems to be due to a combination of soccer's simplicity; the enjoyment, camaraderie, and physical exercise the sport offers; and the lack of expensive equipment or facilities needed to play it, unlike cricket, ice hockey, and American football. As a result, soccer is easily understood and, for the amateur, accessible and affordable—features that also help explain its resilience.[108]

During the twentieth century, sports were taken more and more seriously, with increasing levels of regulation and systemization and stricter enforcement of rules. For many professional athletes today, the notion of "play"—at least as it was described at the start of this chapter—is no longer a significant factor. Sport has become a job, driven by commercial priorities, not a voluntary activity engaged in for its own sake. Consequently, true play factors such as spontaneity, carefreeness, and fun dwindle away—professional sports are a serious business. The result is that professional sports now occupy a rather odd category of human activity. They are neither true play nor real work and are quite distinct from culture and the processes that create culture. Unlike their origins in sacred festivals, where they had strong ties to well-being and ideas that nourish the soul, modern professional sports are entirely secular affairs. Even though they may be important to participants and spectators, Huizinga argues that the essential "play" factor has all but gone and, because of this, professionalized sports are incapable of being truly "culture-creating" activities.[109]

In the industrial valleys of South Wales, where I grew up, the game of rugby thrived. At that time, it was strictly amateur, and there was a genuine sense of camaraderie among the spectators and players, many of whom we knew personally. There was a friendly rivalry between valley towns, and a win generated a feeling of community pride. Since this sport turned professional in 1995, however, the tone and spirit of the game has noticeably changed, and from a personal perspective, sadly, my interest has waned.

When the two interrelated factors of commercialization and professionalization intrude into the arena of play—in toys, games, and sports—priorities shift. Not only does the spirit of play become eroded but the standing of the amateur also becomes diminished.

Authentic forms of play are participated in for their own sake. They are separate from and extra to serious work. The most popular forms are truly recreational and fun, and approached with an attitude of carefreeness, spontaneity, and creativity. Some are individual; many are communal; the best are simple, local, and ad hoc, with no requirements for consumption.

17 RESILIENT SPIRIT

Spirit and *spirituality* refer to an intuitively apprehended sense that life has meaning. Over the centuries, all kinds of practices, texts, and understandings have arisen from this idea. In general, they concern the inner development of the individual, the harmony of the community, and ideas and practices considered to be life-enhancing. Essentially, it is an area that addresses the age-old question "How should we live?"

In this chapter, we will consider artifacts and activities that respond to enduring questions about life's meaning and purpose. We begin with ritual, which has been a distinctive feature of human societies through the ages. This is followed by pilgrimage, which was popular in medieval Europe and has been witnessing a considerable revival in recent times. We will also look at shrines for both private and public use and their changing fortunes over the years, as well as at sanctuary and the contemporary Japanese practice of *shinrin-yoku.*

RITUAL

The Whitsunday processions in May were an annual ritual when I was growing up. Hundreds of people from all the churches and chapels in the area walked in unison through the streets. There were banners and flags and hymn singing, and the whole community came together in common cause and celebration. Throughout the year, in addition to the weekly church services, there were other rituals like harvest festival, Easter, and Christmas, and those that marked rites of passage, particularly baptisms, weddings, and funerals. More secular rituals were also common—Remembrance Sunday, when scouts, guides, and the town's dignitaries gathered to lay wreaths at the cenotaph in honor of those who died in war; and Eisteddfod, the annual festival on March 1, St. David's Day, honoring the patron saint of Wales and celebrating the country's culture and language.

Whether religious or secular, ritual is one of the defining elements of being human. It has a depth of meaning that becomes actualized through shared, performative experiences, and it helps generate a sense of identity, belonging, stability, and orientation.[1] Ritual is a focal constituent of cultural and social life and has always been so, at least until modern times.[2] And because of its inherent moral teachings, regular participation in ritual means that "one accustoms oneself to inward virtues by outward habits."[3]

In contemporary societies, many traditional forms of ritual have fallen into decline and become marginalized from mainstream activities. This is primarily a result of the progressive effects of post-Enlightenment reason, which recognized that not everything old and traditional was necessarily good, including ignorance, pseudoscience, superstition, and prejudice.[4] The ascendancy of reason, however, also led to a devaluing of more intuitive, imaginative understandings of the world.[5] Ritual was rejected as credulous, irrelevant, and dull; myth became synonymous with falsehood; and in the post-Reformation Protestant churches, some rites of passage were downgraded or eliminated altogether.[6] This resulted in what Charles Taylor characterizes as "a mechanistic, meaning-shorn universe."[7] Yet even in the most secularized of societies, the vestiges of ritual always remain.[8] Generally, however, secular-humanist alternatives lack recognition of not only transcendence but also the layers of history, tradition, and meaning of the older sacred rituals. Modern substitutes based in naturalistic materialism and scientific understandings of the universe have also been accompanied by a sense of meaninglessness and doubt.[9]

As part of a broader reassessment and critique of the modern project, there has recently been a renewed interest in ritual and greater recognition of its function and importance.[10] Ritual deals with perennial human concerns and teaches us how we should live by transforming "a historical memory into mythos, something that happens all the time, by liberating it from the past and bringing it into the present."[11] Ritual is imaginative and poetical rather than literal and factual and, like many of the artifacts we have looked at in earlier chapters, we must be cautious about defining and classifying it too tightly. The roots of ritual lie in a worldview unfettered by narrow categorizations. Such categorizations can effectively obstruct the kinds of joined-up thinking needed for understanding the interrelated systems, relationships, ecologies, and interdependencies of human and nonhuman forms of life. Ritual can be understood as a multivalent phenomenon that combines a range of elements, values, and interpretations into a coherent whole. It relies on our pattern-recognition abilities such that, through its practices, raw materials become synthesized into ideas that, like poetry, may have a variety of connotations and meanings.[12] Ritual is closer to art than science and can include different combinations of pageant, ceremony, drama, routinized actions, rites, readings, music, and song (figure 17.1). A primary function of ritual is that it teaches us how to live together in harmony by overcoming egoism and fostering habits of empathy, compassion, and charity. By transcending self-interest and considering others, not in terms of their occupation or social position but as persons like us, we grow as individuals.

The wisdom teachings contained in sacred texts were originally developed within oral cultures and were meant to be spoken aloud as a part of ritual, and their lessons acted out through ethical behaviors. They should be understood not as accurate accounts of historical events but as intuitive forms of imaginative, artistic expression. Therefore, criticizing them as irrational or implausible would be like criticizing Bob Dylan because the answer has never actually been proven to be "blowin' in the wind."[13] And just like a song or poem, there is a performative element to these teachings. When reinforced through ritual, their truths become experienced intuitively, and thence they begin to affect our outlook and our behavior. Through physical movements and gestures, as well as sights, sounds, smells, and vocal responses, and by repeating these again and again, we embody the teachings, knowledge, and ideas—they become part of who we are. It is through such *enactment*—ritually and ethically—that we learn the meaning and transformative power of ritual.

Figure 17.1 *Ritual*
a service at the Basilica of Saint Pius X
Lourdes, France

Many regular, repetitive practices became devalued in the modern era, including ritual and ceremony as well as many applied activities such as craft apprenticeships. All these represent important forms of learning because they allow us to absorb understandings at a deeper level, not just rationally. When we learn through physical practices, the body becomes involved in and part of the learning, and this enables us to acquire *bodily-kinesthetic knowledge.*[14] Moreover, this is not a one-way process in which brain activity directs bodily movement; rather, these two components are functionally *interdependent.*[15] In ritual, information and knowledge are incorporated into creative, applied art forms that allow them to be absorbed both emotionally and through repeated bodily routines.[16] Frequent participation cultivates an attitude or mode of consciousness that is related to the holistic, imaginative ways of knowing associated with the "right brain." Here, the meaning of the words recited in ritual is not so important. The sounds and physical actions repeated daily or weekly are always the same—monotonously so—but it is this very monotony that silences the more dominant, rational "left brain" to allow deeper, more intuitive, holistic insights and ways of perceiving the world.[17] Similar insights are experienced by artists when they are engrossed in the creative act.[18]

While the truths contained in these teachings may be timeless, the rituals through which they are enacted should not remain static. To stay relevant to each successive generation, ritual has to be continually reinterpreted and adapted to meet the changing circumstances in which people find themselves. In this way, ritual maintains its currency and potency; if it fails to do this, it becomes ossified and lifeless and falls into disuse.

Ritual is a far less prominent feature of public life today than it was even a generation or two ago, and with its decline, its role in binding communities together has withered.[19] With its passing, society has inevitably become more atomized. Increasing numbers of people are living alone, and we spend much of our work and leisure time in front of screens. This shift toward solitary living, especially when set against the backdrop of rapid environmental deterioration, adds to a pervasive sense of uncertainty and unease.

It is hardly surprising, therefore, that in recent years, some have been looking again at the role and benefits of ritual. The need has never been greater for community-based, shared practices that are both formative and transformative.

Nonetheless, for many people, ritual is no longer a significant part of their lives. Traditional forms of ritual that continue to struggle on, often in much deteriorated form, would undoubtedly benefit from creative renovation. There is also a need to develop new kinds of ritual that are both meaningful and suited to contemporary mores. Here, creative disciplines like design should be able to make a useful contribution—but they may be ill-equipped to do so. Since the beginning of the twentieth century, designers have focused primarily on instrumental factors because of their involvement in developing market-led products and services. Our behaviors and our ways of understanding ourselves in relation to others and the world have been affected by these instrumental priorities, but they differ considerably from those associated with ritual, which have complex, multifarious patterns of meaning and significance.

The fact that ritual practices have been sidelined in modern societies for years means that their teachings and practices are no longer part of the collective consciousness.[20] If designers are to offer any kind of meaningful contribution, therefore, they will have to bear in mind the sheer magnitude of the task.

PILGRIMAGE

And I shal apparaille me . . .
In pilgrymes wise,
And wende with yow I wile,
Til we fynde Truthe;
And caste on my clothes
Y-clouted and hole,
My cokeres and my coffes,
For cold of my nailes;
And hange myn hoper at myn hals
In stede of a scryppe.
A busshel of bred corn
Brynge me therinne;

For I wol sowe it myself,
And sithenes wol I wende
To pilgrimage, as palmeres doon,
Pardon for to have.
—William Langland, fourteenth century[21]

Pilgrimages were being made to Britain's great stone circles and henges some three thousand years ago. On the other side of the world, Hindu pilgrims were traveling to Benares in India. The Temple of Jerusalem and the Tomb of Rachel near Bethlehem have been destinations for Jewish pilgrims for well over two millennia. Christians were visiting sites associated with the New Testament from the beginning of the second century, and by the fourth century the practice had become well established. In Islam, the Hajj is an annual pilgrimage to the Kaaba in Mecca, with many also visiting Medina, the City of the Prophet.[22]

During medieval times in Britain, there were pilgrimages to local shrines; to the large regional cathedrals that housed holy relics and images, such as Durham, Ely, and Hereford; and to national shrines like Canterbury, Walsingham, and St. Winefride's Well in Flintshire, which claims to be the oldest pilgrimage site in continual use in the country, with records dating back 1,300 years.[23] Longer routes took people to the sacred sites of Europe, especially Rome and Santiago de Compostela, and to the Holy Land.

This extensive web of interconnected pilgrimage routes meant that the land itself became imbued with a sense of the sacred[24]—an idea that is still common among the world's Indigenous and Aboriginal peoples.

The Reformation brought pilgrimage to an abrupt end in many parts of northern Europe. In 1538, Henry VIII and Thomas Cromwell banned the practice in Britain, and hundreds of sacred places were desecrated, looted, and destroyed, leaving the country and the national imagination all the poorer.[25]

In recent times, pilgrimage in Europe has undergone a considerable revival, with Santiago de Compostela in Spain, Lourdes in France, and Fatima in Portugal attracting hundreds of thousands, even millions, of pilgrims each year (figure 17.2). The British Pilgrimage Trust was established

Figure 17.2 *Cathedral of Santiago de Compostela*
Galicia, Spain

in 2014 as a charity dedicated to the renewal of pilgrimage and its promotion as a form of cultural heritage that benefits physical and mental health, spiritual well-being, and community.[26] Through these kinds of initiatives, the presence of spiritually significant sites and pilgrimage routes and the notion of sacred geographies are being recognized as important constituents of cultural heritage.[27]

Pilgrimage is about embarking on a journey—it involves leaving one's familiar comforts and traveling through unknown territory. Typically, destinations are places associated with holy figures and events significant to one's own spiritual tradition. Fundamentally, this outer, physical journey serves as a metaphor for the inner journey and the seeking of meaning. It is, therefore, a journey of transition—from one place to another and from one state of being to another, spurred along the way by the prospect of arriving at a place of particular spiritual import.[28]

Pilgrimage is a good example of a resilient practice. It is a global phenomenon that has existed for thousands of years. It is a pursuit that is available to everyone, whether religious or secular. Traditionally, those with few resources of their own would be given alms, food, and accommodation at their destination.[29] Even today, hoteliers at pilgrimage sites often feel a strong sense of responsibility to keep their prices low so as to accommodate a broad range of pilgrims. When pilgrimage is limited to walking, it has low environmental impact and is also a low-consumption activity, constrained by how much one can carry. Pilgrimage on foot is also beneficial to physical health, as well as to mental health because it is a time of reflection, fellowship, and inspiring destinations.

Visitors to sacred sites also help support the local economy—the hospitality industry, shopkeepers, artisans, and guides. They also make donations and purchase souvenirs and religious items, usually a cockle or scallop shell, the traditional symbol of the pilgrim.[30] But today, as in the past, many of the major sites suffer from overcommercialization. In contrast, local pilgrimage routes are shorter, more affordable, and less commercialized, and they connect people more closely to the traditions of their own landscape.

My own place of pilgrimage is not a famous shrine or grand cathedral. It is a sacred site not far from where I grew up. It lies deep in the Black

Mountains of Wales. A single-track road from Crickhowell rises up behind the town and follows the hillside for some miles before descending to the village of Llangenny, where it follows the river to Llanbedr. From here, the views open up onto fields and hills before the road again rises and narrows to a dappled track hemmed in by banked hedgerows and overhanging trees. Eventually, I descend to a deeply shaded hollow below Crug Mawr hill.

Arriving at this remote corner of Wales, I feel I am coming home. Here, among the trees, with the gentle sound of flowing water filling the air, all is cool, green, and damp. Shallow stone steps lead down to a path along the bank of Nant Mair (Mary's Brook), and a little way along, barely distinguishable from the drystone wall it abuts, is an ancient well (figure 17.3). For a thousand years, it has been a holy place. Ffynon Ishow is the well of Celtic convert and sixth-century hermit and martyr St. Issui, or Ishow, who lived here until he was killed by a robber to whom he had offered hospitality. Many miracles have been credited to St. Issui, during his lifetime and ever since, and it is said that the holy well is able to cure diseases. In the eleventh century, we are told, a pilgrim with leprosy was restored to health by its waters. In thanks, he left a bag of gold to construct a shrine chapel in the saint's memory. It was built on the site of the saint's hermitage on the hillside above the well, and St. Issui is believed to be buried under its altar. And even in our highly secularized age, healings continue to be attributed to the waters of this remote well.[31]

The little chapel later became part of the fourteenth-century church of St. Issui, a simple stone structure with a well-preserved rood screen. The intricate carvings of the screen, fashioned from Irish bog oak, were saved from the ravages of the Reformation by the very isolation of the place. When I stand beneath the rood screen today, looking at the simple altar, the timelessness of this place seems almost palpable. And as I turn to leave, facing me is a large wall painting created in red ocher and soot. It depicts a skeleton with hourglass, scythe, and spade—a reminder, a memento mori, of the fleeting nature of human life.

Standing at the porch, the sun filling the graveyard with its warmth, I look across the little valley to sheep grazing on the opposite hillside. They were here, no doubt, when Issui chose this place for his ascetic life, and when

Figure 17.3 *St. Issui's Well*
Powys, Wales

Gerald of Wales visited in 1188 with Baldwin, Archbishop of Canterbury, who preached from the steps of the graveyard cross in a recruitment drive for the Third Crusade.[32] Sheep will be here still when I am long gone and others stand in this spot looking out at the same scene, having come to the holy well just below the hill and made it their own special place of pilgrimage.

DOMESTIC SHRINE

A domestic shrine may be a small cabinet or niche, or simply a dresser or table that is used to display a group of items for religious veneration. It is a place set apart from ordinary, everyday affairs so that an individual or a household can express feelings of reverence toward a god, a saint, or ancestors (figure 17.4).

Domestic shrines date back to Neolithic times. They have been found at excavations in Europe, Turkey, and Egypt and among Mycenaean, Greek, Roman, pagan, and Christian cultures.[33] Today, they are often an integral feature of homes in Catholic Spain, Latin America, and some parts of the United States.[34] In Hinduism, a domestic shrine signifies a purified space.[35] In Japanese Buddhism, a small cabinet, known as a butsudan, typically contains representations of divinities and ancestral memorial items. Nowadays, however, there is a highly competitive market in commercially produced butsudan that harmonize with interiors, but often depart significantly from tradition.[36] And in Mexico, the Indigenous Nahua people of Sierra Norta de Puebla venerate ancestors by offering incense, flowers, and prayers at domestic altars.[37]

These types of shrines tend to be looked after and primarily used by women, with practices and rituals being passed on from mother to daughter and daughter-in-law.[38] Although still common in many places, their importance has declined with modernization, secularization, and the fact that more women now work outside the home. In India, this has led to a growth in street shrines.[39]

A sacred place in the home, set apart and displaying images, statues, and other objects is clearly a highly resilient form of material culture that is accompanied by equally resilient practices. While each may be different,

Figure 17.4 *Domestic Shrine*

handmade wall niche of Our Lady of Fatima, mass-produced plastic statuette of the Virgin Mary, rosary, Bible, rosebud, and candle

their general aesthetic and notions of affiliation, connection, respect, and veneration remain virtually unchanged, irrespective of time, culture, or specific belief system.[40]

WAYSIDE SHRINE

When wandering country roads and byways or crossing mountain passes in Europe, the traveler will invariably come across a wayside shrine. It may be a large crucifix sheltering under a canopy or a niche set in a wall, with a statue of the Virgin, a holy picture, and flowers. It might mark the place where someone died, or it could be a marker on a pilgrimage route, or it may have been erected simply as an act of piety. For Christians, these shrines serve as something of an anchor, a place along the way for pause and quiet reflection, a place of comfort. Wayside shrines are also common in Japanese Shintoism, and in India, shrines honoring Hindu saints and deities are ubiquitous features of the landscape.[41] Research into their role in Mumbai suggests that for women especially, street shrines often play an integral role in their daily lives and religious experiences and are regarded as an extension of their lived spaces. They also make the streets feel safer and more welcoming.[42]

A more recent phenomenon along roadsides in Britain and North and South America are more ephemeral shrines made from a variety of materials. They may include religious items, but often they are entirely secular. I recently encountered one at a junction in Yorkshire where a cyclist had been killed. There were bunches of flowers in cyclists' water bottles, bicycle wheels festooned with more flowers, two cycling shirts with messages written in felt pen, and photographs of the deceased.

The purpose and meaning of these informal shrines can be interpreted in a number of ways. In keeping with traditions that transcend both time and culture, they are a ritualization of absence and a public memorialization of the loss of an individual.[43] Usually placed as close to the site of a death as possible, by their very nature they represent "the boundary between life and death."[44] In the process, they temporarily transform ordinary, everyday places into sacred spaces that are both commemorative and celebratory. They also implicitly raise a public concern about, for example, careless driving

Figure 17.5 *Wayside Shrine*
Patagonian Highway (Ruta Nacional 40), Argentina

or dangerous road conditions; in this sense, they also serve as a warning. Their audience is the passerby, so they invite unselective public participation, witness, and social transformation. Hence, they can be understood as sites of pilgrimage, places of commemoration and communication, and commentaries about public issues. Unlike graveyards, which are separate, enclosed spaces, these vernacular shrines are spontaneous intrusions into, and disruptions of, our everyday lives. They implore us to acknowledge the individuals involved and the ensuing grief and repercussions—they demand that the anonymous statistic be seen as a human being, an individual who was loved and is mourned.[45]

The intention behind the example from Patagonia shown in figure 17.5 is ambiguous. It is set back quite a distance from the road—a path to it is marked out with old plastic bottles. Is it a memorial commemorating an untimely death or simply an act of piety? The question itself recognizes that the readings and associations of the observer will inevitably be different from those of the creator. Whatever the maker's intention might have been, it is a grassroots public artifact concerned with ritual, spirituality, and commemoration. As such, it is both a silent witness and a challenge to many of the dominant, often rather alienating themes of our age.[46]

DEFACED STATUES

In Hereford Cathedral, an old stone tomb is ornately carved with robed figures, but they have been badly vandalized—their faces have been hacked away. In this damaged state, however, they are physical manifestations of the changing religious sensibilities of sixteenth-century England (figure 17.6). In 1538, during the Protestant Reformation, the cathedral's carvings and ornamentation were subjected to deliberate acts of disfigurement or removal.[47] All over the country, altars were removed, holy relics destroyed, wall paintings whitewashed over, and statues smashed or burned—these kinds of holy artifacts were regarded as far too "popish"—that is, reflective of the beliefs and traditions of Roman Catholicism.

The figures on the Hereford tomb had been skillfully and beautifully crafted from stone. They were designed for longevity, and their present

Figure 17.6 *Defaced Statues*
Hereford Cathedral, United Kingdom

mutilated state tells a story. Over the course of their long history, people's views and understandings about what is appropriate and acceptable have changed. And this history gives the fabric of our society depth and meaning.

Today, nearly five hundred years after they were first installed, sensibilities have shifted again. The cathedral's shrines to St. Thomas of Hereford and St. Ethelbert have been refurbished, thirteen new icons tell the story of St. Ethelbert, and a holy relic of St. Thomas has been donated to the cathedral by the Roman Catholic abbots of Downside and Belmont Abbeys.[48]

Changing mores and the narratives this can bring to our material culture will never occur when artifacts are designed for disposal. When they are constantly being replaced, there is no opportunity for our material environment to accumulate such meanings.

SANCTUARY

The word *sanctuary* comes from the Latin *sanctus*, meaning "holy," "consecrated," or "sacred." It originally referred to open land where the Divine was believed to be present. In the fourth century, the idea was enshrined into Roman law, and at the Council of Orléans of 511 CE, it became recognized by the Church.

In England, the right of sanctuary was made part of common law ca. 600 CE, during the reign of King Æthelberht.[49] This right meant that fugitives accused of any offense other than treason or sacrilege could seek protection by reaching a church's door and grabbing the ring-shaped handle; as a consequence, a church-door handle became known as a sanctuary ring or a sanctuary knocker.[50] The church offered a place of safety for up to forty days, after which the accused could either give themselves up for trial or confess and promise to leave the realm. Choosing the latter also meant that offenders forfeited all their worldly possessions and their spouses, and if they ever returned, they would be regarded as outlaws.

This legal right of sanctuary lasted a thousand years, until it was abolished in 1623 for criminals and in 1723 for civil cases.[51] Even so, many people in Britain and elsewhere still take the view that churches, mosques, and other holy places are, or should be, inviolable, and instances in recent times where this has not been respected have caused widespread moral outrage.[52]

A more general understanding of "sanctuary" is as a place set apart from the busyness of our everyday activities. This might be a sacred place of worship, or it could be a place that is special to a particular individual, perhaps in nature, where they go to be alone and reflect. Typically, these places will have an atmosphere of peace and tranquility, as in this example from Plato: "What a lovely secluded spot! The plane tree here is tall and spreading, the agnus offers shade and is in full bloom and gives the place the sweetest perfume. The stream flowing under the plane tree is particularly charming, with the coolest of water to judge by my foot. The place seems by the figurines and statuettes to be sacred to certain Nymphs and to Achelous. . . . But best of all is that the grass grows on a gentle slope and is thick enough to rest one's head upon."[53] Places of sanctuary provide us with opportunities to temporarily step away from the everyday rush of the world, to restore a sense of inner calm and well-being; they help remove the layers of clutter to reveal the "underlying contours—the deep needs, the ingrained resistances, the hopes and loves."[54]

Spending time in such places requires nothing in the way of expenditure, they do not depend on consumption, and they are environmentally benign. If human-made rather than a place in nature, their design, creation, and care help build local knowledge, skills, and capacity, and if associated with a place of worship, they can contribute to a sense of spiritual well-being, community, and cultural identity.

Sadly, however, as we continue to pursue forms of progress and growth that are locked into material consumption, natural places are being relentlessly impinged upon by urban development and the demands of industry and commerce. In the process, the sense of apartness and the specialness of such places are compromised, even destroyed. And because they are not commercially productive, calls for their conservation are frequently dismissed as unimportant. Three recent examples from England demonstrate how sites of sanctuary—religious and natural—are being ruined by encroaching developments.

The first is the seventh-century Saxon church of St. Peter-on-the-Wall, one of the oldest churches in England. It is still regularly used for worship and is a Grade I listed building, which means it is of exceptional interest and may not be demolished. It is located close to the sea in a remote corner of Essex next to the Dengie National Nature Reserve. This is an area of mudflats and saltmarshes that, between tides, provides extensive feeding grounds for all kinds of birdlife.

Despite its Grade I listing and the nature reserve being of special scientific interest, the area is under threat from a proposed nuclear power station, which will dominate the skyline and overwhelm the chapel and nearby community. The perimeter of the power station and its sea defenses will be just one field—about two hundred meters from the chapel. Due to its enormous size, local people claim it will destroy the sweeping vistas, the natural qualities, and the spiritual atmosphere of the place, which has long been a sanctuary for people and wildlife. To counter these claims, the power-generation company said that it will be "exploring landscaping to screen the chapel from the development."[55]

A second example comes from the northwest of England. In the village of Cleator in Cumbria, there is a sacred grotto that replicates the Sanctuary of Our Lady of Lourdes. The communities in this area were once dependent on the mining and iron industries, which were hard hit by the Great Depression of the 1920s and 1930s. To help the local people, the village priest started a national appeal and used some of the funds to construct a grotto, rewarding the volunteers who built it with food and clothing vouchers. It was opened in 1927 and quickly became a focus for pilgrimage for the diocese, not least because the economic situation at that time meant most people were unable to travel long distances.[56] The grotto, which is still in regular use, is built on consecrated land and has a vow of silence. In early September, hundreds of people visit it in an annual pilgrimage (figure 17.7). But a new housing development has been proposed next to the site, which will adversely affect the historical, sociocultural, and spiritual significance of the grotto as well as its tranquility. To allay objections, the developer has said that "landscaping could reduce its impact."[57]

Figure 17.7 *Sanctuary*
Our Lady of Lourdes
Cleator, Cumbria, United Kingdom

The third example is much more widespread in its effects. Phase One of England's high-speed rail project, known as HS2, runs between London and Birmingham, a distance of 140 miles.[58] Estimated journey times will be reduced by twenty to thirty minutes and project costs will exceed £40 billion.[59] In the process, dozens of irreplaceable ancient woodlands have been completely destroyed and others severely impacted.[60] Many others will suffer from noise, pollution, and disturbance. The Woodland Trust says the project as a whole represents "a grave threat to the UK's ancient woods."[61]

Similar encroachments and losses are occurring in other countries. In the United States, Canada, Australia, and elsewhere, lands and locations held sacred by Aboriginal peoples are being regularly destroyed by mining operations, pipelines, and other activities.

The cumulative effects of such developments are plain to see. Places of sanctuary, where for centuries people have found a sense of peace and solitude, are being rapidly lost in the name of progress, impacting people, wildlife, and overall biodiversity. Such cases raise important questions for us all: Are we prepared to support progress, speed, and convenience at any cost? Or should we choose somewhat slower, less consumptive, less energy-demanding lifestyles in order to conserve natural and other special places?

To answer these questions, it is important to acknowledge that there is another kind of progress entirely, which does not result in continual destruction. I am referring here to "inner" progress, which occurs when we reflect on the larger existential questions of what it means to be human and choose to seek a deeper sense of meaning in our lives. It is for this kind of pursuit that places of sanctuary are so important. They provide us with the environments and the opportunities for spiritual renewal. They may be traditional places of worship, or they may be natural places, but as they continue to disappear, so do our prospects for being able to truly flourish.

SHINRIN-YOKU

Shinrin-yoku is the Japanese practice of "forest bathing." Although a relatively recent phenomenon, it is a modern incarnation of traditions that have deep roots in Japanese culture and strong associations with Shintoism, Buddhism, and Zen spirituality. For centuries, appreciation of the natural environment has been reflected in the recurring themes of haiku poetry. The master of this form was Matsuo Bashō (1644–1694), who strove to express a vision of the eternal through the temporal.[62] He achieved this by immersing himself in nature and closely observing its ways—the sunlight, the morning mist, trees, leaves, raindrops, and blossoms:

> Spring rain–
> under trees
> a crystal stream.[63]

Bashō explained the process this way: "Go to the pine if you want to learn about the pine, or to the bamboo if you want to learn about the bamboo. And in doing so, you must leave your subjective preoccupation with yourself. Otherwise you impose yourself on the object and do not learn."[64] The idea of leaving behind one's everyday concerns and preoccupations—or perhaps being released from them—is echoed by the English poet John Clare (1793–1864), who spent time in Epping Forest while recovering from mental illness:

> Still the forest is round me
> Where the trees bloom in green
> As if chains ne'er had bound me
> Or cares had ne'er been[65]

The term *shinrin-yoku* was introduced in the early 1980s by the director of the Japanese Forest Agency, Tomohide Akiyama. It means spending time in the forest, walking slowly among the trees, immersing oneself in nature, and directly experiencing the colors and textures of bark and leaves; the smell of pine and cedar; hearing the breeze through the branches, water murmuring in a forest stream, and birdsong (figure 17.8). While the practice began from an intuitive sense that it was good for one's well-being, in the years since its introduction, scientific investigations have confirmed its many therapeutic benefits. It can lower pulse rates and blood pressure; reduce stress levels and associated illnesses; and improve one's sense of well-being.[66]

Figure 17.8 *In the Forest*
Sechelt, British Columbia, Canada

All the artifacts and activities we have discussed in this chapter arise from peoples' enduring questions about ultimate purpose, meaning, and how we should live. One of the most resilient responses to these questions is that of ritual.

Whether religious or secular, ritual has always been a fundamental characteristic of humanity. The physical routines and forms of communication it involves are invariably permeated by religious or philosophical beliefs and teachings, which include moral principles. Through regular participation and habituation, we learn about what is right and wrong and how to behave in relation to others. In this way, the sociocultural experiences typical of ritual help us live in harmony with each other and the natural world.

We have also seen that the roots of ritual lie in a nonmodern worldview—one unfettered by narrow categorizations that compartmentalize knowledge and activities into discrete sectors. Such divisions tend to restrict our outlooks. We fail to see the world as an integrated whole and so blind ourselves to its interrelationships and fragile interdependencies.

The waning of public ritual in modern times, and the shift toward more solitary ways of living, add to a pervasive sense of uncertainty and unease. Individualism and the atomization of society lead to social divisions and, sometimes, the development of extreme perspectives, which are often reinforced by interactions on social media.

In addition to ritual, traditions like pilgrimages, outdoor shrines and memorials, and more contemporary, secular equivalents like *shinrin-yoku*, can imbue natural landscapes with special or sacred qualities. They all recognize the importance of our deeper, spiritual needs and offer opportunities for contemplation, quiet reflection, and more thoughtful modes of being. As such, they can be focal points of meaning, comfort, witness, and even safety. Perhaps, too, they are needed more than ever today, at a time when we have to seriously rethink our ways of living, what we value most, and what is of inherent value and worth taking care of for its own sake.

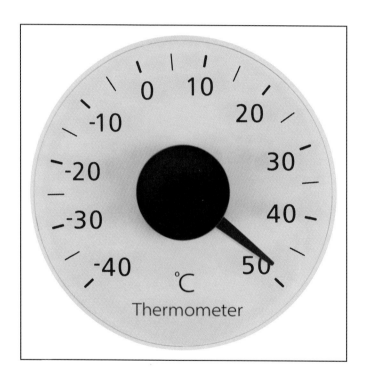

18 DESIGN FOR GOOD

Kenneth Clark, the former director of London's National Gallery, is perhaps best known for his 1960s television series and accompanying book *Civilisation*, which looked at the history, art, and philosophy of the West from the fall of Rome to the beginning of the twentieth century. Despite the title of the series and his broad grasp of Western development, however, Clark was hesitant to define the term *civilization*. He did say it was easy to distinguish from barbarism and suggested a set of interrelated values that characterize it—including modesty, decorum, good sense, tranquility, order, and beauty.[1] These attributes represent the very opposite of coarseness, cruelty, corruption, and other such hallmarks of "uncivilized" ways of life.

In broad terms, civilization can be understood as an advanced form of intellectual, social, and cultural development that includes but is not limited to the arts. In civilized societies, the arts and other creative endeavors can, and arguably should, embody human values that are consistent with ideas of goodness and virtue, as well as implicitly or explicitly be critical of behaviors and activities that transgress these indispensable features of social harmony. Even so, we should be under no illusions that civilized society is capable of preventing or is free from barbarism; history tells us otherwise. As we shall see, civilization and barbarism tend to coexist; like optimism and pessimism, they represent contradictory but inseparable characteristics of human nature. However, while there may be little evidence to suggest that positively conceived endeavors have much effect on thwarting brutality and malign tendencies, this is no reason to stop engaging in creative activities that strive toward the good. We should pursue them for their own sake, simply because they are good, not for some other instrumental reason.

The Seeds of Oppression and Brutality: Autocratic and totalitarian regimes usually attempt to eradicate forms of creative work that do not support their ideologies. This frequently means silencing people through fear, control of the press, confinement, punitive action, or worse.[2] Typically, among the first to be targeted are a society's intelligentsia—academics, teachers, artists, and scientists. Anyone capable of engaging in thoughtful critique is muzzled, particularly those involved in activities that help shape cultural and political opinion.[3]

Silencing, oppression, and violence also occur in Western democracies. Following the 9/11 attacks in New York in 2001, the then US president ignored international law so as to better facilitate retribution. Prisoners were sent to the notorious Guantánamo Bay detention camp in Cuba, which was declared a "law free zone" unconstrained by either the scrutiny of the courts or the American Constitution.[4] So-called fake news has been used by a subsequent president to condemn and belittle the press. And the US website Turning Point calls upon students to report instances of what they perceive to be left-wing bias by their lecturers, whose names are then published.[5] As a consequence, academics "have faced threats of death, rape and harm to their children after being singled out" by the site's "Professor Watch."[6] Turning Point is also present in the United Kingdom, and its equivalent "Education Watch" has received endorsements by a number of prominent members of the British parliament.[7] Such tactics can have a chilling effect on academic freedom and those principles and liberties that Western democracies are so quick to say they uphold.

The Coexistence of Civilization and Barbarism: Paradoxically, human society seems to be perfectly capable of compartmentalizing cultural appreciation and barbarism and living simultaneously with both. As G. K. Chesterton said, "The broad truth is that barbarism and civilisation have always dwelt side by side in the world."[8] It is not the case, he argued, that we have gradually progressed from an era of barbarism to an era of civilization. Even in earliest times, humanity was already "civilized," Babylon and Egypt being two ancient examples of which we have reasonably reliable and detailed records. And in one of his typical inversions of common preconceptions, he suggested that societies do not become despotic because they are barbarous, but very often they find their way to despotism because they are civilized.[9]

The cultural achievements of Babylon and Egypt, as well as ancient Greece, are rightly celebrated, but these societies also relied heavily on slavery. Centuries later, the same was true of Britain, France, Spain, Portugal, and the Netherlands, all of which actively participated in the slave trade. From the fifteenth to the nineteenth centuries, millions of enslaved people from Africa were transported to the Americas. In addition to the unconscionable exploitation and abuse, the United Nations puts the number of resulting deaths at around fifteen million.[10] European expansionism also meant that Indigenous peoples were dying in their millions all over the world—through deprivation, infectious diseases, brutal policy decisions, and deliberate acts of killing. In North America, those who survived were confined to reservations, while their traditional lands were given away or sold at minimal cost to European settlers. Meanwhile, cultural production in England was at its height, with people enjoying the works of Austen, Blake, Defoe, Milton, Shelley, Wollstonecraft, and Wordsworth.

In the twentieth century, there were similar instances of culture and callousness existing together. Sybille Steinbacher's research tells us that in the Auschwitz concentration and extermination camp, alongside the ruthless depravities and murders being carried out on a daily basis, "a wide variety of cultural events kept all the SS men in a good mood. Light entertainments, pleasant music and jolly gatherings provided distraction and amusement. . . . And there was no shortage of classics in Auschwitz: In February 1943 the Dresden State Theatre presented a programme entitled 'Goethe Then and Now'. . . . Mass murder and respectability were not opposites but were closely interwoven."[11] This seemingly contradictory juxtaposition becomes possible when those who are perceived as the enemy are stripped of their humanity and demonized. The language of euphemism plays a significant role in justifying the crimes and making them seem acceptable. The Nazis used terms like "the removal of human ballast" and "significant population-related structural cleansing" to disguise the realities.[12] On arrival at the camp, prisoners were given numbers, their own clothes were replaced by striped prison suits, and their heads were shaved.[13]

In the late twentieth and twenty-first centuries, successive US administrations have referred to their enemies variously as the "Evil Empire," "uncivilized," "animals," and "sick and deranged" and used the term "collateral damage" to refer to the deaths or injuries of civilians caught up in their overseas campaigns. This kind of language aims to dehumanize and obscure the faces of the perceived enemy and casualties of aggression, and it allows "society en masse to participate in acts of violence or to accept . . . massive civilian casualties without so much as a moral blink of the eye."[14] As art lovers in New York were enjoying Italian illuminated manuscripts and the works of El Greco and Paul Klee at the Metropolitan Museum of Art, members of the US Army were carrying out atrocities in Iraq, and the numbers of people being rounded up and confined in Abu Ghraib prison near Baghdad were increasing exponentially. Detainees were subjected to various kinds of humiliation and torture, and some died from shocking levels of abuse.[15] More recently, undocumented immigrants coming across the southern border from Mexico were repeatedly referred to as animals, drug dealers, criminals, and rapists.[16]

Injustice and tyranny are often far closer than we think or like to admit, even to ourselves. The language of euphemism, propaganda, and persuasion can have powerful effects. It enables us to turn a blind eye, and, in doing so, civilization and barbarism continue to coexist. Many of our own cultural opportunities and experiences are dependent on uncivilized ways of doing business. At our fingertips, we have the ability to access the world's information resources; to communicate with others around the world; to view images of great artworks; to listen to music, poetry, and literature; and to stream movies and live theater performances. All these things rely on technologies whose manufacture, advancement and affordability frequently depend on highly destructive processes underpinned by business norms that are indifferent to human suffering and the long-term effects. Unscrupulous labor practices associated with the electronics industry have been widely reported.[17] And we are well aware that our technologically advanced but excessively wasteful lifestyles are the result of pillaging the natural world, despoiling the oceans, and poisoning the very air we breathe. These practices, which also include the creation of digital applications deliberately designed to foster addiction-like behaviors and encourage consumption, are driven by an ideology founded on dubious and limited notions of progress, growth, and profit. Far too many of our large-scale production- and service-based activities, which we take for granted and regard as perfectly normal are, in reality, modern forms of barbarism because they are inextricably bound up with physical, psychological, or sexual exploitation; cruelty; greed; and corruption.

Finding a Voice through Art, Poetry, Literature, and Other Cultural Productions: Down the years, artists and creatives of all kinds have made works that reveal, condemn, or mourn acts of inhumanity, intimidation, and oppression. In doing so, they have produced some of the world's most memorable literature, artworks, and designs.

In World War I, the enormous loss of life and horrendous conditions in the trenches yielded the poetry of Rupert Brooke, Robert Graves, Wilfred Owen, and Siegfried Sassoon. In response to the brutalities of Nazism, Kathrine Kressmann Taylor wrote her brief but stunning indictment *Address Unknown* (1938), and Albert Camus responded with *La Peste* (1947). Years later, in 1976, the Polish composer Henryk Górecki produced his heartrendingly sad and beautiful *Symphony of Sorrowful Songs*, the second movement of which features a prayer found scratched on the wall of a Gestapo cell by an eighteen-year-old female prisoner.[18]

The artist Ai Weiwei, who relocated to Europe after being jailed in his home country of China, has said, "An artist must also be an activist—aesthetically, morally, or philosophically. That doesn't mean they have to demonstrate in street protests, but rather deal with these issues through a so-called artistic language. Without that kind of consciousness—to be blind to human struggle—one cannot even be called an artist."[19] This is true not just for fine artists but for all creatives—novelists, poets, musicians, and designers. Whatever form the work takes, the resulting creation is never neutral—it is an aesthetic, moral, and philosophical statement, and, as such, it expresses a position. It can explicitly or implicitly support or advance the prevailing condition, or it can critique, oppose, or reveal alternative possibilities. American conceptual artist Barbara Kruger uses imagery, text, and collage techniques to challenge power conventions and the way mass media and consumer culture present the female body. Her bold artwork includes images and words such as "I shop therefore I am" and "When I hear the word culture I take out my checkbook."[20] British designer Vivienne Westwood speaks out against perceived injustices and immoral activities with fashion models bearing prominent slogans declaring, "We sold our souls for consumption" and "You think you own the world."[21] Another British designer, Katharine Hamnett, creates clothing ranges with the words "Buy less, choose well," "No more fish in the sea?," and "Save the Future."[22]

Despite these examples, we should not be under any misapprehension that creative endeavors that strive toward the good are capable of preventing uncivilized behaviors; to do so would be naive.

Why design for good? As we have discussed in earlier chapters, Western society has long been enamored with and driven by instrumental rationality, where the focus is on achieving a specific, desired end, and only those activities deemed to be useful are valued.[23] With this type of mindset, the means—the actions one takes and the reasons for taking them—are motivated predominantly by the pursuit of the sought-after objective; it is this final outcome that matters. Instrumental rationality is a mode of thinking that also puts great store in efficiency, especially economic efficiency, but it tends to ignore or downplay other motivations and consequences. In the process, important human values, such as compassion and charity, as well as such invaluable aspects of human life as community, tradition and identity become diminished or even disparaged. Greater weight is put on accountability, usually through quantification, to demonstrate that the objective has been achieved. This has resulted in metrics, rankings, ratings, and hierarchies being created across all walks of life. Levels of bureaucracy and accountability expand enormously, which are not just incredibly time-consuming and expensive but also inherently divisive. Areas that ought to be working cooperatively for the benefit of society as a whole end up being pitted against one another. By reducing complex human situations to a series of quantifiable metrics, institutions and the people in them come to be seen as winners or losers, some being ranked as "outstanding" while others are categorized as "failing"; some prominently announcing their position in the top ten, while others are left to feel mediocre or somehow inadequate. Inevitably, the measures used for such exercises tend to be selective, often favoring those with the most powerful and/or privileged voices. This has the effect of changing and distorting the purpose of an activity, affecting both the means and the results, and making the overall benefits to society questionable. Educational institutions as well as those organizations meant to support and affirm the creative arts start to focus more on what their "customers" want, rather than on sound educational principles or creativity, exploration, and cultural contribution. The language shifts from that of the common good, human heritage, and intrinsic value, to that of commerce, economic development, "creative industries," and competitiveness.[24]

When our activities are shaped by and for the market, we cease to be seen as whole persons and become mere consumers. Similar methods of cost-benefit analysis are applied to the natural environment, with disastrous consequences. Nature is turned into a commodity and an investment that is expected to yield financial returns, which means it has to be owned and made productive. The problem is that what appears to be cheap in terms of cost-benefit analysis is generally expensive for broader society.[25] Private markets do not provide public accountability, nor do they build on or take into account the public good—their measure is limited to the profitability of companies. When the market model is applied to public education, health care, and the arts, accountability is achieved by introducing layer upon layer of additional processes, standards, tests, and targets. There is little evidence that these lead to any significant improvement,[26] but they do result in staff being diverted from their primary duties and becoming embroiled in endless form-filling.

Fundamental ethical precepts are not confined to any particular society or time period, they are universal. While different societies may have different customs of behavior, manners, and dress, basic moral principles are grounded in a long heritage of people living together and their collective communal experiences. As such, these precepts and principles can be taken as self-evidently true and regarded as necessary elements of any civilized society. Critically, unlike the "ends" that are the focus of instrumental rationality, these moral obligations cannot be reached as conclusions.[27] Rather, they are premises, and it is *this* that provides the basis and justification for designing for the good. Creative endeavors that are motivated by ideas of goodness and virtue ought to be pursued for their own sake, whether or not they are attached to any other, practical end. This is reason enough, simply because it is the right thing to do—its value is intrinsic. Moreover, doing the right thing and striving to uphold notions of goodness and virtue in creative endeavors that have practical value—such as those in which designers are typically involved—can help steer the processes and procedures, and hence the outcomes, in directions that are more comprehensively good for people and planet.

19 TRUISM

Cubism

Futurism

Scientism

Secularism

Literalism

Hedonism

Naturalism

Narcissism

Modernism

Minimalism

Capitalism

Objectivism

Rationalism

Industrialism

Individualism

Universalism

Utilitarianism

Neoliberalism

Fundamentalism

Postmodernism

Postindustrialism

Deconstructivism

Environmentalism

Temporalism

20 $(C_2H_4)_n$ FEVER

I must go down to the seas again, to the lonely sea and the sky,
To the polyethylene terephthalates, polyvinyl chlorides and
    polypropylenes,
The low and high density polyethylenes, the polystyrenes and
    polylactic acids,
To the flung polycarbonates, acrylics and polyoxymethylenes with
    their aqueous formaldehydes, alcohols and acetic anhydrides.
And all I ask is a merry yarn from a laughing fellow-rover,
And quiet sleep and a sweet dream 'til the long trick's over.[1]

21 DESIGN AFTER A PANDEMIC

Some six months into the COVID-19 pandemic, the United Nations published its *Research Roadmap for the COVID-19 Recovery*. The report's principal message was that the pandemic crisis had thrown new light on, and intensified the impact of, preexisting global disparities, vulnerabilities, and unsustainable practices. Recovery, it said, would require significant efforts across a wide range of areas in order to

- strengthen health-care access, services, and systems;
- safeguard and expand social programs and basic services in areas such as food, shelter, and education;
- protect food supply, care services, livelihoods, and small-scale enterprises;
- reinforce multilateral collaborations, investment, debt relief, and regional trade cooperation;
- ensure environmental resilience; and
- improve social cohesion through dialogue, advocacy, empowerment, equitable service delivery, and good governance.[1]

This long and ambitious list rightly acknowledges the sheer magnitude of the pandemic's impact. The scale and scope of the UN agenda reveals critical vulnerabilities as well as the fundamental interdependencies among people, nations, systems, and the natural environment. By recognizing a need for action on a global level, it calls for a reimagining of societies by placing greater emphasis on human rights as well as transformative changes that can help ensure a more positive and hopeful future for everyone.

However, despite the timeliness and good intentions of the UN report, I was perturbed to read its subtitle, *Leveraging the Power of Science for a More Equitable, Resilient and Sustainable Future*, and that, in the UN's view, science offers the world the best chance for a positive way forward. This claim gave me pause. First, because, misleadingly, "science" was used to embrace a far wider range of disciplines, including engineering and the humanities—representing areas such as literature, history, and religion—which are obviously not sciences.[2] Second, because there is no mention of creativity and only a fleeting nod to the arts. The main emphasis is firmly on demonstrating "the power of global science" and encouraging the implementation of a range of science-based strategies, such as scaling up data infrastructure and implementing rapid learning systems and knowledge mobilization.[3]

In dealing with pandemics and other health crises, we rely on advancements in science and rightly praise the Herculean efforts made by research scientists in developing vaccines and medicines. No thinking person would dispute the enormous contributions of science, especially in health care. But in framing the path to recovery as the UN report does, there is a real danger of simply repeating the same mistakes of the past by addressing the deeper and broader questions with exactly the same kind of progress-entrenched thinking that has caused so much harm to people, other species, and natural environments.

Modern societies have long believed in the self-generated myth of "progress," driven primarily by the contributions of science and understood as a continual, upward trajectory of improvement and betterment. The United Nations, in privileging the place of science over other areas of human knowledge and expertise, appears to be maintaining and reinforcing this patently false assumption. The belief in progress has been crumbling for some time. The future no longer holds much promise—it is more a place of fear than of hope.[4] As philosopher John Gray has said, the hollowness of today's secular faith in progress was made all too plain in the face of a virus that caused vast loss of life, untold hardship, family separation, and losses of livelihood, income, education and opportunity.[5] The pandemic exposed the weaknesses of globalization and of outsourcing manufacturing and reducing our own production capabilities. And it allowed us to recognize more acutely those societal roles that matter most when it comes to keeping our communities functioning in difficult times, including health workers, carers of the elderly, supermarket staff, delivery drivers, refuse collectors, and foodbank volunteers.

The UN's wide-ranging set of recovery goals cannot be achieved solely through the contributions of science; a far more holistic approach is needed—one that also depends on the expertise of educators, historians, philosophers, linguists, policy makers, and those in the creative arts, including the applied arts. And it requires the kind of joined-up thinking that is so fundamental to traditional forms of knowledge, which some scientists are already recognizing.[6] Only by envisioning more creative, imaginative ways forward and adopting more holistic, integrated, and context-appropriate approaches will we be able to ensure that our scientific knowledge and technological capabilities are accompanied by—and in some cases tempered by—humane, ethical, and socially equitable forms of development.

If we are to truly build a more sustainable, inclusive, and resilient future for everyone, we must pay far more attention to the perspectives and belief systems of others; to priorities and aspirations that rise above mundane pragmatism; to values that transcend self and selfishness; and to compassion, empathy, charity, benevolence, and conservation. Greater consideration for *these* enables us to position the contributions of science within a larger vista of human significance and meaning. They help ensure that our efforts are guided by values that overcome self-interest and emphasize concern for neighbor and nature and are respectful of the particularities of place, context, and tradition.

Effective transformation and improvement will also involve a change in our personal attitudes and aspirations. We have, perhaps, become too eager to *do*—we are constantly organizing, developing, launching, announcing, researching, ideating, innovating, and advancing. But in all this rushing, we seem to have lost the ability to simply *be*. It was once said of D. H. Lawrence that "his genius lay in his capacity for being, a capacity so few people seem to have. . . . One tries to believe that he was a forerunner, the first sample of a type to come, of those who will defeat industrialism and the mechanization of life, and who will lead humanity out of the impasse where it perishes now."[7] Given that these words were written long before our current environmental crisis, they were, indeed, prophetic. Today more than ever, any sensible road to recovery must involve far less *doing* and much more *being, seeing, listening, contemplating, and appreciating*. Such a route would allow us to benefit from the latest scientific knowledge while also making our subsequent actions more considered and more positive for all. If we were less eager to intervene, things would be better able to unfold at their natural pace and in their own way. For instance, empirical studies of passive rewilding on abandoned farmland have shown that, within a few decades, native woodlands can become reestablished with a rich diversity of species. Seeds are dispersed by the wind or distributed by seed-caching and berry-eating animals. Within fifty years, and at very low cost, newer woodlands can be resilient to variable weather conditions and the presence of herbivores, and close to the height structure of older woods[8]—all with little or no human intervention.

Kierkegaard argued that the ethical *is* the universal, and the highest purpose of the individual is to rise above one's particularity to pursue the ethical life and become the universal. Those who set their own wishes aside in the interests of others relinquish the finite in order to grasp the infinite.[9] For designers, this approach does not mean giving up one's sense of creative expression simply to do the bidding of someone else. It means setting aside egotistic tendencies in design practice in order to make a more meaningful contribution—design both as offering and obligation. Perhaps this can never be entirely achieved, but surely a nobler goal is to design with this higher sense of purpose than to be constrained by the smaller, lower horizons of self. Moreover, such a path does *not* advocate some sort of one-size-fits-all universal design—quite the opposite. This is egoless design that strives to fit seamlessly and harmlessly into the world by taking into account the constraints and circumstances of the specific. Designers must observe, listen, and familiarize themselves with the particularities of context.

But how can they assure themselves that they are justified in their courses of action? They cannot surrender their responsibility to others, by handing it over to "society" or the state. Humoring the wishes of others or simply complying with regulations means never having to face the ethical questions that are so critical to contemporary design. If designers waive their responsibilities, they do not allow themselves to grow—either as practitioners or as individuals. Furthermore, designers cannot fall back on "judging the outcome" of their work. At the beginning of a project and throughout most of the process, there is no outcome. Designers have to deal with the ethical dilemmas that arise in the midst of the creative undertaking, where myriad individual decisions collectively determine the outcome; this cannot be done after the fact. If designers on the verge of action were only prepared to make decisions according to the outcome, they would never be able to begin.[10]

For good or bad, all the small decisions that designers make along the way become embedded in, and indistinguishable from, the outcome itself. Therefore, they have to have some means of assuring themselves that they are beginning from the right starting point, and they have to be vigilant at each step of the development process. Achieving this requires a combination of relinquishment and trust—relinquishment of self-oriented priorities and trust in a bigger, higher vision. It means holding on to this higher ethic during the creative process in order to make good decisions *without* knowing all the information, *not* seeing the full picture and *not* knowing precisely what the outcome will be. Mistakes will inevitably be made—we *will* fall short—but doubts and anxieties of failing cannot paralyze us or stop us from reaching higher.

The UN roadmap refers to a range of large-scale issues and dilemmas that lie beyond the scope and remit of any single designer—strengthening health care, expanding social programs, building multilateral collaborations, improving social cohesions, and so on. Nevertheless, designers have a part to play, and whatever their particular area of contribution, they will be faced with practical questions about the details of form, function, usability, and affordability. It is useful, therefore, to focus the discussion less on grand schemes in some undefined future and more on the nitty-gritty activities of the present—all guided by a strong inner ethic. This is where the designer operates, where theory meets practice.

These issues are especially important if we are to learn from the COVID-19 pandemic. In the early stages of lockdown, there were dramatic reductions in air pollution; skies free of jet trails; views across the landscape that were clear and bright; wild animals roaming our city streets; and a world that was noticeably quieter, where we were able to hear the birds again. We were given an opportunity to pause, to see the world anew and ourselves more clearly—stripped of the busyness, distractions, and headlong rush that modern life had become—a life with no time and perhaps no inclination to look, listen, or even really think.[11]

The social separations imposed by the pandemic also allowed us to realize the importance of family, friends, neighbors, and community and their part in making our lives richer, simply through their presence. In moving forward, we must realize our vulnerabilities and work far more vigilantly to restore hope in our collective future. We should not aim to simply return to our previous ways. There are urgent challenges that need to be tackled.

A few years ago, I was spending August just north of Victoria on Vancouver Island. On the morning after my arrival, I woke up coughing and continued to do so all that day and the next. I assumed I'd caught a bug on the journey over. The weather was warm but hazy. And I couldn't stop coughing.

A friend rang from her home on Gabriola Island, a few hours north. As we talked, I had to pause to cough again, to which she said, "The smoke's been pretty bad here these last few days, are you getting much of it down your way?" And suddenly, the "heat haze" and coughing were explained. I checked the provincial updates—hundreds of forest fires were burning in mainland British Columbia, and their smoke was filling the air here, over sixty miles away.

In recent years, the Pacific Northwest has been experiencing record-breaking temperatures, with increased numbers of forest fires burning at greater intensities. Thermometers nudged 120 degrees Fahrenheit, and the air was so dry that water dropped from the firebombers evaporated before reaching the flames. Whole communities were consumed, air quality was compromised for millions, and hundreds died from the excessive heat. Infrastructure was also affected—train cables melted and roads and sidewalks buckled and cracked.

Band-Aid solutions to deal with these conditions included setting up cooling centers (essentially, air-conditioned convention centers, community halls, and other indoor spaces with mattresses on the floor); installing community misting stations; and opening up air-conditioned libraries to offer respite from the heat and smoke.

The inordinately high temperatures also caused the deaths of hundreds of millions of coastline creatures—effectively, large tracts of shellfish were cooked in situ. And, increasingly, many areas are experiencing water shortages and large expanses of land are turning to desert—reducing wildlife habitats and food supplies for all kinds of animal life.

The latest scientific reports tell us that without far more serious commitment to change, the impacts of global warming will only worsen. Without coordinated action, there are likely to be devastating consequences. Needless to say, the impacts will affect our infrastructures; businesses; supply chains, especially food and medical provisions; jobs; and ways of life.[12] If we fail to voluntarily implement suitable policies, significant change will be forced upon us in ways that will inevitably be far worse because we will be unprepared.

We must rethink the nature of design for resilient, sustainable ways of living—not at the level of grand but vague visions but with a renewed commitment to people and place. When we engage at this level, in activities that involve face-to-face relationships, we are able to see each other as full human beings, and we become more aware of the concrete impacts of our decision-making. This, to use the phrase of Victor Papanek, is "design for the real world"—open, honest, done in good conscience, and fully accountable.

We must guard against repeating the errors of modernity, which sought to impose all-encompassing visions of how the world should be, irrespective of the instincts, aspirations, and wishes of ordinary people.[13] Designers can make valuable contributions by bringing their thoughtfulness, attention to detail, aesthetic sensitivity, and sense of moral rectitude to the creation of all those things we use in our everyday lives. They can also pursue a form of design that is closely attached to and respectful of place, thereby helping create a world in which we feel we belong. This suggests a form of design that draws on tried and tested ways and offers a greater sense of permanence and stability. It is design that builds capacity and expertise within the community and contributes to useful, fulfilling employment.

In the research I have been leading in recent years, we have found that many small maker enterprises are already doing this. They tend not to be motivated by money or constantly increasing the size of their business. Instead, they want to contribute to their community, to build sustainable ways of working, and to create responsible, environmentally friendly outcomes. Designing with, supporting, and encouraging these types of businesses can have a wide variety of interconnected benefits. Local, context-appropriate design can help

- make the most of local resources and other local assets;
- foster all kinds of community-led solutions;
- create local, inclusive forms of employment;
- reduce transportation needs and air pollution;
- reduce waste and public expenditure on disposal and clean up; and
- contribute to a robust, resilient, and highly diversified economy.

As Wolfgang Sachs has said, "It is only from places that variety crops up, because it is in places that people weave the present into their particular thread of history. . . . In culture as well as in nature, diversity holds the potential for innovation and opens the way for creative, non-linear solutions."[14] Through such means, we have the opportunity to build collaborative forms of multigenerational enterprises that are capable of preserving and sustaining those things we value most.[15] This means eliminating excess, overproduction, and waste and focusing on those aspects that allow our designs to become tangible expressions of people, place, and tradition, as well as manifestations of cultural meaning and sufficiency.

Design opportunities for contributing to such change obviously include such things as the creation of low-impact products and services; greener housing, transport, and infrastructure; and, generally, more passive, environmentally benign ways of working and conducting our affairs.

During the COVID-19 pandemic, we also saw very confusing and constantly changing messaging from government. So, clearly, there is a need for far better communication design, and the development of effective communication strategies that will ensure that people are aware of the necessary changes and are willing and prepared to alter their behaviors.

There are also opportunities to design new types of curricula and programs for schools and universities to improve understanding and awareness and to progress change in an holistic, thoughtful manner.[16] In order to ensure a well-balanced approach, it will be particularly important to produce imaginative, well-designed materials for non-STEM subjects, which in the United Kingdom, at least, have been badly served in recent years.

We should also acknowledge that we have designed and produced far too much. In moving forward, we must also commit to *not* designing things, as their production would only increase the pressure on natural systems. Instead, we can create objects, activities, and social initiatives that help foster community cohesion and self-reliance, as well as programs for restoration, raising public awareness and involvement, and other forms of constructive, positive change.

A blank page
an artificial emptiness
waiting to be filled

Choosing to refuse
rejecting the premise
of *ex nihilo*

Stepping back
silently acknowledging
what already is

Seeing purpose
in perspective in context
in the world

An intentional act
of *not* creating *not* imposing
one's will

The page remains
unmarked its implications
unenforced

A stillness ensues
an apposite emptiness
fills the void

23 A TALE OF THREE BIRDS

When they had completed their studies, two friends decided to set up a design business together. During the first year, things went well, and they accumulated a number of commissions. Yet they found they were unable to do the kind of work they believed in while also satisfying the wishes of their clients, who were often influenced by the latest trends. So they decided to visit an old artisan whose work they greatly admired and ask for some advice.

Arriving at the workshop, and once introductions were over, the three sat down to talk. One of the designers said: "To us, your work seems to have a timeless quality about it and a sense of integrity that we greatly admire. How do you achieve this while also satisfying the demands of your customers? How do you manage to separate your work from the fads and fashions of the market and stay true to yourself and your own creativity?"

The old man considered the question—he walked slowly around the workshop, looking at his tools, thinking about his craft. After pondering for a long time, he replied: "The questions you ask are not so easy to answer because these things are difficult to put into words. At some point, you have to let the work speak for itself. When I was young, I had similar questions, and I sought advice from my old teacher. Instead of answering directly, she told me this story, which she said was an old fairy tale, though I have never been able find it."

Once upon a time, in a faraway land, the people were happy because the realm had been at peace for as long as anyone could remember. The country was ruled by the good King Armonia, who was much loved by his subjects.

The time came when the king's son, Prince Moda, was to be married to the fair Princess Bella. The king had been told that nothing delighted the princess more than the sweet song of the birds. So, to please her on her wedding day, he asked his chamberlain to send out a proclamation to the birds of his realm inviting them to come to the palace so one could be selected to perform for the princess at the marriage feast.

Heralds rode out to the villages, meadows, and forests across the land, blew their long trumpets, and announced the good news. Very soon, birds of all shapes and sizes began to arrive at the palace, and the chamberlain, after conferring with each one, chose three to appear before the king.

Sitting on his throne, the king received the first bird. It was small of stature, wore a drab brown suit, and acted as if its thoughts were elsewhere. With low expectations, he bade the bird sing. When it began, the king was greatly surprised, for its high melancholy warble was entrancing, and it filled the whole chamber. The king was transfixed. When he came to himself, he thanked the bird, which silently withdrew. Turning to his aide, the king inquired as to the name of this dull-looking bird with the remarkable voice. He was told it was a nightingale.

The second bird to come before the king could not have been more different. It strode in haughtily with head held high and wore a crown almost as fine as the king's own. Its puffed-out chest glimmered blue and green and blue again as it moved, and, behind, it bore a long, resplendent train. With high expectations of a song as impressive as its looks, the king bade it sing. The bird raised its tail into a magnificent fan with a pattern of a hundred eyes, but when it opened its mouth . . . the sound that filled the chamber was like a screeching harpy, unbearable to the ear. The king's eyebrows shot up in astonishment—he was stunned into silence, and simply gestured for the bird to leave. Turning to his aide, the king inquired as to the name of this majestic bird with the startlingly ugly voice. He was told it was a peacock.

The third bird to appear was neither dull nor haughty. It came in with a jaunty hop, hop, hop and was smartly turned out in a formal black suit and bright orange beak. It looked up at the king with head tilted to one side, curious as to what would happen next. The king couldn't help but smile. Without any expectations, he bade it sing. The bird looked about the chamber, tilting its head this way and that, and flew up to the top of the tallest cabinet, and from this elevated spot began to sing. The bird's fluted refrain rang out, rich and mellow. One song flowed into another, and another, each quite different from the last. The king raised his hand. The bird flew down and cheerfully hop, hop, hopped out of the room. Turning to his aide, the king inquired as to the name of this smart-looking bird, who could sing so many different songs. He was told it was a blackbird.

The chamberlain waited to receive the king's decision, and, after a brief pause, the king spoke, "The first bird—the dowdy nightingale—certainly has a lovely voice, quite enchanting, but its attire and distant manner are quite unsuited to such a grand occasion.

The second bird—the pompous peacock—comes clad in impressive regalia but its self-important attitude masks a hideous voice, so this one, also, is quite unsuitable.

The third bird—the graceful blackbird—has a lovely voice, his soothing serenade is glorious and clear, and he has an extensive repertoire. Not only that, his appearance is elegant and his manner charming.

I have made my decision; the blackbird will be the one to sing at the wedding feast."

As the old artisan came to the end of the story, he added: "This is all I can tell you. It is as far as I can take you—you have to walk the rest of the way yourselves."

The two young friends thanked him and returned home, somewhat bemused—the advice, if it was advice, seemed irrelevant to their day-to-day work. Nevertheless, in the months that followed, their designs took on a different quality and character. For some reason, which they couldn't explain, they also felt much happier, even though some of their old clients fell away and their orders declined. But as time went on, their reputation grew, new clients appeared, and now their business is flourishing more than ever.

The limits of reason, progress, and our preoccupation with innovation have been discussed from various perspectives in earlier chapters. The economic system that has evolved from these priorities has encouraged us all to become habitual consumers. And the globalization of markets accompanied by aggressive advertising is resulting in a hegemonic uniformity. In the process,

- the natural world has been ruined;
- the diversity of the world's cultures has been eroded;
- immorally high levels of wealth have become concentrated in the hands of the few, thereby depriving everyone else and the public purse of their fair share;
- individual horizons have become obscured by materialistic clutter; and
- the future, once a place of hope and possibility, has become far more ominous—a place we contemplate with a sense of unease and foreboding.

The foundations of a worldview built on reason and progress are quickly crumbling. People are attending with renewed respect and appreciation to the distinctiveness of place and the rich cultural legacy of local knowledge, language, practices, and artifacts. As we saw in chapter 3, scientists from a wide range of disciplines are now looking to Indigenous knowledge systems to learn about climate, biology, and local ecologies. Place-based artifacts and foods are receiving renewed interest; agroecological principles have been developed that take into account, among other things, local knowledge, traditions, and human values;[1] and social scientists and designers are seeking understanding and finding inspiration in the multilayered nature of traditional beliefs and practices. Within all this variety, we find imagination, ingenuity, surprise, sophistication, and deeply meaningful examples of sociocultural heritage.

One of the major deficiencies of our current, linear way of thinking is our constant prioritization of what comes next, the new, and the latest fads and fashions. This has led to an endless series of "innovative" solutions, which have a way of riding roughshod over the context-based realities of peoples' lives while simultaneously yielding evermore globally distributed "techno-fixes" aimed at maintaining and expanding consumption-oriented aspirations. Clearly, this has to change if we are to develop more resilient ways of living. An entirely different outlook is needed, one firmly located in the places we live, in how we live, and in the place-based opportunities afforded to us.

The artifacts and activities discussed in previous chapters have proved their resilience over long periods of time and, by and large, are based on local needs and resources. They have been continually adapted to suit changing circumstances, and some have maintained a place in human culture for millennia. While they represent only a small selection of the possibilities available, they are enough to provide us with a serviceable grasp of how resilience is manifested, its nature and characteristics, and the values and priorities it represents. And while resilience is not quite the same thing as sustainability, the two concepts are closely aligned. If something has demonstrated its resilience over many generations, we can be reasonably sure that it will have important practical, sociocultural, and/or spiritual meanings, and these will usually be expressed in ways that are in harmony with the natural environment.

A consideration of these artifacts and activities tells us much about those things that really matter—that are permanent aspects of the human condition. All of them are consistent with perennial human values, ethical understandings, social equity, and inclusivity (figure 24.1). They allow us to achieve something we regard as necessary or desirable in a manner that is relatively simple and accessible. They may not do this in the most convenient or quickest way, certainly compared with the alternatives offered by more

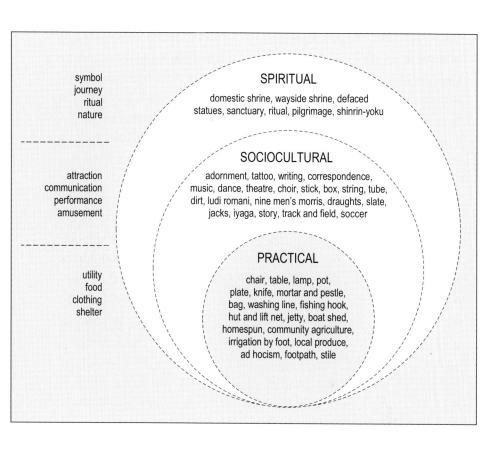

symbol
journey
ritual
nature

- - - - - - - - - -

attraction
communication
performance
amusement

- - - - - - - - - -

utility
food
clothing
shelter

SPIRITUAL

domestic shrine, wayside shrine, defaced
statues, sanctuary, ritual, pilgrimage, shinrin-yoku

SOCIOCULTURAL

adornment, tattoo, writing, correspondence,
music, dance, theatre, choir, stick, box, string, tube,
dirt, ludi romani, nine men's morris, draughts, slate,
jacks, iyaga, story, track and field, soccer

PRACTICAL

chair, table, lamp, pot,
plate, knife, mortar and pestle,
bag, washing line, fishing hook,
hut and lift net, jetty, boat shed,
homespun, community agriculture,
irrigation by foot, local produce,
ad hocism, footpath, stile

Figure 24.1   *Resilient Precedents–Artifacts and Activities*

technological, automated means, but they neither require such significant quantities of materials and energy nor lead to such damaging consequences. I say this not as an argument for abandoning modern technologies and returning to some past state but simply to demonstrate that these examples *do* illustrate what resilience and sustainability actually look like. Consequently, they should at least give us pause to challenge our own assumptions and question many of our current norms.

CHALLENGING ASSUMPTIONS

When we consider the present state of the world, where there is not only suffering from climate change and rapid environmental destruction but also declining levels of happiness among those living in some of the richest countries, it is all too clear that our contemporary ways of living are out of kilter not just with the planet but also with our own best interests. Moreover, this has been the case for a long time. If we are to change, we have to challenge many of the assumptions that have created this situation and brought the world to the brink of environmental collapse. In the following sections, we will consider how our expectations can be reconfigured in order to address resilience and sustainability more effectively.

Progress: The modern notion of progress is commonly understood in terms of economic development and growth, but this is a very particular interpretation and one that was created by the West. It takes for granted that, irrespective of cultural or historical differences, many countries around the world need to "catch up" to the ideals and lifestyles exemplified by Europe and the United States. These so-called underdeveloped countries need to be "improved" through Western economic intervention and the globalization of markets.[2] It is a model that "'consciously aims at a one-dimensional uniformity and seeks to eliminate all differences and traditions in a superficial quest for unity. . . . If a certain kind of globalization claims to make everyone uniform, to level everyone out, that globalization destroys the rich gifts and uniqueness of each person and each people'. This false universalism ends up depriving the world of its various colours, its beauty and, ultimately, its humanity. For 'the future is not monochrome'."[3]

Today's notion of progress is culturally and socially exploitative and highly destructive of natural ecosystems. It promotes Western goods, is fundamentally antilocal, and takes the world toward a bland monoculture. It is also invasive and hegemonic, trampling over local traditions that often hold deep knowledge of place and local ecologies. If considered at all, past and present are just the means to an end—everything is about what comes next. We mistakenly believe that once we get to the future, we will finally be happy—but, of course, this is an unobtainable goal, and, in the meantime, we fail to really live.[4]

True progress does not mean simply continuing along this path and persisting in those very things that have caused so much damage. It means learning from the past, from the wisdom of the ages, and building on this legacy; being guided by charity and compassion toward others; and caring for nature. These things can and should affect our aspirations and expectations and they ought to inform the artifacts we make and how we produce, maintain, and dispose of them. However, doing these things *well* means transcending the dominance of instrumental rationality that has characterized modern times and advocates the most efficient rather than the most effective and appropriate way to achieve a goal.

Efficiency: If people were inclined to believe the rhetoric of politicians and corporate marketing, they would be forgiven for thinking that modern society prides itself on its efficiency. This fallacy has arisen by conflating efficiency with the putative benefits of the market, facilitated by privatization, the reduction of business taxes, deregulation, and the minimization of government intervention. Many believe that this is the only system that works—but it clearly does not work for everyone, and it will not be able to continue for much longer because its impacts are so dire. True efficiency means using resources, energy, and time in ways that are not wasteful while having working methods that are both effective and ethical, thus ensuring due care for people and nature.

Innovation: We can see from the precedents discussed earlier that the kinds of products and practices that have been most resilient down the ages reflect moderate, local, and sustainable ways of living that are affordable, widely accessible, and inclusive. On the whole, they require little in the way of sophisticated technologies.

Innovation, which is simply the introduction of a new idea or method, has become a critically important ingredient of modern, consumerist economic systems. Today's products are not just associated with high levels of consumption but are far more technologically complex than their predecessors. To maintain sales, new models of cars, phones, appliances, and thousands of other products are constantly coming on the market, and most are knowingly designed to be short-lived. When these products incorporate the latest technologies, their functionality will inevitably become quickly outmoded. While science is constantly developing new knowledge about how the world works, problems arise when this knowledge is transformed into fleetingly useful products that are distributed around the world in their millions. This interpretation of innovation is ruinously myopic.

Work: Many people find that they are working long hours within highly competitive systems of employment. And while a few are paid very high sums for perhaps twenty to thirty days of work a year, many have to hold down two or even three jobs just to make ends meet. Such long hours and economic disparities exist because we have been led to believe that we can only be happy if we have the very latest things. Hence, we can only be happy if we have money and are able to consume—but in this system, there is no such thing as enough. Consequently, we all tend to be busy from dawn to dusk. As Pascal once observed, this seems an odd way to pursue happiness.[5]

In practice, convenience, "labor saving," and speed turn out to be rather different from what we had assumed. Simple and slow are better for people and planet—echoing the words of the sixth-century philosopher Boethius, who said that our attainment of true happiness is prevented because we go against the ways of nature: "What in nature is simple and undivided is split by human error, which diverts it from the true and perfect towards the false and imperfect."[6] Instead of contemplating and appreciating the natural world as a unified whole, we separate things out and examine, analyze, and exploit the parts. Such narrow perspectives inevitably create problems because we fail to consider connections and interrelationships. This is precisely the reason why, in the business world, the well-known "triple bottom line" of sustainable development has been ineffective. First, it offered an incomplete characterization of reality. Second, in its implementation, its three categories—environmental, economic, and social impacts—were separated out and dealt with and reported independently. As a consequence, the interrelationships among them went unacknowledged.[7]

The traditional halibut hook discussed in chapter 14 is an especially good example of an object that expresses a more holistic way of thinking. In this one object, we see a seamless integration of function, craft, art, myth, spirituality, ritual, heritage, environmentalism, sustenance, and change.

Aspiration: Modern aspirations constantly stoked by the machinations of marketing tend to be self-oriented, small-minded, and drearily arid—we want to appear more youthful than our years; we want a bigger house, a newer car, the latest gadget, a luxury holiday. Such aspirations are all acquisitive, lamentably vacuous, and entirely at odds with any meaningful understandings of happiness and resilience.

At their core, they are also supported by contemporary education and university research, which as discussed in chapter 2, consistently privileges science and technology, thereby implicitly devaluing the arts and humanities. This has led to understandings of value that are seriously distorted and prejudicial. The creative arts and values-based thinking are vitally important for developing empathy, building relationships, ensuring a fair and just society, and making meaning. A more holistic, well-balanced worldview gives our lives a greater sense of depth, purpose, and stability and provides us with a more substantive idea of happiness. The great wisdom traditions of the world are consistent in teaching that the source of this way of seeing ourselves and the world lies *within* us—we have to look into our hearts—not out there at material goods and extrinsic rewards.

We should not underestimate the social and environmental costs of such materialistic aspirations, including the serious effects on our mental health and the pervasive sense of uncertainty and anxiety caused by the climate crisis.[8]

Consumption: Close on the heels of these damaging ideas about progress and efficiency comes the ideology of consumerism, which holds that a continual increase in the consumption of goods is economically beneficial. The sheer power of corporate marketing tends to eclipse those things that are critical to one's sense of identity and belonging. Culture, community, tradition, a sense of continuity and stability, good-quality livelihoods, the natural environment[9]—all become collateral damage left in the wake of the juggernaut that is consumerism. When our own sense of identity is undermined, we become easily convinced by superficial slogans and meaningless brands, and are all too ready to build new identities through acquisition. This is what marketing is all about. It creates opportunities for continuous, but always fleeting, consumption by making us feel dissatisfied with everything we already have. It has come to completely dominate modern economies and our beleaguered world. And because obsolescence and disposal are inherent to this system, it results in excessive waste, resource exploitation, ecocide, and, for all of us, a continual sense of discontentedness and meaninglessness.

Any criticism of this ideology is quickly and vehemently suppressed by those who profit most from it and those who are ideologically persuaded by its shortsighted rewards. Criticizing or even discussing alternatives to this system has been prohibited in the British school education system through a statutory curriculum recently introduced by government.[10] It is a policy that has been widely condemned on the grounds that it inhibits free speech and could disallow teaching and discussion of large parts of British history as well as the works of prominent voices such as designer William Morris, philosopher Iris Murdoch, and political activist Thomas Paine.[11]

THREE TYRANNIES

These different elements of modern society—from assumptions about progress, innovation, and efficiency to ideas about work, aspiration, and consumption—can be summed up as three interconnected tyrannies that, together, lock us into a self-destructive path:

- *The tyranny of the majority*—Our silent acceptance and passive complicity are a large part of the problem. We comply because we see everyone else complying—we are "joined in a massive consensus" that is both "implicit and unconscious."[12] Our current ways of living have to be actively called into question, and a very different, far less consumptive path has to be developed.

- *The tyranny of materialism*—This manifests itself as ever-increasing acquisition and waste. As Mahatma Gandhi wrote, "This struggle is for freeing the world from the monstrous tyranny of material greed; it is a struggle to prove that money is not God."[13]
- *The tyranny of short-term thinking*—Immediate opportunities for profit continually trump long-term thinking. For years, we have considered it more cost-effective to simply postpone any significant action on climate change. We have stood by and watched the world go to rack and ruin.[14] But as D. H. Lawrence wrote, "The sky-scraper will scatter on the winds like thistledown . . . This is an interregnum."[15]

TOWARD A NEW PHILOSOPHICAL OUTLOOK

The dominant worldview and the concerns and preoccupations it upholds are, for all practical purposes, still steeped in the values and priorities of modernity. And they are entirely out of kilter with environmental care, social equity, and the welfare of people.

Reason without compassion is a cold and merciless master. If we are to steer a different course, we will need to retrieve ways of thinking and ways of doing that are in congruence with the natural world. To achieve a well-rounded outlook and a more balanced way forward, explanatory forms of knowledge, facts, and the contributions of science have to be complemented and integrated with tacit and interpretive ways of knowing and human values. When reason and imagination are *both* valued, they complement one another and offer a much more comprehensive understanding of ourselves and the world. But to achieve this, we have to acknowledge what has been lost.

Over thousands of years, all major cultures developed teachings and ideas about how to live in the world, and these were passed down from one generation to the next. Values, notions of meaning, beliefs, and practical information were continually being taught, carried forward, and adapted. In oral cultures, this knowledge was contained in stories, myths, and sacred teachings. Their purpose, however, was not simply to impart factual information. Through metaphor, symbol, and ritual, they also conveyed tacit forms of knowledge concerning an individual's inner development. When these teachings were eventually written down, they were intended to be read aloud—to be performed, perhaps within a ritual. And just as a functional object like a halibut hook could provide a basis for storytelling in an oral culture, in earlier times, texts were meant to serve a similar role, as an aide-mémoire, so that the stories and ideas could be adjusted, contextualized, and made relevant.[16] Hence, they were living texts that continually flourished through fresh interpretation—just as a piece of music or a poem begins in written form but comes alive again and again each time it is performed. Hence, every performance will be unique, depending on the artist, the venue, and the audience.

This is quite different from the way we regard texts today, and so we often mistakenly read traditional writings as if they were factual histories and either dismiss them as not being credible or accept them literally. Either way, their true purpose is missed. As John Marincola has said: "Assumptions that we make as members of a society where writing is an everyday part of life may be invalid when applied to the very different cultures of the ancient world. . . . Inquiry, it seems, is not a simple matter of asking questions and getting answers."[17] Within traditional, oral cultures, one of the most important lessons about living a meaningful life concerns our relatedness to others and the world. Sioux theologian Ohiyesa said this was an essential aspect of a child's education. It was an education that encouraged spiritual development, physical health, and sociocultural responsibility and shunned the pursuit of possessions and wealth. From childhood, he was consciously trained

> not to care for money or possessions, but to be in the broadest sense a public servant. After arriving at a reverent sense of the pervading presence of the Spirit and Giver of Life, and a deep consciousness of the brotherhood of man, the first thing for me to accomplish was to adapt myself perfectly to natural things—in other words, to harmonize myself with nature. To this end

I was made to build a body both symmetrical and enduring—a house for the soul to live in—a sturdy house, defying the elements. I must have faith and patience; I must learn self-control and be able to maintain silence. I must do with as little as possible and start with nothing most of the time, because a true Indian always shares whatever he may possess.[18]

In traditional or nonmodern worldviews, empirical facts are transcended, and the world is imaginatively interpreted, thereby revealing a deeper sense of meaning and significance. Not only is such imaginative interpretation a vital ingredient of being human; it is necessary for understanding the world. Even in contemporary society, in which we put such great store in facts and empirical evidence, "we deal with the world as it appears to us, not as it intrinsically is"; the whole notion of "objective truth" is an illusion.[19]

This creative, imaginative element is a critical ingredient of design—the problem lies not in our abilities but in our priorities. To a large degree, our design priorities are not grounded in ideas and intentions that help cultivate a material culture consistent with a world of depth and meaning. In fact, quite the opposite—much contemporary design is intimately involved in creating a continuous outpouring of novelty and superficial amusement that is transient, inherently destructive, and sustained through shortsighted self-interest.

RESILIENCE, TRADITION, AND TOLERANCE

I have spoken extensively in this book about the importance of traditional knowledge and practices in developing more resilient ways of living. Through custom, communal forms of practice, and ritual, tradition helps create a sense of belonging and identity by situating one's individual actions and contributions within a larger continuum of meaning and purpose. Traditions that endure typically involve continuous processes of creativity and change that enable them to remain culturally germane, vibrant, and generative. But the modern eye is often blind to the imaginative, dynamic reality that characterizes so much tradition, prompting Z. S. Strother to ask, "How can we open up our definitions of invention and innovation to include the explosive creativity of teamwork, collaboration, appropriation and competition? What model can scholars use to explore the processes of transformation . . . ?"[20]

Many traditions emerged from communal ways of living within geographically limited areas. As a result, they are often especially well attuned to context and to contemporary notions of sustainability, even though to an outside observer, they may seem insular and incompatible with today's more individualistic outlooks and expectations. One consequence of this is that many traditions are not looked upon favorably by the dominant culture and are under threat—sometimes from encroachment and sometimes from accusations of intolerance and discrimination. On this latter point, criticism may be justified, for when traditions fail to change, they not only ossify but can also become intransigent. But we should also bear in mind that criticism works both ways. In modern society, there is often vested interest in undermining traditional ways of living in order to open up new economic opportunities on the lands of traditional peoples, as we have seen in recent times in Canada, Australia, and the Amazon regions of South America. Commonly, too, there is a lack of understanding and tolerance by outsiders with respect to many traditional perspectives, priorities, and values. While we do not doubt that precolonial societies had their own histories, recognition of this is not the same thing as giving an accurate account of it. Many community-based, noncapitalist, nonconsumerist societies have existed in the world. They have demonstrated models of living that are compatible with sustainability, inclusivity, and resilience. Yet, as John and Jean Comaroff have asked, "Have we really advanced on our old conception of 'traditional' societies, 'cold' cultures? Of local worlds trapped in repetitive cycles of structural time . . . ?"[21]

The modern mind, trained in rational argument and evidence-based truths, is not well-equipped, and perhaps not attitudinally receptive, to the kinds of holistic thinking and polysemous forms of expression that characterize traditional practices. Typical expectations of modern research—such as evidence to corroborate events spoken of in traditional texts—simply do not apply in the realm of mythos. Traditional spiritual and mythological stories are not concerned with conveying facts—this is the role of science. Rather, they are concerned with the world of meaning—with values, trust, charity, and timeless teachings about how we should live in harmony with each other and the world. These texts should not be interpreted literally but always in ways that are guided by kindness, generosity, and empathy—even when this seems to contradict a literalist reading.[22]

Hence, on the one hand, we see that those very qualities of tradition that facilitate local, place-appropriate practices; the accumulation of deep, ecological knowledge; and community and cooperation can also lead to overly conservative, narrow-minded attitudes. On the other hand, a more liberal outlook may be more open to change, but it can also lead to an erosion of one's sense of identity and belonging and a loss of knowledge about and disregard for place. How do we strike the right balance? Clearly, there has to be change and learning on both sides if harmonious ways forward are to be found. More conservative communities can look beyond literalist, uncompromising interpretations to draw on the deeper teachings of love and compassion at the heart of all the world's great spiritual texts, and they can look outward with a receptive attitude of cosmopolitan localism (as discussed in chapter 3). Similarly, those with more liberal views can be more respectful and open to learning about the importance of place, context, and tradition—not least because traditional knowledge and holistic modes of thought are urgently needed to more effectively address today's environmental crisis.

TOWARD A RESILIENT FUTURE

The development of cleaner technologies and repairable, upgradable products can certainly make important contributions, but they are not enough to reverse the environmental harms caused by current ways of living. No matter how "green" they are, mass-produced products still depend on enormous amounts of resource extraction, energy use, production, and waste. We cannot manufacture our way out of global warming.

Transformational change will not be achieved with the same type of thinking that has dominated for so long. Time and again, evidence has been gathered and targets set, only for them to be watered down to get agreements signed. And, inexorably, emissions have continued to rise.

A major cause of environmental destruction is the fact that we consume far too many products. But in our growth-oriented economic system, one of our main solutions seems to be to consume even more, albeit products that are somewhat "greener." However, any small gains offered by such products will have to be accompanied by *significantly reduced levels of overall consumption*. It is also necessary to develop new priorities and approaches based on quite different priorities and values.

A Change of Heart: Current approaches have to be accompanied by developments that help steer behavior change. Ethical ways of living, which are interpretive rather than evidential, have to take a greater role in our activities—especially values that transcend self so as to ensure our activities include care for the world as a whole. These values-based teachings are found in a culture's spiritual and philosophical traditions. They become enculturated into our everyday behaviors through repetitive practices—including ritual and other collective activities such as community agriculture, games, and sports.[23] However, in modern times, not only has adherence to spiritual practices fallen into rapid decline but so have community coherence and collaborative practices. As a result, opportunities for meeting and sharing experiences with others who may hold different views from one's own have declined. In restoring such ways, there is much to learn from traditional knowledge, but this has to be reinterpreted, developed, and expressed in new forms if it is to be relevant and appealing in contemporary society.

Normalizing Moderation: Lifestyles, especially for those living in the richer societies, need to become far more restrained, and moderation has to become the new norm. This means substantial reductions in overall consumption levels, which include choosing to live in smaller spaces that require fewer goods to furnish and less energy for heating or air conditioning. Smaller and fewer cars on the road implies more walking and bicycle use, combined with greater reliance on public transport. Long-distance travel—for business and holidays—has to be drastically curtailed, and, wherever possible, the use of trains rather than planes has to become the norm. In addition to reducing acquisition and product ownership, new business models will have to be adopted to facilitate changing habits while also maintaining a flourishing but more responsible and less rapacious economy.

New Business Models: Business models that do not depend on selling products but entail product leasing or renting have been around for a long time; these tend to be far more compatible with resilience. The provider maintains income from ongoing product services rather than one-time product sales. Consequently, it is in the producer's interest for products to be high-quality, long-lasting, and reliable so that they require minimal service provision. They should also be repairable and upgradable. On this point, the European Union and the United Kingdom recently introduced laws that require manufacturers of electrical goods to make their products repairable for at least ten years.[24] If products are kept in use for longer periods, while being economically viable for the producers/lessors, significant reductions can be made in resource and energy use, product throughput, and waste. The onus is changed—it is the opposite of a system driven by production and sales of short-lived goods. Moving away from product ownership also supports smaller living spaces; when products that are only used occasionally— such as camping equipment, bike trailers, and power tools—are rented rather than purchased, they do not require storage space in one's home.

We should also be aware of the potential pitfalls of such models. Product leasing would undoubtedly enable leaseholders to have access to high-quality, well-made products. However, this model could also maintain hierarchies of conspicuous wealth, which is an upward driver of a culture based on "more." Greater restraint and moderation in this area is also a necessary part of an outlook grounded in moderation. These things have not changed much since the time of Seneca (first century BCE) who put it this way: "It is not necessary to ransack the depths of every sea or to load our bellies with the meat of slaughtered creatures or to extract shellfish from unknown shores of the furthest sea: the curses of gods and goddesses land on the heads of those whose luxury exceeds the limits of an empire already the object of too much envy! . . . If a man holds such things in contempt, what harm can poverty inflict on him? . . . What need of laying waste to forests? What need of plundering the deep? . . . Greed is satisfied by nothing."[25]

Local Capacity-Building: Traditional production methods in small enterprises frequently employ locally sourced skills and materials and are often conducted in ways that are environmentally responsible and magnanimous of spirit. Knowledge, skills, and capacity are developed; employment opportunities are created; monitoring and accountability are integral; and transportation and packaging are reduced. Highly agile forms of production can result from local networks and a combination of cooperation and competition among those with different skills and abilities, as discussed in chapter 14. This form of production, which can create varied and fulfilling work at the local level, is still very much in evidence in many parts of the world, such as the hundreds of small interdependent furniture-making enterprises in Damietta, in the Nile delta region of Egypt. Within such working methods, the more tedious, less skilled processes can be effectively brought up to date using small-scale, digital manufacturing tools. And, as we saw in chapter 14, local, diversified forms of food production are capable of far higher yields per square meter than the vast monocultures created by the large agro-industry conglomerates. Small-scale, organic agriculture also produces healthier soils and sustains greater biodiversity.

An emphasis on local capacity-building can provide a sense of purpose, self-reliance, and self-determination. It helps keep wealth within the community, contributes to decentralization, and gives people a say in their own future—all of which build self-confidence, as well as a more distributed, resilient economy. Locally based production also acknowledges and affirms people, community, and place. It recognizes the provenance of material goods and foods as well as the efforts and skills of those who produce them, and it anchors and orients us within a larger context of belonging. Consequently, it is inherently more respectful and appreciative of people and planet.[26] These relationships *mean* something, they matter to us. But sadly, in recent times they have tended to be pushed aside in the name of "progress," economic globalization, and the pursuit of profits—irrespective of the human and environmental costs. We have now reached a point where these costs are far too high—it is time for this model to be fundamentally changed and for the things that give our lives meaning to be restored. To this end, Alasdair MacIntyre writes: "When recurrently the tradition of the virtues is regenerated, it is always in everyday life, it is always through the engagement by plain persons in a variety of practices, including those of making and sustaining families and households, schools, clinics, and local forms of political community. And that regeneration enables such plain persons to put to the question the dominant modes of moral and social discourse and the institutions that find their expression in those modes."[27]

These days, in conducting research in a wide variety of areas, academics often carry out projects with local communities, and this is invariably regarded as a good thing. However, we must sound a note of caution. The attitudes of people who live in established communities, with familiar, stable, interdependent relationships are quite different from those "of the more transient scholars, who all come with an agenda that connects to other settings and other communities; the issues are different for those who are not living with stability."[28] University researchers working with communities are not part of those communities—they are not fully involved or familiar with the prevailing ways and relationships and their interventions can create instability by introducing innovations and initiatives that disrupt and undermine existing forms of self-reliance and local capacity.

Connecting and Caring: All the precedents I have discussed here are, in one form or another, about our relatedness to other people. This is crucial, not just to cultural activities but to all aspects of life. It is also a vital ingredient of sustainability.

Those living in the wealthier nations who currently enjoy the benefits of low-cost products and foods imported from poorer countries have a responsibility to the people in those regions. Richer nations can support local capacity-building so that people living in less-wealthy countries can build self-reliance, rather than be dependent on production for export, often under exploitative conditions. However, to avoid the hegemonic ills of the past, any support requires sensitivity to context, two-way knowledge exchange, long-term commitment, and transparent collaborative implementation. Such programs could have environmental and social benefits and would go some way to reducing inequity, exploitation, and mass migration.

Localization that is widely connected to others, including internationally, is facilitated today like never before because of digital communications. This enables production to be suited to local conditions while also being informed by a wider perspective. This type of local production is capable of overcoming the dangers of overcentralization, the homogeneity of globalization, and the potential prejudices of a narrow parochialism. It helps build a diversity of mutually enriching, place-based practices, designs, and outcomes that are all attuned to the particularities of place.[29]

This is not the only aspect of relatedness we should be considering. Equally important is our relatedness to nature, but the truth of the matter is that we are becoming less and less able to understand or experience the meaning of this relational connection. Through urbanization, labor-saving machines and technological marvels, we have disconnected and insulated ourselves from the world. Relatedness to nature means a deep, living, breathing connection; it has to be a connection that is caring and respectful so that both we and the natural environment are able to flourish.

When we conquered nature, or thought we had, we severed this relatedness. A relationship in which one party seeks to subjugate and exploit the other is simply abusive. If we are to repair this connection, one of the first things we have to do is recognize and work to overcome the physical and mental barriers we have erected between ourselves and the natural universe. To this end, many of the artifacts and activities considered in earlier chapters offer direction. By and large, the elements used are natural—stone, wood, clay, wool, flax, fire, earth, even bone. Such materials and their associated practices help reconnect us through aesthetics; through their visual and tactile qualities, their sounds, tastes, and smells; and through a renewed recognition of the need for nurturing, caring for, and complying with the rhythms and durations of nature. As J. M. McCarthy said: "The rocks and the animals and the image of Pan himself combine to displace the Cartesian orthodoxy of an inert world at the feet of an active human subject. In its place [is] nature as a complex, material realm where vigorous things interpenetrate human experience."[30]

Creating Good Work: Our working lives are increasingly sedentary and bound up in the tedium of online reporting, form-filling, and key performance indicators. People and institutions are ranked according to highly selective metrics that distort reality. And working methods increasingly have to fit within predetermined systems. Inexorably, work becomes stripped of initiative, vitality, and joy. For years, these impositions have been affecting teaching, nursing, and medical practices, and they are seriously impacting universities. When our day-to-day tasks are reduced to negotiating poorly designed online systems, creative approaches that do not fit easily into the system tend to be dropped, and spontaneity is all but eradicated.

The creation of good work is essential for effective learning as well as for our physical and mental health and our general sense of well-being. Work practices can provide a stable basis for living and a force for the good in society. Good work means making a meaningful, creative contribution within an environment of respect, trust, and commitment—without conflict or hierarchy, because there is nothing to prove. With stability grows familiarity, an "at ease" with skills and relationships that become second nature; such ways involve humility, interdependence, and a sense of responsibility to others, community, and place.

DESIGN FOR RESILIENCE

The artistic, poetic, mythological, spiritual, and philosophical—these have always been present in human societies because through them we confront life's big questions. They are also fundamental to creative practices like design. Neither scientific investigation nor rational explanation can provide tangible evidence to "prove" their truths. But when imaginative, creative works resonate with us at a deeply intuitive level, we feel and indeed know them to be self-evidently true. To make a more substantive contribution, design has to better recognize the role of these areas of human knowledge in the creative design process.

The process of designing is inherently holistic—it has more to do with synthesis than analysis. To invoke it, we have to allow ourselves to think in broader, more intuitive ways, and we have to experience it directly through engagement in practice. In its essence, design is not an intellectual process, though it requires intellectual thinking from time to time. Being a creative process, it calls upon the imagination and, in many ways, is more like daydreaming—we feel outside ourselves and outside of time—we become lost in the work, which absorbs every thought, every second. If we start to rationalize, we snap out of it. Discussing the writing of F. Scott Fitzgerald, Ernest Hemingway wrote: "His talent was as natural as the pattern that was made by the dust of a butterfly's wings. At one time he understood it no more than the butterfly did and he did not know when it was brushed or marred. Later he became conscious of his damaged wings and of their construction and he learned to think and could not fly any more because the love of flight was gone and he could only remember when it had been effortless."[31] Similarly, Henry Shukman says of D. H. Lawrence: "It is an oddity about Lawrence that somehow the books at which he labored most directly, such as the novels, are arguably not his best. Rather, when he was relaxing, as it were doodling, leaning back against the tree at his ranch where he loved to write, a notebook in his lap, it seemed his vivid genius was in full flood, and he was most able to capture a mood or atmosphere, a character, a relationship."[32]

These insights tell us much about the nature of the creative process and also how ill-suited to it are the rigid formats and expectations of our formal education system. Creativity is concerned with skill building and experience, both of which are achieved through repetitive, performative modes of learning and the interaction between hand, eye, and mind. It has elements of play and ritual to it (see chapters 16 and 17), and these require the right kind of conditions, such as "relaxing . . . leaning back against the tree," for the process to unfold; we cannot force it.

The distinctive nature of design makes it especially well-suited to address complex issues like resilience and sustainability through a process of thinking-and-doing that is interpretive and integrational and can take into account broad, systemic issues. To do this, however, design has to move beyond stale arguments about *form follows function* and efficiency. The products of design are capable of embodying utilitarian, sociocultural, spiritual, and ecological ideas while simultaneously incorporating responsible economic management.

So how should designers proceed? While we might all agree that the broader implications of design decisions and actions have to be taken into account, when in the midst of the process, the designer is unable to make judgments based on the outcome, simply because at this stage it is still unknown. Nevertheless, judgments have to be made. Moreover, to develop designs that are ethical, we cannot simply kowtow to someone else's bidding; we have to be true to our own principles. Each designer has to walk the difficult path of their own inner, ethical development, trust in its veracity, and act accordingly, even without evidence or proof. And while we have to walk this path alone, there is consolation in knowing that many have walked it before us. So even without concrete evidence, we can learn from their accounts and experiences.

There is also something of a paradox here—while there is an essential interiority about this path, inner development is furthered through care for others and nature. And this care is expressed through our day-to-day decisions and actions.

One's inner development helps ensure that the design process does not seek to achieve its objective at any cost. Instead, *means and ends* become an inseparable, ethical whole. When grounded in the philosophical and spiritual teachings of one's own culture, this process of *design praxis* aims to improve the prevailing situation, not least by ensuring that the outcomes are contextually and culturally appropriate.[33]

Intergenerational forms of knowledge accumulate over time and are continuously adapted to remain relevant to each generation. Material culture and designs can develop in the same way. Through knowledge, skills, and processes that are handed down and through trial and error, artifacts and architectures have evolved in response to changing needs and circumstances. Through this process, learning from the past is brought into the present and built upon. Over time, the contributions of many different people result in highly refined, effective, and often very beautiful artifacts that are usually remarkably well-suited to their purpose, express a sense of moderation and restraint, and achieve an elegant fit with their environment. They synthesize natural materials with making, ritual, tradition, and reverence and fuse functional necessity with meaningful decorative symbolism that is respectful of, and indeed honors, all of creation.

In recent years, there has been a great deal of design scholarship about the need to develop more sustainable, inclusive, and resilient ways of living.

But it is important to acknowledge that not everything about design can be written down. In this book, a wide variety of issues have been raised, including critique, scale of production, appreciation, localization, and so on. However, we should not be attempting to deal with each of these issues in isolation. More challengingly, they have to be addressed all together in an integrated fashion. However, imaginative integration cannot be reduced to a lockstep process diagram. Instead, these various issues inform the nature and spirit of design engagement.

This integrated, *means-and-ends* process is necessary to effectively combine function, expressiveness, and multidimensional depth into design outcomes. As a professional discipline, mainstream design can and should be doing much more to creatively address the pressing issues of our time, and this kind of informed, holistic process provides the necessary foundation for doing so. In taking it seriously, designers can demonstrate leadership and offer hope.

IMPLICATIONS FOR DESIGN

Among the various precedents discussed earlier, the Hewn Trestle Table, the New Delft Plate, and the L'al Yak Bag are all rooted in long-standing traditions, but their production processes and aesthetics have been updated to suit contemporary needs. The heritage of the Pusser's Dirk clasp knife lies in the age of sail and Britain's seafaring tradition. Its design has been adapted to suit today's needs by employing modern materials and by resizing to conform to contemporary regulations.

A rather different approach is represented by the halibut hook, which, despite its long tradition and its relationship to ecological practices, has been superseded by mass-produced alternatives. In recent times, the traditional hook has been transformed into large, colorful, and intricately crafted objets d'art. While no longer practical, they do enable individual carvers to refine their creative skills while also making a decent living, and they express and sustain important aspects of Indigenous culture. On the other hand, the traditional functional hooks, which held an important place in the day-to-day practices of the living culture, have been transformed into rather expensive collectors' pieces, and this raises several concerns. First, the object's role is effectively diminished in terms of its practical, cultural, and spiritual meanings. Second, they are created for and dependent on a market that is *external* to the culture of origin. And, third, they have become "sociopositional" in nature—markers of taste and wealth. This aspect, which is common to many modern products, is particularly problematic because it is one of the key drivers of consumption.

Some of the precedents, such as the washing line and ad hocism, need no design interventions. The first works perfectly well as it is, and the second cannot be consciously designed.

It is also important to keep in mind that highly refined craft skills can be employed to create objects and environments that fall into the category of kitsch, as discussed in chapter 8. Again, rich traditions become diminished, in this case to superficial tropes and clichés, which shield us from reality by smothering it in sentimental coziness. Yet, despite their lack of substance, kitsch objects and environments are very effective, if manipulative, means of driving consumption. Consequently, they are antithetical to the values and principles of resilience.

To determine if and how designers can make a constructive contribution to resilience, they have to be informed, sincere, and judicious—*and they have to struggle*. Meaning in life is found in suffering—in the striving for a worthwhile sense of purpose and a task freely chosen, as discussed in chapter 7. This is, or should be, our principal driving force—to possess the *why* of life. And this is fundamental to design—to immerse ourselves fully in the creative process is to engage in life itself, with all of its caprice and possibility but also with all of its uncertainty, risk, doubt, and suffering. In many respects, this process is illogical and uncertain, and yet . . . it is a recognition that our main goal should be life itself, not the thing that is created, which once attained is complete, finished, lifeless, and hence the beginning of a kind of death.

Humility and Restraint: Many of the artifacts considered, such as the pot and the sickle, have had a place in human culture for hundreds if not thousands of years. They have been continually developed and improved until their designs have a reached a state of essentiality. The resulting artifacts are moderate and beautiful, and through stories and myths, they have acquired a deep cultural significance.

To think that contemporary design can bring anything substantively new to such artifacts seems presumptuous. So, key qualities of design for resilience should be humility, restraint, and a relinquishment of ego. The first question we should ask is "Does design have anything of consequence to offer?" The answer may well be "No."

Making Special: Mass-produced ubiquity has made many things ordinary, throwaway, unvalued—a condition that applies not just to material goods. Buying a record or going to the cinema were once eagerly awaited occasions. Immediate access to virtually any film or piece of music via the Internet is convenient and cheap, but the anticipation, socialization, and opportunities to create memorable experiences are greatly diminished. When everything is commonplace, nothing is special. Quality, discernment, and the conviviality of shared experiences are replaced by quantity and effortlessness, which ultimately engender indifference and ennui.

To address this, designers have the opportunity to contribute to new kinds of "special"—artifacts, spaces, and experiences that are meaningful to people and set apart from daily routines. This applies not just to materials things but also to practices.

Appreciation: To appreciate what we have, we first have to know about it, so an important contribution by designers can be the effective presentation and communication of locally available goods and services. Discovering the opportunities available in one's area and becoming aware of their relationship to local traditions adds to the richness of life. In doing so, we implicitly demonstrate greater appreciation for the sense of belonging that emerges from tried-and-tested ways of doing. Appreciation also includes a renewed realization of the pleasures of conviviality and making time for family and friends, and here simple pastimes that require little in the way of expense, equipment, or technology can provide a basis for being together.

Appreciation also requires discernment. For instance, in recent years, there has been renewed interest in walking the great pilgrimage routes of

Europe. In theory, this practice can be environmentally benign, but many people now complete these routes over several years by flying in annually to hike short portions. While local pilgrimage routes are less well known, they still exist, and walking one of these requires less time and expense and no air travel.

Meaning Making: Our most resilient artifacts and activities tend to be quite simple and unpretentious. Resilient forms of material culture are also things that are meaningful in terms of their purpose, which might be utilitarian, sociocultural, and/or spiritual. And they often have little or nothing to do with the market system. The precedents considered here have far more to do with making meaning than making money. They are also consistent with sustainability because, in addressing human needs over such long periods of time, they have had to respond in some manner to who we are as full human beings.

Design for resilience means creating a material culture that not only is lasting and has enduring usefulness but also—through its continued presence—is able to acquire other kinds of meaning. Artifacts become metaphors, stories are told, and, over time, there is the accretion of memories and symbolism. These things give material culture depth and significance. Many of the artifacts and activities discussed here have multiple meanings and many interwoven relationships to people and the world. They embody and express utility, ecology, community, myth, spirituality, and philosophical understandings while simultaneously incorporating skills and economic management. Such a complex array of constituents surpasses anything offered by short-lived consumer products.

Hence, the precedents point to meaningful ways of breaking our addiction to consumption—an addiction on which our current economic and political systems rely.

These unassuming examples are illustrative of *the major systemic transformation* that is needed to seriously commit to sustainability, inclusivity, and resilience. They imply a root and branch reform of priorities, values, motivations, and drivers—a fundamental turning away from our current, highly destructive ways of life.

Improvisation: One of the lessons emerging from this discussion is that resilience often does not involve design at all; at least not design as a professional service, which is how we tend to think of it today. Resilience means acting more intelligently and restoring a sense of balance and moderation. Perhaps most of all, it means recognizing and appreciating the beauty, abundance, and possibility of what we already have. A more imaginative use of locally available resources not only avoids waste but also allows things to acquire the patinas and meanings of age. A defaced statue, a shed made from an upturned boat, a piece of worm-eaten pine made into a game board—such things enrich our world and our lives. Through improvisation and the accumulation of significance, a postconsumerist material culture helps move us away from the destructiveness of globalized banality.

In answer to specific needs, ad hoc solutions possess a spontaneous, relaxed utility that is quite indifferent to the affectations of good taste. They express an almost unconscious purposefulness that seamlessly blends creativity, intuition, and rational thought. As such, they are rather revealing in that they represent both sides of our nature—emotion and imagination holistically combined with logic and reason. There is also a sense of freedom to them, a lean spontaneity that defies rules and methods. They can be characterized as "making do" and "good enough"—sufficient for the purpose and entirely free of professionalism, brands, marketing, packaging, pretense, and, typically, expense.

Aesthetics: To be consistent with the principles of resilience and sustainability, an artifact's aesthetic has to emerge from the essence of what it actually is, rather than be something consciously added on or styled by a designer. The aesthetic of a thing goes deeper than mere surface—it is an inherent articulation of values, priorities, and meanings. When it is reduced to a superficial exercise in facade, it is an artificial imposition, a presumption, and this, too, is expressive of values—but not values compatible with resilience.

Transformation: To readers who might think the precedents I have considered in this book imply a future too far removed from current ways of living to be feasible, I reply that to achieve resilience, the scale of systemic change will have to be transformational on many levels. This includes a much greater focus on localization; far less consumption; more communitarian ways of living; and greater emphasis on purposeful, meaningful activities that do not involve depletion of the earth's resources. However, even this scale of change may be too little too late. Immediate, transformational change of this magnitude is exactly what the majority of climate scientists are calling for if we are to have any chance of avoiding catastrophic planetary effects.[34]

PRINCIPLES OF DESIGN FOR RESILIENCE

Living in ways that are modest, sufficient, inclusive, and resilient has never been an easy message to hear, but it has been the consistent message of philosophers and spiritual leaders down the ages, from the Buddha, Socrates, and Jesus to Mahatma Gandhi. With the natural world in a truly tragic state, happiness on the decline, and anxiety on the rise, it is a message worth repeating, taking seriously, and working toward. Evidence from climate science alone suggests that heeding this wisdom is more urgent today than at any other time in our history.

Bringing together the various thoughts, ideas, and propositions from the foregoing, we are now in a position to summarize what they all amount to. The magnitude of the task before us should not be underestimated. It means reconfiguring our notions of progress and decoupling them from growth. It means questioning the costs of convenience—and recognizing the benefits of a deeper engagement in and with the real world and the flow of life. And it means taking seriously the real costs of materials and processes that are in fundamental conflict with nature and the health of all of us. Greater humility and circumspection would not go amiss—we would do well to acknowledge that, first, we never have the whole picture and, second, we do not know what the long-term effects might be. This calls for prudence or what some may call basic common sense. There is an urgent need to adopt the right kind of attitude and spirit to ensure that, from the outset, our design activities are responsible and positive for people and the natural environment. Adherence to the following principles will, I trust, offer a constructive way forward.

Ten Principles of Design for Resilience

Design for Resilience is

1. **Beautiful**: embodying an aesthetics of goodness, integrity, and care for people and planet
2. **Enduring**: functionally, physically, aesthetically, and psychologically
3. **Restrained**: manifesting self-control, moderation, and responsibility
4. **Equitable**: informed, socially just, and ethical
5. **Situated**: grounded in the particularities of place
6. **Enabling**: fostering decision-making and development at the local level
7. **Trustworthy**: conscientious and reliable; creativity permeated by moral commitment
8. **Farsighted**: acting judiciously and with forethought to avoid further damage to nature
9. **Holistic**: bringing together utility, aesthetics, context, and values
10. **Transformational**: fundamentally restorative, so communities and nature can recover

We have discussed many artifacts and activities that have endured over very long periods of time. On the whole, they have been environmentally benign and socially constructive. They result from centuries of gentle, sensitive work shaping things to serve human needs in ways that frequently yield a particular kind of beauty—one that is entirely suited to context—neither entirely human-made nor entirely natural, but a harmonious melding of both that does not violate or exploit. All of which shows that we can live on and from the earth without disfiguring it. Critically, too, these artifacts and activities demonstrate that design for resilience is both possible and viable.

While these precedents may not comply with modern ideas about amenity and technological possibility, they have, nevertheless, proved their importance and endurance in sustaining human societies and enabling them to function and flourish. Implicitly, too, they foster a deeper appreciation of and respect for nature.

We are living through the realities of a world suffering from the increasingly severe impacts of a fast-changing climate. We have been slow to recognize that a fundamental shift in our ways of living is needed. Designers have the training, the ability, and the potential to step up and make substantial contributions that enable such change. In doing so, they will be supporting practical programs for positive transformation and offering hope for a future that lasts.

Acknowledgments

I am grateful to the Arts and Humanities Research Council and the Faculty of Arts and Humanities at Lancaster University for their continued support of the numerous research projects that have informed the contents of this book. Thanks also to the various peer reviewers who have provided such helpful feedback on earlier manuscripts. My sincere thanks go to Professor Martyn Evans at Manchester Metropolitan University, with whom, over many years, I have collaborated on research projects in the United Kingdom, the United States, and China. I also thank Victoria Hindley and everyone at the MIT Press, who have worked so hard to bring this book to fruition. Finally, as always, I thank my wife, Helen, for her repeated proofing and copyediting of successive versions and for her unwavering support.

Appendix 1: Merrill's Rules of *Rota*

The original rules of *Rota* are unknown, but E. T. Merrill suggests the following, for two players with three counters each.[1]

The Aim
The first player to align their three counters in a straight line wins.

How to Play
- The players toss a coin or decide between themselves who begins.
- The first player places a counter on the board either at one of the intersection points where the spokes of the wheel meet the outer circle or at the center point.
- The second player then places a counter on any one of the unoccupied points.
- The players continue alternately until all six counters have been placed on the board.
- The first player then moves one of his counters to an adjacent, unoccupied position—along a spoke or along the arc of the circle.
- The second player makes a similar move.
- They continue in this way until one player aligns his three counters into a straight line along a single diameter—this is the winning move.
- Two counters may not occupy the same intersection point on the board.
- No "capturing" or "jumping" is permitted.
- At their turns, players cannot decline to move.

Playing Suggestion
It seems that the player who begins is at an advantage. As the duration of each game is rather short, a series of games is recommended with players taking it in turns to start.

Appendix 2: Schädler's Rules of *Latrunculi*

The original rules of play of *latrunculi* have been lost, but in recent times, various authors have proposed rules based on clues found in contemporary writings. Those suggested by Ulrich Schädler are probably the most cited:[1]

- For a board of 8 × 8 squares, each player has 16 pieces, with sides differentiated by color or motif.
- Players take turns to place a piece on a vacant square.
- When the pieces are all placed, players take turns to move them orthogonally (i.e., at right angles, not diagonally) on the board to a free square.
- A piece can leap another piece of either color if the square beyond is free; several leaps can be taken in one turn, as in draughts.
- The aim is to trap your opponent's piece between two of your pieces so it is blocked and unable to move. The trapped piece is turned upside down.
- In the following turn, if your two trapping pieces are still free, instead of moving another piece, you can remove the trapped piece from the board. However, the trapped piece is immediately set free if one of your two trapping pieces is itself trapped.
- You can move a piece between two of your opponent's pieces only if, in doing so, you are able to trap one of these two enemy pieces.
- The winner is the player who has two or more pieces left on the board when the opponent is reduced to only one.

Appendix 3: Rules of Nine Men's Morris

This game is for two players. Each has nine stones of one color. The stones are placed on the twenty-four points of the board—that is, the corners of the squares and the intersections where the lines meet or cross the sides of the squares.

The Aim

The winner is the player who reduces the opponent's stones to two or blocks the opponent from making a move.

How to Play

- The players flip a coin to decide who begins.
- Players take turns to place their stones on any empty point. In placing the stones, the aim is to make a "mill," which is created when three pieces form a line. Each time a player is able to make a mill, they can remove one of the opponent's stones, but they should only take a stone from a mill made by their opponent if there are no other stones available.
- When all the stones have been placed, a player can move one of their stones to an adjacent point if it is vacant. If, in doing so, this makes a mill, the player can again remove one of their opponent's stones.
- When a stone is removed, it is out of play for the duration of the game.
- A player can "open" one of their mills by moving one of the three stones off the line. In a subsequent turn, it can be "closed" again, thus creating a new mill and entitling the player to remove another of the opponent's stones.[1]

Appendix 4: Rules of Jacks

Natural knucklebones have four long and two short sides, each bone measuring about 25 × 20 × 12 mm, and are thought to be a precursor to dice. Whether played with bones or stones, a game typically uses five pieces, sometimes more. Players progress through various throws and catches, or "figures," which are performed in a chosen sequence. The names of the figures vary from place to place, but the moves are more or less the same everywhere.

One ancient figure involves the player tossing all five pieces into the air, then trying to catch them on the back of the hand, then tossing them up again and catching them in the palm. In another sequence, the pieces are dropped onto the playing surface. For the first figure, called "ones," a single piece, thereafter called the "Jack," is tossed into the air, then another piece is picked up and the Jack caught before it falls—all in the same hand. The caught piece is put down with the others, and the player moves on to "twos." The Jack is tossed again, two pieces are picked up, and the Jack is caught before it falls. Play continues for "threes" and "fours." If at any point a piece is dropped or the Jack is not caught, that player is "out" and play passes to the next person. When their turn comes around again, they have to repeat the "ones" sequence before progressing on to any other figures. There are many other figures, but these are perhaps the most common.[1]

Notes

CHAPTER 1

1. K. Armstrong, *St. Paul: The Misunderstood Apostle* (London: Atlantic Books, 2015), 72.

2. J. Murray, "Half of Emissions Cuts Will Come from Future Tech, Says John Kerry—US Climate Envoy Says People Will Not Have to Give Up Quality of Life to Achieve Some of Net Zero Goals," *The Guardian*, May 16, 2021, https://www.theguardian.com/environ ment/2021/may/16/half-of-emissions-cuts-will-come-from-future-tech-says-john-kerry, accessed May 18, 2021.

CHAPTER 2

1. R. Scruton, *Modern Philosophy: An Introduction and Survey* (London: Mandarin, 1996), 281.

2. R. Raymond, *Out of the Fiery Furnace: The Impact of Metals on the History of Mankind* (University Park: Pennsylvania State University Press, 1986), 187.

3. Letter from Queen Victoria to the King of the Belgians, May 3, 1851, *The Letters of Queen Victoria*, vol. 2, ed. A. C. Benson, 2009, https://www.gutenberg.org/files/24780/24780-h /24780-h.htm, accessed September 13, 2022. Italics in original.

4. Raymond, 188.

5. J. Heskett, *Industrial Design* (London: Thames and Hudson, 1980), 49.

6. Heskett, 49.

7. J. Ruskin, "Ad Valorem," in *Unto This Last* (London: J. M. Dent & Sons, [1860] 1907), 189–190.

8. W. Morris, "Useful Work and Useless Toil," in *News from Nowhere and Selected Writings and Designs* (London: Penguin, 1885), 33–134.

9. F. Dostoevsky, *Notes from Underground*, trans. M. Ginsburg (New York: Bantam, [1864] 1992), 24–25, 156. See also F. Dostoevsky, *Crime and Punishment*, trans. C. Garnett (Ware, Hertfordshire, UK: Wordsworth Editions, [1866] 2000), 472n40.

10. R. Chapman, "Fyodor Dostoyevsky, Eastern Orthodoxy, and the Crystal Palace," in *Historic Engagements with Occidental Cultures, Religions, Powers*, ed. A. R. Richards and I. Omidvar (New York: Springer, 2014), 35–36.

11. W. P. Pomerleau, *Twelve Great Philosophers: An Historical Introduction to Human* Nature (Lanham, MD: Rowman & Littlefield, 1997), 430.

12. K. Armstrong, *St. Paul: The Misunderstood Disciple* (London: Atlantic Books, 2015), 5.

13. D. Nakashima, I. Krupnik, and J. T. Rubis, eds., *Indigenous Knowledge for Climate Change Assessment and Adaptation* (Paris: UNESCO Publishing; Cambridge: Cambridge University Press, 2018); N. J. Turner, M. Boelscher Ignace, and R. Ignace, "Traditional Ecological Knowledge and Wisdom of Aboriginal Peoples in British Columbia," *Ecological Applications* 10, no. 5 (2000): 1275–1287.

14. G. Nicholas, "It's Taken Thousands of Years, but Western Science Is Finally Catching Up to Traditional Knowledge," *The Conversation*, The Conversation Trust, Melbourne, February 15, 2018, https://theconversation.com/its-taken-thousands-of-years-but-western-science-is -finally-catching-up-to-traditional-knowledge-90291.

15. C. S. Lewis, *The Abolition of Man* (New York: HarperCollins, 1944), 70.

16. Lewis, 70–71.

17. P. Dormer, *The Meanings of Modern Design* (London: Thames and Hudson, 1990), 19–20.

18. K. Sato, *Alchimia: Contemporary Italian Design* (Berlin: Taco, Verlagsgesellschaft und Agentur mbH, 1988); *Atelier Alchimia*, https://atelieralchimia.com/, accessed July 28, 2020.

19. S. Barnes, "How the Memphis Movement Went Against 'Good Taste' to Inspire Designers Today," *My Modern Met*, April 17, 2018, https://mymodernmet.com/what-is-memphis -design/; P. Sparke, *An Introduction to Design and Culture: 1900 to the Present*, 2nd ed. (Oxford: Routledge, 2004), 195.

20. A. McKie, "Concerns over 'Deeply Subjective' Criteria for Extra English Places," *Times Higher Education*, June 4, 2020, https://www.timeshighereducation.com/news /concerns-over-deeply-subjective-criteria-extra-english-places.

21. McKie, "Concerns over Deeply Subjective' Criteria."

22. G. Harris, "UK Government Approves 50% Funding Cut for Arts and Design Courses: Education Secretary Gavin Williamson Says Money Will Be Directed towards Stem Subjects," *Art Newspaper*, London, July 22, 2021, https://www.theartnewspaper.com/news /uk-government-sanctions-50-funding-cut-for-arts-and-design-courses.

23. N. Cross, "Achieving Pleasure from Purpose: The Methods of Kenneth Grange, Product Designer," *Design Journal* 4, no. 1 (April 28, 2015): 48–58.

24. J. Cox, "Move Over STEM: Why SHAPE Skills Will Add True Value to Tomorrow's Workforce," *Forbes*, July 2, 2020, https://www.forbes.com/sites/josiecox/2020/07/02/stem-skills -education-value-future-of-work-shape/; V. Thorpe, "University and Arts Council in Drive

to Re-brand 'Soft' Academic Subjects," *Guardian*, June 21, 2020, https://www.theguardian.com/education/2020/jun/21/university-and-arts-council-in-drive-to-re-brand-soft-academic-subjects.

25. A. Walker, *In Search of our Mothers' Gardens* (New York: Harcourt Brace Jovanovich, 1983), 264.

CHAPTER 3

1. E. F. Schumacher, *Small Is Beautiful: A Study of Economics as if People Mattered* (London: Abacus, Sphere Books, 1973), 9, 21.

2. R. H. Tawney, *Religion and the Rise of Capitalism* (London: Penguin, [1926] 1990), 276.

3. Wye Valley, Angidy Valley, Monmouthshire County Council, Usk, https://www.wyevalleyaonb.org.uk/exploring-wye-valley-aonb/wye-valley-on-foot/download-walk-leaflets, accessed September 12, 2022.

4. C. J. Rzepka, "Pictures of the Mind: Iron and Charcoal, 'Ouzy' Tides and 'Vagrant Dwellers' at Tintern, 1798," *Studies in Romanticism* 42, no. 2 (2003): 155.

5. Wye Valley, "Industrial Wye Valley," *Wye Valley AONB: Area of Outstanding Natural Beauty*, Monmouth, https://www.wyevalleyaonb.org.uk/exploring-wye-valley-aonb/heritage/industrial-wye-valley/, accessed August 6, 2020.

6. J. Pickin, "The Iron Works at Tintern and Sirhowy," *Gwent Local History: The Journal of Gwent Local History Council*, The National Library of Wales, Aberystwyth (1982): 3, 6, https://journals.library.wales/view/1337678/1338230/4#?cv=4&m=11&c=0&s=0&manifest=https%3A%2F%2Fdamsssl.llgc.org.uk%2Fiiif%2F2.0%2F1337678%2Fmanifest.json&xywh=-1915%2C-98%2C6210%2C3801, accessed March 26, 2021.

7. W. Wordsworth, "Lines Written a Few Miles above Tintern Abbey on Revisiting the Banks of the Wye During a Tour, July 13, 1798," *Selected Poems* (London: Penguin, [1798] 2004), 63, lines 51–58.

8. Rzepka, "Pictures of the Mind," 153–158, 169–183.

9. Wordsworth, "Lines Written a Few Miles above Tintern Abbey," 61–62, lines 9–15.

10. N. Chidumayo and D. J. Gumbo, "The Environmental Impacts of Charcoal Production in Tropical Ecosystems of the World: A Synthesis," *Energy for Sustainable Development* 17 (2013): 86–94.

11. Rzepka, "Pictures of the Mind," 160–161.

12. The Heritage Crafts Association, "Tanning (oak bark)," *The HCA Red List of Endangered Crafts*, https://heritagecrafts.org.uk/tanning-oak-bark/, accessed September 12, 2022.

13. Wye Valley, "Industrial Wye Valley."

14. Rzepka, "Pictures of the Mind," 163–169.

15. R. H. Tawney, *Religion and the Rise of Capitalism* (London: Penguin, [1926] 1990), 41.

16. E. Manzini and M. K. M'Rithaa, "Distributed Systems and Cosmopolitan Localism: An Emerging Design Scenario for Resilient Societies," *Sustainable Development* 24 (2016): 278.

17. Schumacher, *Small Is Beautiful*, 28, 52–59, 203, 226.

18. Manzini and M'Rithaa, "Distributed Systems," 280.

CHAPTER 4

1. C. Cough, "Musical Acoustics—Stringed Instruments," in *Springer Handbook of Acoustics*, ed. T. D. Rossing (New York: Springer Science+Business Media, 2007), 554–601.

2. S. Walker, "Progressive Design Practice," in *Design Realities: Creativity, Nature and the Human Spirit* (Oxford: Routledge, 2019), 283–292; H. G. Gadamer, *Truth and Method*, 2nd ed. (London: Continuum, [1989] 2004), 355; A. J. Godzieba, ". . . And Followed Him On The Way" (Mk 10:52): Identity, Difference, and the Play of Discipleship," Catholic Theological Society of America, 69th Annual Convention, San Diego, CA, June 5–8, 2014, https://ejournals.bc.edu/index.php/ctsa/article/view/5501/4983, accessed September 12, 2022.

3. A. Walker, *In Search of Our Mothers' Gardens* (London: The Women's Press, 1984), 31–32.

CHAPTER 5

1. R. L. Stevenson, "The Adventure of the Hansom Cab," in *The Complete Stories of Robert Louis Stevenson*, ed. B. Menikoff (New York: Modern Library, [1878] 2002), 69.

2. A. de Jong, ed., "Discover Amsterdam's Social Initiatives: The Best Gifts for the Holiday Season," *Holland Herald*, December 2019, 46.

3. de Jong, "Discover Amsterdam's Social Initiatives," 47.

4. CBC, "Saskatchewan Town Parlays Paper Clip Fame into Film Deal," *Canadian Broadcasting Corporation*, Toronto, ON, January 27, 2009, https://www.cbc.ca/news/entertainment/saskatchewan-town-parlays-paper-clip-fame-into-film-deal-1.862449; Town of Kipling, "Red Paperclip Story," *Town of Kipling*, Saskatchewan, 2014, https://townofkipling.ca/p/red-paperclip-story, accessed September 12, 2022.

5. S. Collini, *Speaking of Universities* (London: Verso, 2017), 129–130.

6. OfS, "All Information about Grade Inflation," *Office for Students*, Bristol, https://www.officeforstudents.org.uk/advice-and-guidance/regulation/grade-inflation/, accessed January 18, 2021.

7. Collini, 147–148.

8. Lao Tzu (ca. 6th century BCE), *Tao Te Ching*, trans. Gia-Fu Feng and J. English (New York: Vintage, 1989).

CHAPTER 6

1. Gov.UK, "Find and Compare Schools in England Search for Primary, Secondary and Special Needs Schools and Colleges Near You, and Check Their Performance," London, https://www .gov.uk/school-performance-tables, accessed March 26, 2021.

2. REF, "Research Excellence Framework," *UK Research and Innovation*, Swindon, Wiltshire, 2020, https://www.ref.ac.uk/, accessed March 26, 2021; TEF, "Teaching Excellence and Student Outcomes Framework," *Gov.UK*, London, updated March 3, 2022, https://www.gov .uk/government/collections/teaching-excellence-framework, accessed September 12, 2022; KEF, "Knowledge Excellence Framework," *UK Research and Innovation*, Swindon, Wiltshire, 2021, https://re.ukri.org/knowledge-exchange/knowledge-exchange-framework/, accessed March 26, 2021.

3. This chapter was inspired by Dostoevsky's *Notes from Underground*, the Russian title of which (in Roman script) is *Zapiski iz Podpol'ya*.

CHAPTER 7

1. R. Wall Kimmerer, *Braiding Sweetgrass: Indigenous Wisdom, Scientific Knowledge and the Teachings of Plants* (London: Penguin Random House, 2013), ix, 5, 26–27.

2. wildflowers.uk, "Holy Grass," *British Wild Flower Plants*, North Burlingham, Norfolk, https://www.wildflowers.uk/holy-grass-c6x17748334, accessed May 31, 2020.

3. plantlife.or.uk, "Holy-Grass," *Plantlife*, Salisbury, Wiltshire, https://www.plantlife.org.uk /uk/discover-wild-plants-nature/plant-fungi-species/holy-grass, accessed May 31, 2020.

4. In developing this description of the creative act, I would like to acknowledge debt to a short extract from C. Mopsik, *Lettre sur la sainteté. Le secret de la relation entre l'homme et la femme dans la cabale, étude préliminaire* (Paris: Verdier, 1986), 14–15, in the English translation of J.-Y. Leloup, *The Gospel of Philip: Jesus, Mary Magdalene, and the Gnosis of Sacred Union*, trans. J. Rowe (Rochester, VT: Inner Traditions, 2003), 21–22.

5. N. Cross, "Design Research: A Disciplined Conversation," *Design Issues* 14, no 2. (Summer 1999): 9–10.

6. S. Black, D. G. Gardner, J. L. Pierce, and R. Steers, "Design Thinking," *Organizational Behavior*, OpenStax Books-PressBooks, Creative Commons, 2019, https://opentextbc.ca /organizationalbehavioropenstax/chapter/design-thinking/, accessed June 14, 2020.

7. L. Irani, "Design Thinking: Defending Silicon Valley at the Apex of Global Labor Hierarchies," *Catalyst: Feminism, Theory, Technoscience* 4, no. 1 (2018): 1–19, https://catalystjournal .org/index.php/catalyst/article/view/29638/pdf, accessed June 14, 2020.

8. *Oxford English Dictionary, s.v. "Innovation,"* https://www-oed-com.ezproxy.lancs.ac.uk /view/Entry/96311?redirectedFrom=innovation&, accessed September 12, 2022; *Oxford English Dictionary, s.v. "Invention,"* https://www-oed-com.ezproxy.lancs.ac.uk/view /Entry/98969?redirectedFrom=Invention&, accessed September 12, 2022; *Online Etymology*

Dictionary, D. Harper, "Originality," https://www.etymonline.com/word/originality#ety monline_v_29888, accessed September 12, 2022.

9. C. S. Lewis, *The Abolition of Man* (New York: Harper Collins, 1944), 39.

10. R. Wall Kimmerer, *Braiding Sweetgrass: Indigenous Wisdom, Scientific Knowledge and the Teachings of Plants* (London: Penguin Random House, 2013), 17.

11. R. Fry, "Appreciative Inquiry," *The SAGE Encyclopedia of Action Research*, ed. D. Coghlan and M. Brydon-Miller (London: SAGE, 2014), 44.

12. Fry, 44.

13. Fry, 45.

14. F. Dostoevsky, *Notes from Underground* (New York: Bantam Books, 1864), 39.

15. V. E. Frankl, *Man's Search for Meaning*, 3rd ed. (New York: Touchstone, Simon & Schuster, 1984), 110.

16. G. Allport, preface to *Man's Search for Meaning*, 3rd ed., by V. E. Frankl (New York: Touchstone, Simon & Schuster, 1984), 10.

17. Frankl, *Man's Search for Meaning*, 46–55, 104, 115.

18. Fry, "Appreciative Inquiry," 48.

19. F. Dostoevsky, "Notes from the Underground," in *The Best Short Stories of Fyodor Dostoevsky*, trans. D. Magarshack (New York: Modern Library, 2001), 106.

20. Wall Kimmerer, *Braiding Sweetgrass*, 336–337.

21. J. M. Watkins, B. J. Mohr, and R. Kelly, *Appreciative Inquiry: Change at the Speed of Imagination* (Hoboken, NJ: Center for Creative Leadership, 2011), 37–38; Fry, "Appreciative Inquiry," 46–47; D. Whitney and A. Trosten-Bloom, *The Power of Appreciative Inquiry: A Practical Guide to Positive Change*, 2nd ed. (San Francisco: Berrett-Koehler Publishers, 2010), 8.

22. Whitney and Trosten-Bloom, *Power of Appreciative Inquiry*, 7–8.

23. M. C. Bol, "The Case of the City Different," in *Design Roots: Culturally Significant Designs, Products and Practices*, ed. S. Walker, M. Evans, T. Cassidy, J. Jong, and A. Twigger-Holroyd (London: Bloomsbury, 2018), 261–262.

24. Whitney and Trosten-Bloom, *Power of Appreciative Inquiry*, 9.

25. P. Gay, *Modernism: The Lure of Heresy—From Baudelaire to Beckett and Beyond* (London: Vintage, 2007), 4.

26. G. Santayana, "Flux and Constancy in Human Nature," in *The Life of Reason* (New York: Dover, 1905; Project Gutenberg, 2005), vol. 1, chap. 12, https://www.gutenberg.org /files/15000/15000-h/15000-h.htm#vol1CHAPTER_XII_FLUX_AND_CONSTANCY _IN_HUMAN_NATURE.

27. F. Nietzsche, *Twilight of the Idols and The Anti-Christ*, trans. R. J. Hollingdale (London: Penguin, [1889] 1990), 33. Italics in original.

28. Frankl, *Man's Search for Meaning*, 104.

29. J. Hick, *An Interpretation of Religion: Human Responses to the Transcendent* (New Haven, CT: Yale University Press, 1989), 129–171.

30. S. Walker, *Designing Sustainability: Making Radical Changes in a Material World* (Oxford: Routledge, 2014), 93, 118–119.

31. S. Walker, *Design Realities: Creativity, Nature and the Human Spirit* (Oxford: Routledge, 2019), 268–294.

CHAPTER 8

1. R. Poynor, "Where Are the Design Critics?," *Design Observer*, September 25, 2005, https://designobserver.com/feature/where-are-the-design-critics/3767/.

2. J. Elkins, *What Happened to Art Criticism* (Chicago: Prickly Paradigm Press, 2003), 7–8.

3. Elkins, 11–12.

4. M. Malpass, "Criticism and Function in Critical Design Practice," *Design Issues* 31, no. 2 (Spring 2015): 65.

5. T. Triggs, "Writing Design Criticism into History," *Design and Culture* 5, no. 1 (2013): 37.

6. Red Dot, "Wenheyou Laochangsha Lobster Restaurant," *Red Dot Design Award*, Design Zentrum Nordrhein Westfalen, Essen, Germany, 2019, https://www.red-dot.org/project/wenheyou-laochangsha-lobster-restaurant-40652, accessed December 9, 2019.

7. R. Scruton, "Kitsch and the Modern Predicament," *City Journal* (Winter 1999), http://www.city-journal.org/html/9_1_urbanities_kitsch_and_the.html.

8. A. Dorfman, *The Empire's Old Clothes: What the Lone Ranger, Babar, and Other Innocent Heroes Do to Our Minds* (New York: Pantheon, 1983), 7, 35–173.

9. T. Kinkade and R. Barnett, *The Thomas Kinkade Story: A 20-Year Chronology of the Artist* (Boston, MA Bulfinch Press, 2003).

10. T. W. Adorno, *Aesthetic Theory*, trans. R. Hullot-Kento (London: Bloomsbury Academic, [1970] 1997), 44.

11. U. Eco, *Travels in Hyperreality*, trans. William Weaver (London: Picador, Pan London, 1986), 28.

12. D. Hirst, *Treasures from the Wreck of the Unbelievable* (Venice: Other Criteria, Marsilio Publishers, 2017, exhibition catalogue).

13. J.-J. Rousseau, *Reveries of the Solitary Walker* (London: Penguin, [1782] 2004), 69.

14. Rousseau, 70.

15. J. Jones, "Damien Hirst: *Treasures from the Wreck of the Unbelievable* Review—A Titanic Return," *The Guardian*, April 6, 2017, https://www.theguardian.com/artanddesign/2017 /apr/06/damien-hirst-treasures-from-the-wreck-of-the-unbelievable-review-titanic-return.

16. L. Cumming, "Damien Hirst: *Treasures from the Wreck of the Unbelievable* Review—Beautiful and Monstrous, *The Observer*, April 16, 2017, https://www.theguardian.com/artanddesign/2017 /apr/16/damien-hirst-treasures-from-the-wreck-of-the-unbelievable-review-venice.

17. Jones, "Damien Hirst."

18. R. Scruton, *An Intelligent Person's Guide to Modern Culture* (South Bend, IN: St. Augustine's Press, 2000), 86.

19. A. Sooke, "Damien Hirst, *Treasures from the Wreck of the Unbelievable*, Review: This Spectacular Failure Could Be the Shipwreck of His Career," *The Telegraph*, April 6, 2017, https:// www.telegraph.co.uk/art/what-to-see/damien-hirst-treasures-wreck-unbelievable-review -spectacular/.

20. "Trompe L'oeil and Art Trickery at Our Places," *National Trust*, Swindon, https://www .nationaltrust.org.uk/features/trompe-loeil-and-art-trickery-at-our-places, accessed July 8, 2020.

21. Harewood, "Gallery," *Harewood House*, Leeds, https://harewood.org/explore/house/gallery/, accessed July 8, 2020.

22. R. Hughes, *Nothing If Not Critical: Selected Essays on Art and Artists* (New York: Alfred A. Knopf, 1990), 9.

23. B. Adib-Yazdi, Design Leads to Outdoor Adventure at Bass Pro Shops, *National Real Estate Investor*, July 1, 2000, https://www.nreionline.com/mag/design-leads-outdoor -adventure-bass-pro-shops.

24. Scruton, *An Intelligent Person's Guide*, 93.

25. T. W. Adorno, *Aesthetic Theory*, trans. R. Hullot-Kento (London: Bloomsbury Academic, [1970] 1997), 414.

26. J. M. Wirth, "Kitsch," in *Commiserating with Devastated Things: Milan Kundera and the Entitlements of Thinking* (New York: Fordham University Press, 2015), 125–126.

27. Adorno, *Aesthetic Theory*, 412.

28. I. Kant, *Fundamental Principles of the Metaphysics of Morals*, trans. T. K. Abbott (Mineola, NY: Dover, [1785] 2005), 14.

29. Wirth, "Kitsch," 102–103.

30. I. Strauss, "Globalization and Taxation: Trends and Consequences," Global Labour Column, Corporate Strategy and Industrial Development (CSID), University of the Witwatersrand, no. 98 (May 2012), http://www.global-labour-university.org/fileadmin/GLU_Column /papers/no_98_Strauss.pdf.

31. Alexander, *The Timeless Way of Building* (New York: Oxford University Press, 1979), xiv, 7.

CHAPTER 9

1. J. Gross Stein, *The Cult of Efficiency* (Toronto: Anansi, 2001), 3–5, 13.

2. R. H. Tawney, *Religion and the Rise of Capitalism* (London: Penguin, 1926), 277.

3. F. Chaib, "Shortage of Personal Protective Equipment Endangering Health Workers Worldwide," *World Health Organization*, Geneva, March 3, 2020, https://www.who.int /news-room/detail/03-03-2020-shortage-of-personal-protective-equipment-endangering -health-workers-worldwide.

4. M. Heffernan, *Uncharted: How to Map the Future Together* (London: Simon & Schuster, 2020), 199.

5. BBC, "US West Coast Fires: I Don't Think Science Knows about Climate, Says Trump," *BBC News Online*, September 15, 2020, https://www.bbc.co.uk/news/world-us-canada-54144651.

6. J. Murray, "Half of Emissions Cuts Will Come from Future Tech, Says John Kerry—US Climate Envoy Says People Will Not Have to Give Up Quality of Life to Achieve Some of Net Zero Goals," *The Guardian*, May 16, 2021, https://www.theguardian.com/environ ment/2021/may/16/half-of-emissions-cuts-will-come-from-future-tech-says-john-kerry, accessed May 18, 2021.

7. WWF UK and Greenpeace UK, *The Big Smoke: The Global Emissions of the UK Financial Sector*, London, May 2021, 4, https://www.wwf.org.uk/sites/default/files/2021-05 /uk_financed_emissions_v11.pdf.

8. WWF, *Living Planet Report 2020: Bending the Curve of Biodiversity Loss*, ed. R. E. A. Almond, M. Grooten, and T. Petersen, Gland, Switzerland, https://f.hubspotusercontent20.net /hubfs/4783129/LPR/PDFs/ENGLISH-FULL.pdf, accessed September 16, 2020.

9. InfluenceMap, *ExxonMobil Attempts to Influence the European Green Deal*, London, March 6, 2020, 2, https://influencemap.org/report/An-InfluenceMap-Note-ExxonMobil-Lobbies -the-EU-Commission-add01200dc694b00e9ac4bebf660227b.

10. InfluenceMap, 10, 11, 13, 15, 25.

11. P. Keane, "How the Oil Industry Made Us Doubt Climate Change," *BBC News Online*, September 20, 2020, https://www.bbc.co.uk/news/stories-53640382; C. Stager, "Sowing Climate Doubt among Schoolteachers," *New York Times*, April 27, 2017, https://www .nytimes.com/2017/04/27/opinion/sowing-climate-doubt-among-schoolteachers.html.

12. M. Heffernan, *Wilful Blindness* (London: Simon & Schuster, 2019), 332.

13. Heffernan, 248–249.

14. K. Armstrong, *St. Paul: The Misunderstood Apostle* (London: Atlantic Books, 2015), 9.

15. J. de Yepes (16th century), *The Collected Works of St. John of the Cross*, 3rd ed., trans. K. Kavanaugh and O. Rodriguez (Washington, DC: Institute of Carmelite Studies, [1991, 2017], 359, verses 3 and 8.

16. Future Generations, *Well-Being of Future Generations (Wales) Act 2015*, Cardiff, Wales, https://www.futuregenerations.wales/about-us/future-generations-act/, accessed September 10, 2020.

17. Future Generations, *Future Generations Report 2020*, Cardiff, Wales, https://www.futuregen erations.wales/public_info/the-future-generations-report-2020//, accessed September 10, 2020; Heffernan, *Wilful Blindness*, 310–313.

18. GNH, *A Compass Towards a Just and Harmonious Society 2015 GNH Survey Report*, Centre for Bhutan Studies & GNH Research, Thimphu, Bhutan, http://www.grossnational happiness.com/, accessed September 10, 2020.

19. Prosperity for All, *Prosperity for All: The National Strategy—Taking Wales Forward*, Welsh Government, Cardiff, 2017, 2, https://wcva.cymru/wp-content/uploads/2020/01/Prosper ity-for-all.pdf, accessed September 12, 2022.

20. A. Beckett, "The New Left Economics: How a Network of Thinkers Is Transforming Capitalism," The Long Read, *The Guardian*, June 25, 2019, https://www.theguardian.com /news/2019/jun/25/the-new-left-economics-how-a-network-of-thinkers-is-transforming -capitalism.

21. A. Gorz, *Ecologica* (London: Seagull Books, 2010), 26–27.

22. A. MacIntyre, *After Virtue*, 3rd ed. (London: Bristol Classical Press, Bloomsbury Academic, 2007), xii–xvi.

23. MacIntyre, 239.

24. MacIntyre, 204, 227, 239.

25. M. Thatcher, "Interview for *Woman's Own* ("no such thing as society")," September 23, 1987, Margaret Thatcher Foundation, https://www.margaretthatcher.org/document /106689.

26. T. Piketty, *Capital in the Twenty-First Century* (Cambridge, MA: Belknap Press of Harvard University Press, 2014), 571.

27. R. H. Tawney, *Religion and the Rise of Capitalism* (London: Penguin, 1926), 277.

28. E. F. Schumacher, *Small Is Beautiful: A Study of Economics as if People Mattered* (London: Abacus, Sphere Books, 1973), 118, 233.

29. H. Daly, *Ecological Economics and Sustainable Development: Selected Essays of Herman Daly* (Cheltenham, UK: Edward Elgar, 2007), 117–123.

30. M. Sandel, "A New Politics of the Common Good," The Reith Lectures, *BBC Radio 4*, June 30, 2009, https://www.bbc.co.uk/programmes/b00lb6bt.

31. T. Jackson, *Prosperity without Growth: Economics for a Final Planet* (London: Earthscan, London, 2009), 171, 187, 193.

32. Piketty, *Capital in the Twenty-First Century*, 572.

33. BusinessNewsWales, "Welsh Government Wants 30% of Workforce to Work Remotely," *BusinessNewsWales*, September 14, 2020, https://businessnewswales.com/welsh-government-wants-30-of-workforce-to-work-remotely/.

34. R. D. Wolff, *Capitalism's Crisis Deepens: Essays on the Global Economic Meltdown* (Chicago: Haymarket Books, 2016), 294.

35. "Preston, UK Looks to Cleveland and Spain for an Inclusive, Cooperative Economic Model," *Revitalization: The Journal of Urban, Rural and Environmental Resilience*, no. 52 (June 1, 2017), https://revitalization.org/article/preston-uk-looks-cleveland-spain-inclusive-economic-growth-models/; A. Beckett, "The New Left Economics: How a Network of Thinkers is Transforming Capitalism," The Long Read, *The Guardian*, June 25, 2019, https://www.theguardian.com/news/2019/jun/25/the-new-left-economics-how-a-network-of-thinkers-is-transforming-capitalism.

CHAPTER 11

1. K. Armstrong, *The Lost Art of Scripture: Rescuing the Sacred Texts* (London: Bodley Head, 2019), 7.

2. D. Hardoon, "An Economy for the 99%, It's Time to Build a Human Economy That Benefits Everyone, Not Just the Privileged Few" (Oxfam Briefing Paper, Oxfam International, Nairobi, January 2017), 2, https://oxfamilibrary.openrepository.com/bitstream/handle/10546/620170/bp-economy-for-99-percent-160117-en.pdf?sequence=1.

3. C. Levi-Strauss, *The Savage Mind* (London: G. Weidenfeld and Nicolson, 1962), 234.

4. D. Nakashima, J. T. Rubis, and I. Krupnik, "Indigenous Knowledge for Climate Change Assessment and Adaptation: Introduction," in *Indigenous Knowledge for Climate Change Assessment and Adaptation* (Paris: UNESCO Publishing; Cambridge: Cambridge University Press, 2018), 3.

5. W. Davis, foreword to *Lo-TEK: Design by Radical Indigenism*, by J. Watson (Cologne: Taschen, 2019), 13, 14.

6. J. Watson, introduction to *Lo-TEK*, 17.

7. Nakashima, Rubis, and Krupnik, "Indigenous Knowledge," 3.

8. Nakashima, Rubis, and Krupnik, 3–4.

9. N. J. Turner, *Plant Technology of First Peoples in British Columbia* (Victoria, BC: Royal British Columbia Museum, 1998).

10. N. J. Turner, M. Boelscher Ignace, and R. Ignace, "Traditional Ecological Knowledge and Wisdom of Aboriginal Peoples in British Columbia," *Ecological Applications* 10, no. 5 (2000), 1275.

11. B. Pascoe, *Dark Emu, Black Seeds: Agriculture or Accident?* (Broome, Western Australia: Magabala Books Aboriginal Corporation, 2014), 129.

CHAPTER 12

1. N. Gardini, *Long Live Latin: The Pleasures of a Useless Language*, trans. T. Portnowitz (London: Profile Books, 2019), 28.

2. M. Hickman, "Survey of Family Spending Charts Half Century of Consumer Culture," *The Independent*, January 29, 2008, https://www.independent.co.uk/news/uk/home-news /survey-of-family-spending-charts-half-century-of-consumer-culture-775185.html.

3. V. Packard, *The Waste Makers* (New York: Pocket Books, 1960), 59.

4. M. J. Cohen, "Collective Dissonance and the Transition to Post-Consumerism," *Futures* 52 (2013): 49.

5. S. Walker, *The Spirit of Design: Objects, Environment and Meaning* (Oxford: Routledge, 2011), 127–134, 187; S. Walker, *Designing Sustainability: Making Radical Changes in a Material World* (Oxford: Routledge, 2014), 92–93.

6. S. Walker, *Design Realities: Creativity, Nature and the Human Spirit* (Oxford: Routledge, 2019), 268–294.

CHAPTER 13

1. H. D. Thoreau, *Walden and Civil Disobedience* (London: Penguin, [1854] 1983), 70.

2. G. Brecht, "George Brecht: Interview by Michael Nyman," in *George Brecht: Works from 1959–1973*, by T. Kellein, M. Nyman, G. Brecht, and J. Robinson (London: Gagosian Gallery, 2004), 50.

3. "Tomb of Queen Meresankh III," *Ministry of Antiquities*, Cairo, Egypt, https://egymonu ments.gov.eg/en/monuments/tomb-of-queen-meresankh-iii, accessed August 27, 2022; W. Rybczynski, *Now I Sit Me Down* (New York: Farrar, Straus and Giroux, 2016), 6.

4. "Marble Seated Harp Player, 2800–2700 B.C., Cycladic," *The Met*, New York, https://www .metmuseum.org/art/collection/search/254587, accessed April 5, 2021; Rybczynski, *Now I Sit Me Down*, 58.

5. E. J. Wormley, E. Lassen, and J. T. Butler, "Furniture," in *Encyclopædia Britannica*, December 14, 2021, https://www.britannica.com/technology/furniture.

6. W. Shakespeare, *Romeo and Juliet* (1597; Project Gutenberg,), act I, scene V, https://www .gutenberg.org/files/1513/1513-h/1513-h.htm, accessed May 11, 2022.

7. C. Schwarz, "Furniture of Necessity: The Trestle Table," *The Lost Art Press*, April 24, 2012, https://blog.lostartpress.com/2012/04/24/furniture-of-necessity-the-trestle-table/.

8. S. Cox, "Hewn Trestle Table," Studio Team, *Sebastian Cox*, Greenwich, London, https://www .sebastiancox.co.uk/, accessed September 20, 2020.

9. M. Guarnieri, "An Historical Survey on Light Technologies," *IEEE Access* 6 (June 5, 2018): 25881, https://ieeexplore.ieee.org/stamp/stamp.jsp?arnumber=8356031.

10. "Parietal Art: Lighting," *Musée d'Archéologie Nationale*, Lascaux, Domain National Saint-German-en-Laye, Ministère de la Culture, France, https://archeologie.culture.fr/lascaux/en/lighting, accessed March 31, 2021; A. Leroi-Gourhan, "The Archaeology of Lascaux Cave," *Scientific American* 246, no. 6 (June 1982): 104, 107, 109; R. Gittins and P. Pettitt, "Is Palaeolithic Cave Art Consistent with Costly Signalling Theory?: Lascaux as a Test Case," *World Archaeology* 49, no. 4 (2017): 477.

11. C. Heron, S. Andersen, A. Fischer, A. Glykou, S. Hartz, H. Saul, V. Steele, and O. Craig, "Illuminating the Late Mesolithic: residue analysis of 'blubber' lamps from Northern Europe," *Antiquity* 87, no. 335 (March 2013): 179.

12. "Archaeology & Anthropology Collections," Exley Science Center, Wesleyan University, Middletown, CT, https://www.wesleyan.edu/libr/collections/arch-anth/highlights/ancient_oil_lamps.html, accessed March 28, 2021.

13. J. Chevalier and A. Gheerbrant, "Lamp," in *The Penguin Dictionary of Symbols*, 2nd ed., trans. J. Buchanan-Brown (London: Penguin, 1982), 589.

14. J. L. Coleman Jr., "The American Whale Oil Industry: A Look Back to the Future of the American Petroleum Industry?," *Nonrenewable Resources*, 4, no. 3 (September 1995): 273–282.

15. Guarnieri, "An Historical Survey on Light Technologies."

16. P. Alstone and A. Jacobsen, "LED Advances Accelerate Universal Access to Electric Lighting," *Comptes Rendus Physique* 19, no. 3 (2018): 147; J. Melik, "Solutions Sought to End Use of Kerosene Lamps," *BBC News*, September 27, 2012, https://www.bbc.co.uk/news/business-18262217.

17. Alstone and Jacobsen, "LED Advances," 146–147.

18. D. Hawley, *Oman and Its Renaissance*, rev. ed. (London: Stacey International, 1980), 145.

19. J. Živković, T. Power, M. Georgakopoulou, and J. C. Carvajal López, "Defining New Technological Traditions of Late Islamic Arabia: A View on Bahlā Ware from al-Ain (UAE) and the Lead-Barium Glaze Production," *Archaeological and Anthropological Sciences* 11 (2019): 4698.

20. V. Roux and P. de Miroschedji, "Revisiting the History of the Potter's Wheel in the Southern Levant," *Levant* 41, no. 2 (2009): 155.

21. "About Oman: Pottery," *Arabia Felix*, Munich, http://oman-travel.kegiseo.com/about-oman/culture-overview-crafts-architecture-music-arts/handicraft-overview-oman/potterie-overview/, accessed March 20, 2021; Hawley, *Oman and Its Renaissance*, 146–147; Živković, Power, Georgakopoulou, and Carvajal López, "Defining New Technological Traditions," 4708.

22. A. H. Kola, "Oman's Dwindling Heritage of Pottery, *Arab News*, June 26, 2013, https://www.arabnews.com/news/456198.

23. Times New Service, "Bahla Maintains Ancient Tradition of Unique Pottery," *Times of Oman*, January 19, 2019, https://timesofoman.com/article/72222-bahla-maintains -ancient-tradition-of-unique-pottery.

24. "About Oman: Pottery."

25. M. S. van Aken-Fehmers, T. M. Eliëns, and S. M. R. Lambooy, *Het wonder van Delfts Blauw/ Delftware Wonderware* (The Hague: Gemeentemuseum, 2012).

26. J. de Baan, Clients—Royal Delft, https://www.jacobdebaandesignmanagement.com/clients /royal-delft.php, accessed September 12, 2022.

27. O. Jones, "What Is an Oak Swill?," *Owen Jones: Oak Swill Basket Maker*, http://www .oakswills.co.uk/WhatIs.html, accessed November 5, 2020.

28. "Lorna Singleton, Basket Maker, North West England: Maker's Story," The New Craftsmen, London, https://www.thenewcraftsmen.com/makers/lorna-singleton/, accessed November 5, 2020.

29. C. Sagona, "Two-Needle Knitting and Cross-Knit Looping: Early Bronze Age Pottery Imprints from Anatolia and the Caucasus," *Oxford Journal of Archaeology* 37, no. 3 (June 2018): 283.

30. C. Breniquet and C. Michel, "Wool Economy in the Ancient Near East and the Aegean," in *Wool Economy in the Ancient Near East and the Aegean: From the Beginnings of Sheep Husbandry to Institutional Textile Industry*, ed. C. Breniquet and C. Michel (Oxford: Oxbow Books, 2014), 2–3.

31. L. Trivedi, *Clothing Gandhi's Nation: Homespun and Modern India* (Bloomington: Indiana University Press, 2007), 148, 154–155.

32. Trivedi, 34.

33. M. K. Gandhi, *Gandhi Literature: Collected Works of Mahatma Gandhi*, vol. 49, April 3, 1930–August 22, 1930, Gandhi Sevagram Ashram, Sevagram, India, 29, https://www.gand hiashramsevagram.org/gandhi-literature/mahatma-gandhi-collected-works-volume-49.pdf, accessed September 12, 2022.

34. "Our Story," *Cable and Blake: Fabrics of the Lakes*, Kendal, Cumbria, https://www.cableand blake.co.uk/our-story/, August 27, 2022; "Our Purpose," *Herdwick Limited*, Near Sawrey, Cumbria, https://www.herdwick.co.uk/herdwick-tweed-about-us.html, accessed August 27, 2022; "About Us," *The Herdy Company*, Kendal, Cumbria, https://www.herdy.co.uk/about, accessed August 27, 2022.

35. Northern Yarn, *Northern Yarn*, Lancaster, Lancashire, https://www.northernyarn.co.uk/, accessed January 7, 2021; Woolclip, *The Wool Clip*, Caldbeck, Cumbria, www.woolclip .com/, accessed January 7, 2021; Woolfest, *Woolfest*, Cockermouth, Cumbria, www.woolfest .co.uk/, accessed January 7, 2021.

36. L. M. Aun, "Nature's Dryer Revisited," *Washington Post*, August 17, 2006, https://www .washingtonpost.com/wp-dyn/content/article/2006/08/16/AR2006081600394.html; T.

Geoghegan, "The Fight against Clothesline Bans," *BBC News Magazine*, October 7, 2010, https://www.bbc.co.uk/news/magazine-11417677; M. Neil, "19 'Right to Dry' States Outlaw Clothesline Bans; Is Yours Among Them? Real Estate and Property Law," *ABA Journal*, August 14, 2013, https://www.abajournal.com/news/article/20_right_to_dry_states_outlaw _clothesline_bans_is_yours_among_them; "Beware the Illegal Clothesline," *Homestead Dreamer*, Ketchikan, AK, October 21, 2015, https://www.homesteaddreamer.com/2015 /10/21/beware-the-illegal-clothesline/.

37. "Lower Palaeolithic: Olduvai Stone Chopping Tool," *British Museum*, London, https:// britishmuseum.withgoogle.com/object/olduvai-stone-chopping-tool#:~:text=Made%20 nearly%20two%20million%20years,campsite%20in%20Olduvai%20Gorge%2C%20 Tanzania, accessed November 22, 2020.

38. A. Fuad-Luke, *Design Activism: Beautiful Strangeness for a Sustainable World* (London: Earthscan, 2009), 42.

39. C. Jencks and N. Silver, *Adhocism: The Case for Improvisation* (Cambridge, MA: MIT Press, [1972] 2013), vii–xx, 48–111.

40. R. Ramakers, ed., *Simply Droog: 10 + 1 Years of Creating Innovation and Discussion* (Rotterdam: Uitgeverij, 2004), 32, 42–43, 158.

41. J. Fulton Suri, *Thoughtless Acts?: Observations on Intuitive Design* (San Francisco: Chronicle Books, 2005), 98–110.

42. P. De Bozzi and E. Oroza, *Objets Réinventés: La Création Populaire à Cuba* (Paris: Editions Alternatives, 2002), 35–84.

43. V. Arkhipov, *Home-Made: Contemporary Russian Folk Artefacts* (London: Fuel Publishing, 2006), 24–25, 112–113, 160–206.

44. "Saw Doctor's Wagon," National Museum of Australia, Canberra, https://www.nma.gov.au /explore/collection/highlights/saw-doctors-wagon, accessed November 24, 2020.

45. "Picasso," in *New Penguin Dictionary of Modern Quotations*, by R. Andrews with K. Hughes (London: Penguin, [1957] 2003), 447.

CHAPTER 14

1. E. David, *French Provincial Cooking* (London: Penguin, [1960] 1998), ix.

2. T. A. Lyson, *Civic Agriculture: Reconnecting Farm, Food, and Community* (Lebanon, NH: Tufts University Press, 2004).

3. K. Watson, "Home Growing Produces Ten Times the Food of Arable Farms," *Our World*, United Nations University, Tokyo, March 20, 2015, https://ourworld.unu.edu/en/home -growing-produces-ten-times-the-food-of-arable-farms; J. L. Edmonson, Z. G., Davies, K. J., Gaston, and J. R. Leake, "Urban Cultivation in Allotments Maintains Soil Qualities Adversely Affected by Conventional Agriculture," *Journal of Applied Ecology* 51, no. 4 (April 24, 2014): 880.

4. D. Goulson, "A Lot to Learn: Dave Goulson Wonders Whether Allotments Can Save the Earth," *Resurgence and Ecologist*, no. 318 (January/February 2020), https://www.resurgence.org/magazine/article5461-a-lot-to-learn.html.

5. M. White, "Spending Just Two Hours a Week in Nature Is Linked to Better Health and Well-Being," *The Conversation*, Creative Commons, London, July 19, 2019, https://www.weforum.org/agenda/2019/06/spending-two-hours-a-week-in-nature-is-linked-to-better-health-and-well-being.

6. M. J. Roslund, R. Puhakka, M. Grönroos, N. Nurminen, S. Oikarinen, A. M. Gazali, O. Cinek, L. Kramná, N. Siter, H. K. Vari, L. Soininen, A. Parajuli, J. Rajaniemi, T. Kinnunen, I. H. Laitinen, H. Hyöty, and A. Sinkkonen, and ADELE Research Group, "Biodiversity Intervention Enhances Immune Regulation and Health-Associated Commensal Microbiota among Daycare Children," *Science Advances* 6, no. 42 (October 14, 2020): 1, https://advances.sciencemag.org/content/6/42/eaba2578/tab-pdf.

7. "Claver Hill Community Food Growing Project and Nature Trail," *Claver Hill Agricultural Cooperative*, Lancaster, UK, https://ourlancashire.org.uk/groups/claver-hill-community-food-growing-project-and-nature-trail/, accessed October 13, 2020.

8. Fairfield Orchard," *Fairfield Association*, Lancaster, UK, http://www.fairfieldassociation.org/orchard/, accessed October 13, 2020.

9. Deuteronomy 11:10.

10. A. Rofé, *Deuteronomy: Issues and Interpretation* (London: T & T Clark, 2002), 4–5.

11. *Oxford English Dictionary, s.v. "Irrigation,"* https://www-oed-com.ezproxy.lancs.ac.uk/view/Entry/99840?redirectedFrom=irrigation&, accessed September 12, 2022.

12. M. Andresen, "Benefits of Ancient Irrigation Channels Still Trickle Down Spain's Sierra Nevada," *UN Environment Programme*, Nairobi, Kenya, July 31, 2018, https://www.unenvironment.org/news-and-stories/story/benefits-ancient-irrigation-channels-still-trickle-down-spains-sierra-nevada.

13. A. Al-Ghafri, "Water Distribution Management of Aflaj Irrigation Systems of Oman" (PhD diss., Graduate School of Agriculture, Hokkaido University, Sapporo, Japan, March 2004), https://www.unizwa.edu.om/content_files/a91551740.pdf.

14. S. Sherman with B. Dooley, *The Sioux Chef's Indigenous Kitchen* (Minneapolis: University of Minnesota Press, 2017), 106.

15. I. Groman-Yaroslavski, E. Weiss, and D. Nadel, "Composite Sickles and Cereal Harvesting Methods at 23,000-Years-Old Ohalo II, Israel," *PLoS ONE* 11, no. 11 (2016): 2; L. A. Maher, "Persistent Place-Making in Prehistory: The Creation, Maintenance, and Transformation of an Epipalaeolithic Landscape," *Journal of Archaeological Method and Theory* 26 (2019): 1009.

16. E. B. Banning, "The Neolithic Period: Triumphs of Architecture, Agriculture, and Art," *Near Eastern Archaeology* 61, no. 4 (December 1998): 188.

17. S. de Beauvoir, *The Second Sex*, trans. H. M. Parshley (New York: Vintage, [1952] 1989), 75–76.

18 B. D. Shaw, *Bringing in the Sheaves: Economy and Metaphor in the Roman World* (Toronto: University of Toronto Press, 2013), 153.

19. Apuleius (2nd century CE), "Cupid and Psyche," in *The Golden Age of Myth and Legend*, by T. Bulfinch (Ware, Hertfordshire, UK: Wordsworth Editions, [1855] 1993), 105.

20. J. Chevalier and A. Gheerbrant, "Sickle," in *The Penguin Dictionary of Symbols*, 2nd ed., trans. J. Buchanan-Brown (London: Penguin, 1982), 879–880.

21. Pliny the Elder (77 CE), "Historical Facts Connected with the Mistletoe," in *The Natural History of Pliny*, vol. 3, book 14, trans. J. Bostock and H. T. Riley (London: Henry G. Bohn, 1858; Project Gutenberg, March 26, 2019), 436, https://www.gutenberg.org/files/59131/59131-h/59131-h.htm.

22. Shaw, *Bringing in the Sheaves*, 101–102.

23. A. Revedin, B. Aranguren, B., R. Becattini, L. Longo, E. Marconi, M. M. Lippi, N. Skakun, A. Sinitsyn, E. Spiridonova, J. Svoboda, and E. Trinkaus, "Thirty-Thousand-Year-Old Evidence of Plant Food Processing," *Proceedings of the National Academy of Sciences of the United States of America* 107, no. 44 (October 18, 2010): 18815; J. Svoboda, M. Králík, V. Culíková, S. Hladilová, M. Novák, M. N. Fisáková, D. Nývlt, and M. Zelinková, "Pavlov VI: An Upper Palaeolithic Living Unit," *Antiquity* 83, no. 320 (2009): 287; I. Groman-Yaroslavski, E. Weis, and D. Nadel, "Composite Sickles and Cereal Harvesting Methods at 23,000-Years-Old Ohalo II, Israel," *PLoS ONE* 11, no. 11 (November 23, 2016): 4.

24. E. Nyrose, "Wisdom: An Investigation of the Relationship between Some Ancient Religious Concepts of Wisdom and Current Notions of Critical Thinking within Information Literacy," *Journal of Religious & Theological Information* 8, nos. 3–4 (2009): 132; Proverbs 27:22.

25. S. Mithen, W. Finlayson, and R. Shaffrey, "Sexual Symbolism in the Early Neolithic of the Southern Levant: Pestles and Mortars from WF16," *Documenta Prehistorica* 21 (December 2006): 107; Job 31:9–10.

26. J. Zipes, foreword to *Baba Yaga: The Wild Witch of the East in Russian Fairy Tales*, ed. S. Forrester, H. Goscilo, and M. Skoro, trans. S. Forrester (Jackson: University of Mississippi Press, 2013), vii, viii.

27. Forrester, Goscilo, Skoro, "Vasilisa the Beautiful," in *Baba Yaga*, 175.

28. Forrester, Goscilo, Skoro, introduction to *Baba Yaga*, xxx, xxxiv.

29. C. MacCauley, *The Seminole Indians of Florida, Fifth Annual Report of the Bureau of Ethnology to the Secretary of the Smithsonian Institution, 1883–84* (Washington, DC: Government Printing Office, 1887; Project Gutenberg, September 1, 2006), 518, https://www.gutenberg.org/files/19155/19155-h/19155-h.htm.

30. J. O. Dorsey, *Omaha Dwellings, Furniture and Implements Thirteenth Annual Report of the Beaurau [sic] of American Ethnology to the Secretary of the Smithsonian Institution 1891–1892*

(Washington, DC: Government Printing Office, 1887; Project Gutenberg, September 1, 2006), 276, https://www.gutenberg.org/files/19913/19913-8.txt.

31. "Mortar and Pestle, ca. 1780, Wedgwood and Bentley," *The Met*, New York, https://www .metmuseum.org/art/collection/search/206740, accessed September 12, 2022; "Wedgwood & Bentley," *British Museum*, London, https://www.britishmuseum.org/collection/term /BIOG81098, accessed April 14, 2021.

32. "Wedgwood & Bentley."

33. G. Tweedale, "Backstreet Capitalism: An Analysis of the Family Firm in the Nineteenth-Century Sheffield Cutlery Industry," *Business History* 55, no. 6 (September 2013): 875.

34. "History of the Cutlery Industry," The Sheffield Cutlery Map, Museums Sheffield, Sheffield, Yorkshire, http://www.sheffieldcutlerymap.org.uk/history-of-the-cutlery-industry/, accessed March 24, 2021.

35. G. Chaucer (ca. 1400), "The Reeve's Tale," in *The Complete Works of Geoffrey Chaucer*, vol. 4, 2nd ed., ed. W. W. Skeat (Oxford: Clarendon Press, 1900; Project Gutenberg, April 29, 2021), line 13, https://www.gutenberg.org/files/22120/22120-h/22120-h.htm.

36. J. A. Cannon, "Sheffield," in *Oxford Quick Reference: The Oxford Companion to British History*, 2nd ed., ed. J. Cannon & R. Crowcroft (Oxford: Oxford University Press, 2015), http:// ezproxy.lancs.ac.uk/login?url=https://search.credoreference.com/content/entry/oupoxford /sheffield/0?institutionId=3497.

37. D. Defoe, *A Tour through the Whole Island of Great Britain*, ed. Pat Rogers (1724–1726; London: Penguin, 2005), 482.

38. "History of the Cutlery Industry," The Sheffield Cutlery Map, Museums Sheffield.

39. Tweedale, "Backstreet Capitalism," 877, 881–886.

40. R. Scruton, *The Aesthetic of Architecture* (London: Methuen, 1979), 241–242.

41. N. E. Bender, "A Hawken Rifle and Bowie Knife of John 'Liver-Eating' Johnson," *Arms & Armour* 3, no. 2 (2006): 168.

42. *Pusser's Dirk*: "Pusser" is naval slang for purser, the officer responsible for provisions. Hence, *pusser's dirk* refers to the standard issue knife supplied by the purser to members of the crew (*Oxford English Dictionary*), https://www-oed-com.ezproxy.lancs.ac.uk/view /Entry/155153?redirectedFrom=pusser#eid, accessed September 12, 2022; *Bos'n's Mate*: Bos'n or "bosun" is an abbreviation of boatswain, the ship's officer in charge of equipment for the deck crew on sailing ships. Hence, *bos'n's mate* means a "friend," or useful tool, supplied by the boatswain (*Oxford English Dictionary*), https://www-oed-com.ezproxy.lancs.ac.uk /view/Entry/21814?redirectedFrom=Bos%E2%80%99n#eid, accessed September 12, 2022.

43. History of the Cutlery Industry," The Sheffield Cutlery Map, Museums Sheffield; E. Baker, "Few Extras in the Service Kit List," *Navy News* (June 2014): 36, https://www.royalnavy .mod.uk/-/media/royal-navy-responsive/images/navynews/archivepdfs/2010s/2014/navy -news-june-2014-issue-719.pdf; "2 Piece Navy Clasp Knife (Pusser's Dirk)," *Sheffield Knives*,

Sheffield, UK, https://sheffieldknives.co.uk/acatalog/10-114.html, accessed September 12, 2022.

44. J. Malindine, "Northwest Coast Halibut Hooks: An Evolving Tradition of Form, Function, and Fishing," *Human Ecology* 45, no. 1 (2017): 53, 65.

45. Malindine, 53, 56.

46. N. J. Turner, *Plant Technology of First Peoples in British Columbia* (Victoria, BC: Royal British Columbia Museum, 1998), 101, 182–183, 193.

47. Malindine, "Northwest Coast Halibut Hooks," 54.

48. R. Delisle, "The Traditional Wooden Halibut Hook That's Still Snagging Fish Off Alaska," *Smithsonian Magazine*, October 24, 2018, https://www.smithsonianmag.com/science -nature/revival-traditional-indigenous-wooden-halibut-hook-alaska-180970623/; Malindine, "Northwest Coast Halibut Hooks," 53, 57.

49. Malindine, "Northwest Coast Halibut Hooks," 56–57.

50. "Plaice Anatomy," *Musée du Patrimoine du Pays Royannais*, Pontaillac, Toyan, France, www .pays-royannais-patrimoine.com/themes/peche/les-carrelets-sur-ponton/anatomie-du -carrelet/, accessed September 19, 2020; "Squares," *Les Carrelets Charentais*, Departmental Association for the Defense of Leisure and Traditional Maritime Fishing, Sérigny, France, http://www.carrelets-charentais.com/carrelet.html, accessed September 19, 2020.

51. C. Dickens, *David Copperfield* (Ware, Hertfordshire, UK: Wordsworth Classics, 1850), 29.

52. *Sea Harvest*, scenes of the herring harvest filmed at Great Yarmouth, Norfolk, by amateur cameraman Mr. Croxson, Norvic Films, University of East Anglia Film Archive, silent documentary, 3 min., 1936, https://player.bfi.org.uk/free/film/watch-sea-harvest-1936-online, accessed August 27, 2022; "The Herring Boom," *Scottish Fisheries Museum*, St. Ayles, Anstruther, Fife, UK, https://www.scotfishmuseum.org/the-herring-boom.php, accessed August 22, 2020.

53. "The Herring Industry," *Woven Communities*: *Basketmaking Communities in Scotland*, University of St. Andrews and Scottish Basketmakers' Circle, St. Andrews, Fife, UK, http://wovencommunities.org/collection/the-herring-industry/, accessed August 22, 2020.

54. N. Lewis, *The Boatsheds at the Castle*, National Trust, Swindon, Wiltshire, UK, www .nationaltrust.org.uk/lindisfarne-castle/features/the-boatsheds-at-the-castle, accessed August 22, 2020.

55. E. David, *French Provincial Cooking* (London: Penguin, [1960] 1998), xi.

CHAPTER 15

1. R. Scruton, *An Intelligent Person's Guide to Modern Culture* (South Bend, IN: St. Augustine Press, 2000), 1–4.

2. T. Higham, L. Basell, R. Jacobi, R. Wood, C. Bronk Ramsey, and N. J. Conard, "Testing Models for the Beginnings of the Aurignacian and the Advent of Figurative Art and Music: The Radiocarbon Chronology of Geißenklösterle," *Journal of Human Evolution* 62 (2012), 674.

3. D. Rowan, "The Universal Lyre: Three Perspectives," *American Harp Journal* (Summer 2013): 57.

4. A. Draffkorn Kilmur, "The Musical Instruments from Ur and Ancient Mesopotamian Music, *EXPEDITION* 40, no. 2 (1998): 12, https://www.penn.museum/documents/publi cations/expedition/PDFs/40-2/The%20Musical1.pdf; M. L. West, "The Babylonian Musical Notation and the Hurrian Melodic Texts," *Music & Letters* 75, no. 2 (May 1994): 161, including note 1; D. Wulstan, "The Earliest Musical Notation," *Music and Letters* 52, no. 4 (October 1971): 365.

5. J. Eisentraut, *The Accessibility of Music: Participation, Reception, and Contact* (Cambridge: Cambridge University Press, 2012), 177.

6. Eisentraut, 177, 178.

7. H. G. Farmer, "A North African Folk Instrument," *Journal of the Royal Asiatic Society of Great Britain and Ireland*, no.1 (January 1928): 25.

8. H. de Bruin, "Africa," *Atlas of Plucked Instruments: Africa*, The Netherlands, http://www .atlasofpluckedinstruments.com/africa.htm, accessed November 14, 2020.

9. C. Sachs, *The History of Musical Instruments* (New York: W. W. Norton, 1940), 102–103.

10. D. A. Olsen, *World Flutelore: Folktales, Myths, and Other Stories of Magical Flute Power* (Urbana: University of Illinois Press, 2013), 150.

11. Rumi, *Spiritual Verses*, trans. A. Williams (London: Penguin, 2006) 7.

12. Olsen, *World Flutelore*, 66.

13. Olsen, 109, 153; S. Walker, *The Spirit of Design: Objects, Environment and Meaning* (Oxford: Routledge, 2011), 111–124.

14. K. Vatsyayan, "Drama: Indian Dance and Dance Drama," in *Encyclopedia of Religion*, vol. 4, 2nd ed., ed. L. Jones (New York: Macmillan Reference, 2005), 2447, https://link.gale.com /apps/doc/CX3424500830/GVRL?u=unilanc&sid=GVRL&xid=484e30d7.

15. L. Talley, "Sufi Whirling Dervishes," *PBS*, February 1, 2013, https://www.pbs.org/wnet /religionandethics/2013/12/13/february-1-2013-sufi-whirling-dervishes/14517/.

16. "The Haka," *Tourism New Zealand*, https://www.newzealand.com/uk/feature/haka/, accessed November 18, 2020; B. Hokowhitu, "Haka: Colonized Physicality, Body-Logic, and Embodied Sovereignty," in *Performing Indigeneity: Global Histories and Contemporary Experiences*, ed. L. R. Graham and H. G. Penny (Lincoln: University of Nebraska Press, 2014), 207.

17. A. Dils and A. Cooper Albright, "Looking at World Dance," in *Moving History/DancingCultures: A Dance History Reader* (Middletown, CT: Wesleyan University Press, 2001), 92–93.

18. Lucius Annaeus Seneca, *On the Shortness of Life*, trans. J. W. Basore (London: Loeb Classical Library, William Heinemann, 1932), sec. 9, www.forumromanum.org/literature/seneca _younger/brev_e.html.

19. C. Sachs, *World History of the Dance*, trans. B. Schönberg (New York: W. W. Norton, [1937] 1963), 3.

20. "The Origins of Theatre—The First Actor," *PBS*, Arlington, VA, https://www.pbs.org /empires/thegreeks/background/24a_p1.html, accessed April 6, 2021.

21. Aristotle (ca. 335 BCE), *The Poetics*, trans. S. H. Butcher (Project Gutenberg, January 22, 2013), chap. 6, https://www.gutenberg.org/files/1974/1974-h/1974-h.htm.

22. E. Csapo, *Actors and Icons of the Ancient Theatre* (Chichester, UK: John Wiley & Sons, 2010), 3.

23. "The Origins of Theatre—The First Actor," *PBS*; "The Origins of Theatre—The First Plays (continued)," *PBS*, https://www.pbs.org/empires/thegreeks/background/24b.html#:~:text =The%20first%20plays%20were%20performed%20in%20the%20Theatre%20of%20 Dionysus,comedy%2C%20tragedy%20and%20satyr%20plays, accessed April 6, 2021.

24. M. Grant, ed., *Latin Literature: An Anthology* (London: Penguin Random House, 2015), 13.

25. "The Story of Theatre," *Victoria and Albert Museum*, London, https://www.vam.ac.uk /articles/the-story-of-theatre, accessed April 6, 2021.

26. "Story of Theatre."

27. J. Perkovic, "Sarah Kane's Controversial 1990s Play Blasted Feels Prescient in the #MeToo Era," *The Conversation*, Melbourne, August 30, 2018, https://theconversation.com/sarah -kanes-controversial-1990s-play-blasted-feels-prescient-in-the-metoo-era-99759.

28. P. Taylor, "Theatre: Shopping and Fucking Royal Court, London," *Independent*, October 2, 1996, https://www.independent.co.uk/arts-entertainment/theatre-shopping-and-fucking -royal-court-london-1356460.html.

29. "A Christmas Carol Charitable Support 2022," July 6, 2022, The Old Vic, London, https:// www.oldvictheatre.com/stories/a-christmas-carol-charitable-support-2022/, accessed September 12, 2022.

30. "A Brief History of Choral Music," *Calgary Children's Choir*, March 30, 2015, https:// calgarychildrenschoir.com/a-brief-history-of-choral-music/.

31. G. Williams, *Do You Hear the People Sing? The Male Voice Choirs of Wales* (Ceredigion, Wales: Gomer Press, 2015), 5.

32. R. Clarke, "Why Wales Is Known as the Land of Song," *BBC*, October 1, 2018, http://www .bbc.com/travel/story/20180930-why-wales-is-known-as-the-land-of-song.

33. Williams, *Do You Hear the People Sing?*, 122.

34. W. Byrd, *The English Madrigal School: Psalms, Sonnets, and Songs of Sadness and Piety to Five Parts*, vol. 14, ed. Rev. E. H. Fellowes (London: Stainer and Bell, [1588] 1920), viii, https://

brittlebooks.library.illinois.edu/brittlebooks_open/Books2009-05/felled0001engmad
/felled0001engmadv00014/felled0001engmadv00014.pdf.

35. A. J. Batten, "Clothing and Adornment," *Biblical Theology Bulletin: Journal of Bible and Culture* 40, no. 3 (2010): 148; L. Hendry, "Human Evolution: Who Were the Neanderthals?," *Natural History Museum*, London, https://www.nhm.ac.uk/discover/who-were-the-neanderthals.html, accessed January 26, 2021.

36. A. Tuiz, *The Spirit of Ancient Egypt* (Sanford, NC: Algora, 2001), 51–52.

37. M. McCabe, T. de Waal Malefyt, and A. Fabri, "Women, Makeup, and Authenticity: Negotiating Embodiment and Discourses of Beauty," Journal of Consumer Culture 20, no. 4 (2020): 654, 674.

38. A. Hill, "The Challenge of Creating Responsible Jewelry," *Forbes*, August 29, 2018, https://www.forbes.com/sites/andreahill/2018/08/29/the-challenge-of-creating-responsible-jewelry/?sh=2b0236892fe6.

39. S. Bom, J. Jorge, H. M. Ribeiro, and J. Marto, "A Step Forward on Sustainability in the Cosmetics Industry: A Review," *Journal of Cleaner Production* 225 (March 2019): 275–279.

40. H. D., Whitehead, M. Venier, Y. Wu, E. Eastman, S. Urbanik, M. L. Diamond, A. Salin, H. Schwartz-Narbonne, T. A. Bruton, A. Blum, Z. Wang, M. Green, M. Tighe, J. T. Wilkinson, S. McGuiness, and G. F. Peaslee, "Fluorinated Compounds in North American Cosmetics," *Environmental Science & Technology Letters* (June 15, 2021): 538–544.

41. Bom, Jorge, Ribeiro, and Marto, "A Step Forward on Sustainability," 275–277, 280.

42. B. Bower, "Iceman Has the World's Oldest Tattoos," *Science News* 189, no. 2 (2016): 5.

43. Genesis 5:1–2.

44. F. Pesapane, G. Nazzaro, R. Gianotti, and A. Coggi, "A Short History of Tattoo," *JAMA Dermatology* 150, no. 2: 145.

45. J. Cook, J. Banks, and Dr. Hawkesworth, *The Three Voyages of Captain Cook Round the World. Vol. I. Being the First of the First Voyage, Longman & Co. London, 6 September 1821* (1821; Project Gutenberg, December 17, 2017), 189, http://www.gutenberg.org/files/56196/56196-h/56196-h.htm.

46. Pesapane, Nazzaro, Gianotti, and Coggi, "A Short History of Tattoo," 145.

47. "Razzouk Tattoo: Our History," *Razzouk Tattoo*, https://razzouktattoo.com/pages/history, accessed October 3, 2020.

48. D. Kaszas, "Echoes of the Ancestors: Inherited Knowledge and Responsibilities," *Body Language: Reawakening Cultural Tattooing of the Northwest*, Bill Reid Gallery, Vancouver, BC, 2018, 7–25.

49. I. Spar, "Heilbrunn Timeline of Art History: The Origins of Writing," *The Met*, New York, October 2004, www.metmuseum.org/toah/hd/wrtg/hd_wrtg.htm.

50. E. Clayton, "A Brief History of Writing Materials and Technologies," *British Library*, 2019, www.bl.uk/history-of-writing/articles/a-brief-history-of-writing-materials-and-technologies.

51. "Proto-Cuneiform Tablet with Seal Impressions: Administrative Account of Barley Distribution with Cylinder Seal Impression of a Male Figure, Hunting Dogs, and Boars, ca. 3100–2900 B.C., Sumerian," *The Met*, New York, https://www.metmuseum.org/art/collection/search/329081, accessed April 9, 2021.

52. P. Tallet and G. Marouard, "The Harbor of Khufu on the Red Sea Coast at Wadi al-Jarf, Egypt," *Near Eastern Archaeology* 77, no. 1 (March 2014): 4, 8.

53. Clayton, "Brief History of Writing Materials."

54. R. Kellman, E. Nadworny, and A. Cole, "Tools of the Trade: Trace the Remarkable History of the Humble Pencil," *NPR*, October 11, 2016, https://www.npr.org/sections/ed/2016/10/11/492999969/origin-of-pencil-lead?t=1617893487211.

55. D. M. Ewalt, "No. 4 The Pencil," *Forbes*, August 26, 2005, https://www.forbes.com/2005/08/26/technology-writing-pencil_cx_de_0826pencil.html?sh=3ac8e37772bd.

56. *Oxford English Dictionary, s.v. "Blackboard,"* https://www-oed-com.ezproxy.lancs.ac.uk/view/Entry/19691?redirectedFrom=Blackboard#eid, accessed September 12, 2022.

57. Clayton, "Brief History of Writing Materials."

58. Clayton, "Brief History of Writing Materials."

59. Phaidon, "Everyday Icon #3 The BIC Biro," October 19, 2011, https://www.phaidon.com/agenda/design/articles/2011/october/19/everyday-icon-3-the-bic-biro/, accessed April 8, 2021; J. Henley, "BIC over the Moon as Sales Top 100bn," *The Guardian*, September 9, 2005, https://www.theguardian.com/world/2005/sep/09/france.jonhenley.

60. F. Bacon, *11. Of Heresies, Meditationes Sacrae* (1597), Creative Commons, https://en.wikisource.org/wiki/Meditationes_sacrae, accessed April 9, 2021.

61. J. LaDou, "Printed Circuit Board Industry," *International Journal of Hygiene and Environmental* 209 (2006): 211, 218.

62. C.-L. Seow, "Ecclesiastes: Date of Composition, Historical Context, and Interpretation," in *The New Oxford Annotated Bible with Apocrypha: New Revised Standard Version*, ed. M. D. Coogan, M. Z. Brettler, C. Newsom, and P. Perkins (New York: Oxford University Press, 2010), 935–936; Ecclesiastes 1:18.

63. C. H. Scheele, *A Short History of the Mail Service* (Washington, DC: Smithsonian Institution Press, 1970), 11; A. C. Brix, "History: Message-Relay Systems of the ancient world, Postal System, written by the First Secretary, International Bureau of the Universal Postal Union, Berne, Switzerland," in *Britannica* (Chicago: Encyclopædia Britannica, Inc., 2017), https://www.britannica.com/topic/postal-system/History#ref15423, accessed March 4, 2021.

64. "Letters," *Archaeology*, Archaeology Institute of America, Boston, MA, May/June 2016, https://www.archaeology.org/issues/214-features/cuneiform/4368-cuneiform-letters,

accessed March 2, 2021; A. L. Oppenheim, *Letters from Mesopotamia: Official, Business, and Private Letters on Clay Tablets from Two Millennia*, trans. L. Oppenheim (Chicago: University of Chicago Press, 1967), 82–83.

65. "Writing-Tablet 1986, 1001.64," *British Museum*, London, https://www.britishmuseum.org /collection/object/H_1986-1001-64, accessed March 3, 2021.

66. H. Joyce, *The History of the Post Office—From Its Establishment Down to 1836* (London: Richard Bentley & Son, 1893; Project Gutenberg, December 17, 2011), 1, http://www .gutenberg.org/cache/epub/38328/pg38328.txt.

67. "The Penny Black," *Postal Museum*, London, https://www.postalmuseum.org/collections /penny-black/, accessed March 4, 2021.

68. K. Armstrong, *St Paul: The Misunderstood Apostle* (London: Atlantic Books, 2015), 72.

69. B. Radice, trans., "Book Ten: 96 to the Emperor Trajan," *The Letters of the Younger Pliny* (London: Penguin, 1963), 293–295, 166–168.

70. SDSU, *Plinian Eruptions*, SDSU College of Sciences, San Diego State University, San Diego, CA, 2020, http://sci.sdsu.edu/how_volcanoes_work/Plinian.html, accessed March 8, 2021.

71. M. L. King Jr., *Letter from a Birmingham Jail*, African Studies Center, University of Pennsylvania, Philadelphia, PA, 1963, https://www.africa.upenn.edu/Articles_Gen/Letter_Birming ham.html, accessed March 8, 2021.

72. H. Barker, *Family and Business during the Industrial Revolution* (Oxford: Oxford University Press, 2017), 14.

73. M. Berners-Lee, *How Bad Are Bananas: The Carbon Footprint of Everything* (London: Profile Books, 2020), 16, 18, 116–118.

74. K. Manral, *The Face at the Window* (New Delhi: Amaryllis, Manjul Publ. House Pvt. Ltd., 2016), 7.

75. I. Calvino, "Quickness," in *Six Memos for the Next Millennium*, trans. P. Creagh (Cambridge, MA: Harvard University Press, 1988), 33.

76. LEF, "Sunderland Point Community Association—Sambo's Grave Interpretation Panel," *Lancashire Environmental Fund*, Lancaster County Council, Preston, Lancashire, 2020, https://www.lancashire.gov.uk/council/grants/community-project-support/lancashire-envi ronmental-fund/, Project Listing, www.lancsenvfund.org.uk/uploads/6/7/6/4/67640065 /2020_grants_awarded.pdf, accessed May 4, 2021.

77. National Trails, "The Ridgeway: A Walk on Britain's Oldest Road," *National Trails*, Natural England, York, Yorkshire and Humber, 2020, https://www.nationaltrail.co.uk/en_GB /the-ridgeway/itinerary/the-ridgeway-a-walk-on-britains-oldest-road/, accessed August 17, 2020; Ordnance Survey, "Your Right to Roam with Public Rights of Way," *Ordnance Survey*, Southampton, 2018, https://www.ordnancesurvey.co.uk/blog/2018/07/right-to-roam -public-rights-of-way/, accessed August 16, 2020.

78. National Trails, "The Ridgeway."

79. Ordnance Survey, "Your Right to Roam with Public Rights of Way."

80. J. Clare, "The Flitting," in *Major Works*, ed. E. Robinson and D. Powell, Oxford World Classics (Oxford: Oxford University Press, ca. 1835), 251.

81. S. Desmond, "Country Crossings: A Stile Guide," *Country Life*, September 8, 2016, https://www.countrylife.co.uk/country-life/country-crossings-stile-guide-128113.

CHAPTER 16

1. J. Huizinga, *Homo Ludens: A Study of the Play-Element in Culture* (Brooklyn, NY: Angelico Press, [1949] 2016), 1, 28.

2. Huizinga, *Homo Ludens*, 3.

3. S. Brown, with C. Vaughan, *Play: How it Shapes the Brain, Opens the Imagination, and Invigorates the Soul* (New York: Penguin, 2010), 17–18.

4. Brown, 134.

5. Huizinga, *Homo Ludens*, 4.

6. Brown, *Play*, 15.

7. I. McGilchrist, *The Master and His Emissary: The Divided Brain and the Making of the Western World* (New Haven, CT: Yale University Press, 2009), 42.

8. B. Edwards, *Drawing on the Right Side of the Brain*, 4th ed. (London: Souvenir Press, 2012), 109.

9. Wellcome Trust, *Play Well: Why Play Matters* (London: Wellcome Collection, 2019, exhibition booklet), 4–14.

10. Huizinga, *Homo Ludens*, 196–198.

11. Huizinga, 1, 4.

12. D. C. Korten, *The Great Turning: From Empire to Earth Community* (Bloomfield, CT: Kumarian Press Inc.; San Francisco: Berrett-Koehler Publishers Inc., 2006), 337–338.

13. Korten, 338.

14. The Center for a New American Dream, *Kids Unbranded: Tips for Parenting in a Commercial Culture*, October 16, 2014, 4, https://newdream.org/downloads/New_Dream_Kids_Unbranded_Guide.pdf.

15. J. Bakan, *The Corporation: The Pathological Pursuit of Profit and Power* (London: Constable & Robinson Ltd., 2004), 119.

16. G. Orwell, *Keep the Aspidistra Flying* (London: Harvest Books, 1956), 51.

17. Wellcome Trust, *Play Well: Why Play Matters*, 13–15; Lady Allen of Hurtwood, *Play and Playground Encyclopedia* (Ashton, ID: Picture Perfect Playgrounds, Inc., 2020).

18. J. H. Liu, "The 5 Best Toys of All Time," *Wired*, January 31, 2011, https://www.wired.com/2011/01/the-5-best-toys-of-all-time/.

19. Liu, "5 Best Toys of All Time."

20. P. Barkham, *Wild Child: Coming Home to Nature* (London: Granta Books, 2020), 144.

21. Orwell, *Keep the Aspidistra Flying*, 51.

22. O. Laczi, "Neolithic Drawings from the Bestažovca Cave in Western Slovenia," *Proceedings of the 16th International Congress of Speleology* (July 21–28, 2013), 156.

23. H. Matisse, "Matisse Assiduously Pursues His Preparatory Work for the Large Drawings on Ceramics and Stained Glass," Chapel of the Rosary in Vence, masterpiece by Henri Matisse, *Matisse Chapel*, Vence, 1949, http://chapellematisse.fr/FR/reperes-chronologiques-matisse-soeur-jacques-marie.php, accessed January 1, 2020.

24. H. Matisse, Chapel of the Rosary in Vence, masterpiece by Henri Matisse, *Matisse Chapel*, Vence, 1948, http://chapellematisse.fr/, accessed January 1, 2020.

25. L. Grozdanic, "STIK Chair Made from Bundles of Tightly Stacked Twigs Shows the Creative Power of Addition, *INHABIT*, El Segundo, CA, 2014, https://inhabitat.com/stik-chair-a-bundle-of-tightly-stacked-natural-sticks-show-the-creative-power-of-addition/, accessed January 1, 2020.

26. S. Walker, *The Spirit of Design: Objects, Environment and Meaning* (Abingdon, Oxford: Earthscan, 2011), 150–153.

27. A. Portis, *Not a Stick* (New York: HarperCollins, 2008).

28. F. Danks and J. Schofield, *The Stick Book: Loads of Things You Can Make or Do with a Stick* (London: Frances Lincoln Ltd., 2012).

29. Liu, "5 Best Toys of All Time."

30. R. Rauschenberg, "Rosalie/Red Cheek/Temporary Letter/Stock (Cardboard)," 1971, *San Francisco Museum of Modern Art (SFMOMA)*, San Francisco, CA, 2020, https://www.sfmoma.org/artwork/2013.149/, accessed December 31, 2020.

31. M. Gale, *Alfred Wallis* (London: Tate Gallery Publishing Ltd, London, 1995), 17, 26.

32. A. Portis, *Not a Box* (New York: HarperCollins, 2006).

33. Liu, "5 Best Toys of All Time."

34. F. V. Grunfeld, *Games of the World: How to Make Them, How to Play Them, How They Came to Be* (Zurich: Swiss Committee for UNICEF, 1982), 254–259.

35. E. Yong, "An Ancient Toy Could Improve Health Care in the Developing World," *The Atlantic*, Emerson Collective, Washington, DC, January 10, 2017, https://www.theatlantic.com/science/archive/2017/01/button-spinner-health-care/512549/, accessed August 25, 2020.

36. ModernEdition, "By a Thread: String as Contemporary Art Medium," *ModernEdition*, London, http://www.modernedition.com/art-articles/string/string-art-history.html, accessed January 1, 2020.

37. Liu, "5 Best Toys of All Time."

38. BBC, *Blue Peter*, London, https://www.bbc.co.uk/cbbc/shows/blue-peter, accessed December 30, 2020.

39. A. Cowan, "5 Stem Activities with Cardboard Tubes," *Science Buddies*, Sobrato Center for Nonprofits, Milpitas, CA, May 7, 2019, https://www.sciencebuddies.org/blog/cardboard -tube-science-activities, accessed August 24, 2020.

40. "Rube Goldberg Machines," *Institute of Imagination*, London, 2020, https://ioi.london /latest/competition-time-help-create-giant-rube-goldberg-machine-kids-invent-stuff/, accessed December 30, 2020.

41. M. Kielnhofer, "*Interlux Chair*, 2002," *Artnet*, Berlin, http://www.artnet.com/artists /manfred-kielnhofer/interlux-chair-_EWMTJoQqxwo3rzFwXKh6A2, accessed December 30, 2020. Description and images of armchair and upright chair at Behance.net, https:// www.behance.net/gallery/356658/Paper-Tube-Chair, accessed December 30, 2020.

42. Liu, "5 Best Toys of All Time."

43. Liu.

44. Boyle Family, *Boyle Family: An Introduction*, https://www.boylefamily.co.uk/boyle/about/, accessed December 31, 2020.

45. J. Gilbert and R. Knight, with S. Blakeslee, *Dirt Is Good: The Advantage of Germs for Your Child's Developing Immune System* (New York: St. Martin's Press, 2017).

46. L. Garcia-Navarro, "'Dirt Is Good': Why Kids Need Exposure to Germs," *NPR*, July 16, 2017, https://www.npr.org/sections/health-shots/2017/07/16/537075018/dirt-is-good -why-kids-need-exposure-to-germs, accessed August 24, 2020.

47. J. Gilbert and R. Knight, excerpt from "Dirt Is Good," *NPR*, July 16, 2017, https://www.npr .org/sections/health-shots/2017/07/16/537075018/dirt-is-good-why-kids-need-exposure -to-germs.

48. S. Walker, *Design Realities: Creativity, Nature and the Human Spirit* (Oxford: Routledge, 2019), 215, 230–231.

49. S. Tzu (5th century BCE), *The Art of War*, trans. L. Giles, The Internet Classics Archive, VII.21, 1910, http://classics.mit.edu/Tzu/artwar.1b.txt, accessed May 22, 2020.

50. Ovid (ca. 10 CE), "Tristia, Book TII:471–496 His Plea: Dubious Entertainments," *The Poems of Exile*, 71, http://uploads.worldlibrary.net/uploads/pdf/20121106192032ovidpoemsfro mexilepdf_pdf.pdf, accessed May 7, 2020.

51. T. Penn and S. Courts, "Playing Games at Vindolanda," *Vindolanda Charitable Trust— Chesterholm Museum*, Northumbria, 2019, https://www.vindolanda.com/blog/playing -games-at-vindolanda, accessed May 8, 2020.

52. John 19:13; W. Slott, "The King's Game," *Times of Israel*, Jerusalem, April 16, 2018, https:// blogs.timesofisrael.com/the-kings-game/, accessed May 14, 2020.

53. M. Burrows, "The Fortress Antonia and the Praetorium," *Biblical Archaeologist* 1, no. 3 (September 1938), 18–19; S. Awwad, *The Holy Land in Colour* (Herzliya, Israel: Palphot Ltd., [1975] 1993), 13; Matthew 27:27–30; Mark 15:16–20.

54. Slott, "King's Game."

55. J. Daley, "Researchers Are Trying to Figure Out How to Play This Ancient Roman Board Game," *Smithsonian Magazine*, Smithsonian Institution, Washington, DC, January 10, 2018, https://www.smithsonianmag.com/smart-news/we-still-dont-really-know-how-play -ancient-roman-board-game-180967778/, accessed May 16, 2020.

56. J. Straková and J. Petrlik, "Toy or Toxic Waste? An Analysis of 47 Plastic Toy and Beauty Products Made from Toxic Recycling," *Arnika—Toxics and Waste Programme*, Prague, 2017, 3–4. https://english.arnika.org/publications/toy-or-toxic-waste-an-analysis-of-plastic -products, accessed May 19, 2020.

57. E. T. Merrill, "An Old Roman Game," *Classical Journal* 11, no. 66 (1916): 365.

58. Richborough, *Richborough Roman Fort and Amphitheatre*, Richborough, Kent, https://www .english-heritage.org.uk/visit/places/richborough-roman-fort-and-amphitheatre/, accessed August 18, 2020.

59. R. G. Austin, "Roman Board Games. II," *Greece and Rome* 4, no. 11 (1935): 76–82.

60. Ovid (ca. 2 CE), "Ars Amatoria (The Art of Love), Book III," trans. A. S. Kline, https://www .poetryintranslation.com/PITBR/Latin/ArtofLoveBkIII.php, accessed September 12, 2022.

61. E. T. Merrill, "An Old Roman Game," *The Classical Journal* 11, no. 66 (1916): 365–366.

62. R. G. Austin, "Roman Board Games. II," *Greece and Rome* 4, no. 11 (1935): 80.

63. J. Daley, "Archaeologists Uncover an Ancient Roman Game Board at Hadrian's Wall," *Smithsonian Magazine*, May 8, 2019, https://www.smithsonianmag.com/smart-news /archaeologists-uncover-ancientroman-game-board-hadrians-wall-180972133/; U. Schädler, "Latrunculi: A Forgotten Roman Game of Strategy Reconstructed," *Abstract Games* (West Vancouver, BC: Carpe Diem Publishing, 2001), 10, https://www.abstractgames.org/uploads /1/1/6/4/116462923/abstract_games_issue_7.pdf, accessed May 8, 2020.

64. R. C. Bell, *Board and Table Games from Many Civilizations*, rev. ed., vol. 1 (New York: Dover, 1979), 33.

65. T. Penn and S. Courts, "Playing Games at Vindolanda," *Vindolanda Charitable Trust*, Chesterholm Museum, Hexham, Northumberland, 2019, https://www.vindolanda.com/blog /playing-games-at-vindolanda, accessed August 19, 2020; Daley, "Archaeologists Uncover an Ancient Roman Game Board."

66. U. Schädler, "Latrunculi, A Forgotten Roman Game of Strategy Reconstructed, *Abstract Games*, no. 7 (Autumn 2001): 10, https://www.abstractgames.org/uploads/1/1/6/4/116462923 /abstract_games_issue_7.pdf.

67. Daley, "Archaeologists Uncover an Ancient Roman Game Board."

68. Ovid (ca. 10 CE), "Tristia, Book TII:471–496 His Plea: Dubious Entertainments," *The Poems of Exile*, 71, http://uploads.worldlibrary.net/uploads/pdf/20121106192032ovidpoemsfro mexilepdf_pdf.pdf, accessed May 7, 2020.

69. Schädler, "Latrunculi," 10.

70. W. Shakespeare, *A Midsummer Night's Dream* (ca. 1596, Project Gutenberg), act II, scene I, https://www.gutenberg.org/files/1514/1514-h/1514-h.htm#sceneII_1, accessed September 12, 2022.

71. Grunfeld, *Games of the World*, 59; Bell, *Board and Table Games from Many Civilizations*, 93.

72. "Life on Board," *The Mary Rose*, Mary Rose Trust, Portsmouth, https://maryrose.org/life-on -board/, accessed August 28, 2020.

73. A. Leopold, *A Sand County Almanac and Sketches Here and There* (New York: Oxford University Press, 1949), 25.

74. Bell, *Board and Table Games from Many Civilizations*, 71.

75. Bell, 71.

76. P. Davies, "Writing Slates and Schooling," *Australasian Historical Archaeology* 23 (2005): 63.

77. Davies, 63.

78. G. Chaucer, "Part II, Supplementary Propositions," *Chaucer's Works—A Treatise on the Astrolabe*, vol. 3, ed. W. Skeat (1391; Project Gutenberg, February 27, 2014), 45:35, 229a, https:// www.gutenberg.org/files/45027/45027-h/45027-h.htm.

79. "School Slates," *The British Medical Journal* 1, no. 1788 (April 6, 1895): 771; "School Slates," *The British Medical Journal* 2, no. 2346 (December 16, 1905):1607.

80. Davies, "Writing Slates and Schooling," 64.

81. E. G. Budd and L. F. Newman, "Knuckle-Bones: An Old Game of Skill," *Folklore* 52, no. 1 (March 1941): 10.

82. Grunfeld, *Games of the World*, 162.

83. H. C. Küchelmann, "Why 7? Rules and Exceptions in the Numbering of Dice," *Palaeohistoria* 59/60 (2017/2018): 110.

84. A. Good, "Knucklebones," *Archaeological Museum*, Johns Hopkins University, Baltimore, MD, https://archaeologicalmuseum.jhu.edu/the-collection/object-stories/archaeology-of -daily-life/childhood/knucklebones/, accessed April 26, 2021.

85. Homer, *The Iliad*, trans. E. V. Rieu (London: Penguin, [1598] 1950), 414.

86. Herodotus (ca. 430 BCE), *The Histories*, trans. A. de Sélincourt (London: Penguin, 1954), bk. 1:94, 40.

87. Good, "Knucklebones."

88. E. G. Budd and L. F. Newman, "Knuckle-Bones. An Old Game of Skill," *Folklore* 52, no. 1 (March 1941): 9.

89. M. W. Myers, "Knuckle-Bones," *Folklore* 52, no. 3 (September 1941: 237–238.

90. *siller*—northern dialect: silver.

91. *welter*—northern dialect: to tumble or fall in an uncontrolled way.

92. M. Ashley, "The Stuarts," in *The Lives of the Kings and Queens of England*, ed. A. Fraser (London: Weidenfeld and Nicolson, 1975), 231, 234–237.

93. "Cup and Ball," *St Fagans National Museum of History*, Cardiff, Wales, https://museum.wales/traditional_toys/cup_and_ball/, accessed August 22, 2020.

94. Grunfeld, *Games of the World*, 252.

95. *Bilboquet Game Equipement* [sic] (2009), Inuit Target Games, Canadian Heritage Information Network, Government of Canada, Gatineau, QC, http://www.virtualmuseum.ca/edu/ViewLoitDa.do;jsessionid=876C171A0B2749AA8EFF83BD000862FA?method=preview&lang=EN&id=11658, accessed August 23, 2020.

96. Grunfeld, *Games of the World*, 253.

97. E. Avedon, *Inuit Bilboquet*, Virtual Museum of Games, University of Waterloo, Waterloo, ON, updated June 17, 2010, https://healthy.uwaterloo.ca/museum/VirtualExhibits/Inuit/english/bilbo.html, accessed August 22, 2020.

98. J-J Rousseau, *The Confessions*, trans. J. M. Cohen (London: Penguin Classics, [1953] 1781), 195.

99. T. Eagleton, *Culture and the Death of God* (New Haven, CT: Yale University Press, 2014), 45–46.

100. T. Bullfinch, *The Golden Age of Myth and Legend* (Ware, Hertfordshire, UK: Wordsworth Editions, [1867] 1993), 173–175.

101. P. Matthews, introduction to *Historical Dictionary of Track and Field* (Lanham, MD: Scarecrow Press, 2012), 24–27.

102. IOC, "Olympic Games, Athens 1896," International Olympic Committee, Lausanne, Switzerland, https://olympics.com/en/olympic-games/athens-1896, accessed June 29, 2021.

103. Matthews, introduction to *Historical Dictionary of Track and Field*, 34.

104. Matthews, 35.

105. *parkrun*, https://www.parkrun.org.uk/, accessed June 30, 2021.

106. W. Shakespeare, *The Comedy of Errors* (1594, Project Gutenberg), act II, scene I, https://www.gutenberg.org/files/23046/23046-h/23046-h.htm#sceneII_1, accessed September 12, 2022.

107. "Shakespeare's Deadly Game of Football," *Shakespeare Birthplace Trust*, Stratford-upon-Avon, Warwickshire, August 14, 2012, https://www.shakespeare.org.uk/explore-shakespeare/blogs/shakespeares-deadly-game-football/.

108. T. Dunmore, introduction to *Historical Dictionary of Soccer* (Lanham, MD: The Scarecrow Press, Lanham, ML, 21–23.

109. J. Huizinga, *Homo Ludens: A Study of the Play-Element in Culture* (Brooklyn, NY: Angelico Press, [1949] 2016), 197–198.

CHAPTER 17

1. C. Geertz, *Local Knowledge* (London: Fontana, [1983] 1993), 125; B. Stephenson, *Ritual: A Very Short Introduction* (Oxford: Oxford University Press, 2015), 42.

2. M. Eliade, *The Sacred and the Profane*, trans. W. R. Trask (San Diego: Harvest/HBJ, 1957), 184.

3. B. Pascal, *Pensées*, no. 912 (781) (London: Penguin, [1670] 1995]), 281.

4. M. Slater, M., ed., *Charles Dickens: A Christmas Carol and Other Christmas Writings* (London: Penguin, 2003), 275n2.

5. I. McGilchrist, *The Master and his Emissary: The Divided Brain and the Making of the Western World* (New Haven, CT: Yale University Press, 2009), 329.

6. C. Taylor, *A Secular Age* (Cambridge, MA: Harvard University Press, 2007), 614.

7. Taylor, 773.

8. Eliade, *Sacred and the Profane*, 186.

9. Taylor, *Secular Age*, 9, 28, 399, 717.

10. B. Stephenson, *Ritual: A Very Short Introduction* (Oxford: Oxford University Press, 2015), 1–2, 103.

11. K. Armstrong, *The Lost Art of Scripture: Rescuing the Sacred Texts* (London: The Bodley Head, 2019), 94.

12. J. Huxley, "Introduction: A Discussion on Ritualization of Behaviour in Animals and Man, *Philosophical Transactions of the Royal Society of London, Series B*, 251 (December 29, 1966): 260.

13. B. Dylan, *Blowin' in the Wind*, Columbia Records, New York, NY, released in 1962 and included on the 1963 album *The Freewheelin' Bob Dylan*, also on Columbia Records. In each verse the song asks a series of questions about war and peace and answers them with the refrain: "The answer, my friend, is blowin' in the wind / The answer is blowin' in the wind."

14. H. E. Gardner, *Multiple Intelligences: New Horizons in Theory and Practice* (New York: Basic Books, 2006), 10.

15. F. R. Wilson, *The Hand: How Its Use Shapes the Brain, Language, and Human Culture* (New York: Vintage, 1998), 10.

16. K. Armstrong, *The Lost Art of Scripture: Rescuing the Sacred Texts* (London: Bodley Head, 2019), 77–79.

17. Armstrong, 7–10, 50–53.

18. . B. Edwards, *Drawing on the Right Side of the Brain* (Los Angeles, CA: J. P. Tarcher, Inc., 1979), 40, 57.

19. Stephenson, *Ritual*, 10–11, 39.

20. Stephenson, 9.

21. W. Langland (14th century), *The Vision and Creed of Piers Ploughman*, vol. 1, 2nd ed., ed. T. Wright (London: Reeves and Turner, 1887; Project Gutenberg, September 7, 2013), passus 6, lines 3909–3924, http://www.gutenberg.org/files/43660/43660-h/43660-h.htm#passVI. Modern English prose translation: "'I, for my part, . . . will dress myself in pilgrim's clothes and travel with you until we find Truth.' Hereupon, Piers began to don his working-clothes, some of them patch, some still in one piece, his leggings, and the mittens he wore to keep his fingers from freezing. At his back, where pilgrims carry a provision-bag, he hung this ploughman's seed-basket. 'In this,' said Piers, 'I want a bushel-weight of wheat grain. I intend to sow it myself and then set off like a pilgrim to obtain my pardon,'" W. Langland, *Piers Plowman: A New Translation of the B-Text*, trans. A. V. C. Schmidt, Oxford World Classics (Oxford: Oxford University Press, 1992), 65–66.

22. M. Palmer and N. Palmer, *The Spiritual Traveler: England, Scotland, Wales* (Mahwah, NJ: HiddenSpring, 2000), 75, 76.

23. E. Curti, *Fifty Catholic Churches to See before You Die* (Leominster: Gracewing, 2020), 169.

24. E. Duffy, *A People's Tragedy: Studies in Reformation* (London: Bloomsbury Continuum, 2020), 9.

25. "About the British Pilgrimage Trust," *The British Pilgrimage Trust*, London, https://british pilgrimage.org/the-bpt/, accessed December 24, 2020; E. Duffy, *A People's Tragedy: Studies in Reformation* (London: Bloomsbury Continuum, 2020), 2, 30; D. Dyas, "Pilgrims and Pilgrimage: The Reformation Onwards," *The Centre for Christianity and Culture*, University of York, York, https://www.york.ac.uk/projects/pilgrimage/content/reform.html#:~:text =In%20England%2C%20as%20in%20a,of%20pilgrimage%20to%20holy%20places.& text=In%201520%20he%20declared%20'All,no%20obedience%20attaches%20to%20 them, accessed December 26, 2020.

26. "About the British Pilgrimage Trust."

27. Palmer and Palmer, *The Spiritual Traveler*; I. Reader, *Pilgrimage: A Very Short Introduction* (Oxford: Oxford University Press, 2015), 23.

28. I. Reader, *Pilgrimage: A Very Short Introduction* (Oxford: Oxford University Press, 2015), 20–23.

29. E. Duffy, *A People's Tragedy: Studies in Reformation* (London: Bloomsbury Continuum, 2020), 25.

30. Duffy, *People's Tragedy*, 7; E. Knowles, *The Oxford Dictionary of Phrase and Fable*, 2nd ed. (Oxford: Oxford University Press, 2006), https://www-oxfordreference-com.ezproxy.lancs

.ac.uk/view/10.1093/acref/9780198609810.001.0001/acref-9780198609810-e-1636?rskey
=UmhVBA&result=1.

31. St Issui, *National Churches Trust*, London, https://www.nationalchurchestrust.org/church
/st-issui-patricio, accessed September 12, 2022; N. M. Smith, *Britain's Holiest Places* (Bristol:
Lifestyle Press, 2011), 453; Synaxarion, "Saint Issui or Isho or Ishaw," *The Saints of Great
Britain and Ireland*, http://www.synaxarion.org.uk/02WelshSaints/Issui/Issui.html, accessed
December 23, 2020.

32. Smith, *Britain's Holiest Places*, 453; T. Weight, *The Historical Works of Giraldus Cambrensis*
(London: George Bell & Sons, 1894), 366.

33. K. Turner, "Altar, Home," in *Folklore: An Encyclopedia of Beliefs, Customs, Tales, Music, and
Art*, ed. C. T. McCormick and K. K. White (Santa Barbara, CA: ABC-CLIO, LLC, Santa
Barbara, CA, 2010), 45; K. E. Foust, "Egyptian Religion," in *Encyclopedia of Women in World
Religions: Faith and Culture Across History*, vol. 1, ed. S. de-Gaia (Santa Barbara, CA: ABC-
CLIO, LLC, 2018), 38.

34. "Day of the Dead," in *Concise Encyclopedia of Mexico*, ed. M. S. Werner (Chicago, IL: Fitzroy
Dearborn Publishers, 2001), 161.

35. D. Dandekar, "Household Shrines," in *Encyclopedia of Women in World Religions: Faith
and Culture Across History*, vol. 1, ed. S. de-Gaia (Santa Barbara, CA: ABC-CLIO, LLC,
2018), 343.

36. J. Nelson, "Contemporary Household Altars," in *Handbook of Contemporary Japanese Religions*, ed. I. Prohl and J. Nelson (Leiden: BRILL, 2012), 575.

37. K. L. Evans (Three Eagles), "Ancestors (Native American)," in *Encyclopedia of Women in World
Religions: Faith and Culture Across History*, vol. 2, ed. de-Gaia (Santa Barbara, CA:ABC-
CLIO, LLC, 2018), 7.

38. P. Engelmajer, "Laywomen in Theravada Buddhism," in *Encyclopedia of Women in World
Religions: Faith and Culture Across History*, vol. 1, ed. S. de-Gaia (Santa Barbara, CA,
ABC-CLIO, LLC, 2018), 127; Dandekar, "Household Shrines," 344; Turner, "Altar,
Home," 45.

39. Dandekar, "Household Shrines," 343–344.

40. K. Turner, "Altar, Home," in *Folklore: An Encyclopedia of Beliefs, Customs, Tales, Music,
and Art*, ed. C. T. McCormick and K. K. White (Santa Barbara, CA: ABC-CLIO, LLC,
2010), 45.

41. B. Larios and R. Voix, "Introduction. Wayside Shrines in India: An Everyday Defiant Reli-
giosity," *South Asia Multidisciplinary Academic Journal*, no. 18 (2018): 2, http://journals
.openedition.org/samaj/4546, accessed October 30, 2020.

42. A. C. Osterberg, "The Role of Roadside Shrines in the Everyday Lives of Female Devotees in
Mumbai, *South Asia Multidisciplinary Academic Journal*, no. 18 (2018), 14, http://journals
.openedition.org/samaj/4565, accessed October 30, 2020.

43. J. Santino, "Performative Commemoratives, the Personal, and the Public: Spontaneous Shrines, Emergent Ritual and the Field of Folklore," *Journal of American Folklore* 117, no. 466 (Fall 2004): 364.

44. A. C. Collins and A. Opie, "When Places Have Agency: Roadside Shrines as Traumascapes," *Continuum: Journal of Media & Cultural Studies* 24, no. 1 (February 2010): 107.

45. J. Santino, "Performative Commemoratives, the Personal, and the Public: Spontaneous Shrines, Emergent Ritual and the Field of Folklore," *Journal of American Folklore* 117, no. 466 (Fall 2004): 364–370.

46. Santino, "Performative Commemoratives," 369.

47. "Our History," *Hereford Cathedral*, Hereford, https://www.herefordcathedral.org/our-history, accessed August 20, 2020.

48. M. Tavinor, "Pilgrimage and Cathedrals from the 1900s to the Present Day," Pilgrimage and England's Cathedrals: Past, Present, and Future, ed. D. Dyas and J. Jenkins (Cham, Switzerland: Palgrave Macmillan, 2020), 140.

49. L. Mitchell, "Lord, Give Me Sanctuary," *BBC*, London, July 25, 2002, http://news.bbc.co.uk/1/hi/uk/2151213.stm, accessed March 14, 2021.

50. "Our Church," *Adel Parish Church—St John the Baptist*, Leeds, https://www.adelparishchurch.org.uk/church-buildings/our-church.html, accessed March 14, 2021; "The Sanctuary Knocker—Durham Cathedral," *Durham World Heritage Site*, Durham, https://www.durhamworldheritagesite.com/learn/architecture/cathedral/intro/sanctuary-knocker, accessed March 14, 2021.

51. W. M. Marshall, "Sanctuary," in *The Oxford Companion to British History*, 2nd ed., ed. R. Crowcroft and J. Cannon (Oxford: Oxford University Press, 2015), https://www-oxfordreference-com.ezproxy.lancs.ac.uk/view/10.1093/acref/9780199677832.001.0001/acref-9780199677832-e-3782?rskey=FplwYA&result=1, accessed March 14, 2021.

52. Mitchell, "Lord, Give Me Sanctuary."

53. Plato (ca. 370 BCE), *Phaedrus* 230 b2-c6. This rendering adapted from two contemporary translations: Plato, *Phaedrus*, trans. R. Waterfield (Oxford: Oxford University Press, 2002), 7; and Plato, *Phaedrus*, trans. C. Rowe (London: Penguin, 2005), 6–7.

54. R. Williams, *Candles in the Dark: Faith, Hope and Love in a Time of Pandemic* (London: Society for Promoting Christian Knowledge [SPCK], 2020), 4–5.

55. T. Fox, "Interview of Local Resident and User of St. Peter-on-the-Wall, Tim Fox by Edward Stourton," *Sunday*, BBC, London, January 31, 2021, 9′30″–14′40″, https://www.bbc.co.uk/sounds/play/m000rv5h, accessed January 31, 2021; "Chapel," *The Chapel of St Peter-on-the-Wall*, Bradwell-on-Sea, Essex, https://www.bradwellchapel.org/chapel.html, accessed January 31, 2021.

56. "The Grotto, Cleator and Frizington St. Mary & St. Joseph's Catholic Parish," Cleator, Cumbria, https://www.stmarysandstjosephs.com/the-grotto.html#, accessed January 29, 2021;

"St Mary's Church and Grotto," *Visit Cumbria*, Gilcrux, Cumbria, https://www.visitcumbria
.com/wc/cleator-st-marys-church-and-grotto/, accessed January 29, 2021.

57. D. Sandelands, "Protest over Plans near Cleator Grotto," *Whitehaven News*, September 25, 2017, https://www.whitehavennews.co.uk/news/17111877.protest-over-plans-near-cleator -grotto/, accessed January 31, 2021; "Controversial Plans for Houses Near to Church Grotto Given the Go-Ahead," *Whitehaven News*, Carlisle, Cumbria, October 4, 2017, https://www .whitehavennews.co.uk/news/17111806.controversial-plans-for-houses-near-to-church -grotto-given-the-go-ahead/.

58. High Speed Two Ltd, *Phase One: London to West Midlands*, London, https://www.hs2.org .uk/building-hs2/phase-one-london-west-midlands/, accessed March 18, 2021.

59. A. Daniel, "HS2 Q&A: Where Is the Route, How Much Will It Cost and When Will It Open?," *City A.M.*, City A.M. Ltd., London, January 20, 2020, https://www.cityam.com/qa-what -is-the-hs2-route-how-much-will-it-cost-and-when-will-it-open/, accessed March 18, 2021; R. Horgan, "HS2 Has Already Spent a Quarter of £40bn Phase One Target Cost," *New Civil Engineer*, London, October 15, 2020, https://www.newcivilengineer.com/latest/hs2 -has-already-spent-a-quarter-of-40bn-phase-one-target-cost-15-10-2020/#:~:text=The%20 total%20funding%20envelope%20for,5.3bn%20of%20contingency%20funding.

60. Gov.uk, *High Speed Two: Phase One: London-West Midlands Ancient Woodland Strategy*, London, August 2017, https://assets.publishing.service.gov.uk/government/uploads/system /uploads/attachment_data/file/664737/hs2_phase_one_ancient_woodland_strategy.pdf, accessed March 18, 2021.

61. Woodland Trust, "HS2 Rail Link," *The Woodland Trust*, Grantham, Lincolnshire, https:// www.woodlandtrust.org.uk/protecting-trees-and-woods/campaign-with-us/hs2-rail-link/#, accessed March 18, 2021.

62. L. Stryk, introduction to *On Love and Barley* (London: Penguin, 1985), 12.

63. M. Bashō, *The Narrow Road to the Deep North and Other Travel Sketches*, trans. N. Yuasa (London: Penguin, [1702] 1966), 37; M. Bashō, *On Love and Barley*, trans. L. Stryk (London: Penguin, 1985), 26.

64. Bashō, *The Narrow Road to the Deep North*, 33.

65. E. Robinson and D. Powell, eds., "Child Harold—Ballad," in *John Clare: Major Works Including Selections from* The Shepherd's Calendar (Oxford: Oxford University Press, 2004), 279.

66. Y. Miyazaki, *Shinrin Yoku: The Japanese Way of Forest Bathing for Health and Relaxation* (London: Aster, Octopus Publishing Company, 2018); K. Meyer and R. Bürger-Arndt, "How Forests Foster Human Health—Present State of Research-Based Knowledge (in the Field of Forests and Human Health)," *International Forestry Review* 16, no. 4 (2014): 434, 437; Bum Jin Park, Yuko Tsunetsugu, Tamami Kasetani, Takahide Kagawa, and Y. Miyazaki, "The Physiological Effects of *Shinrin-yoku* (Taking in the Forest Atmosphere or Forest Bathing): Evidence from Field Experiments in 24 Forests across Japan," *Environmental Health and*

Preventative Medicine 15 (2010), https://link.springer.com/article/10.1007/s12199-009
-0086-9.

CHAPTER 18

1. A. Sooke, introduction to *Civilisation: A Personal View* by K. Clark (London: John Murray, [1969] 2018), xiv.

2. S. Steinbacher, *Auschwitz: A History*, trans. S. Whiteside (London: Penguin, [2004] 2005), 30; Gov.UK, *Human Rights and Democracy Report 2014*, London, updated April 21, 2016, https://www.gov.uk/government/publications/human-rights-and-democracy-report-2014 /human-rights-and-democracy-report-2014#contents, accessed March 21, 2020.

3. "Chinese Artist Ai Weiwei Describes His 81 Days in Prison—And the Extreme Surveillance, Censorship, and 'Soft Detention' He's Endured Since," *Artspace*, December 20, 2018, https://www.artspace.com/magazine/interviews_features/qa/the-most-shocking-image-i -can-remember-is-seeing-myself-in-the-mirrorchinese-artist-ai-weiwei-55832; Pen Reports, *Pen International*, https://pen-international.org/defending-free-expression/policy-advocacy /reports, accessed March 21, 2020; F. Aigbogun, "It Took Five Tries to Hang Saro-Wiwa," *Independent*, London, November 13, 1995, https://www.independent.co.uk/news/world /it-took-five-tries-to-hang-saro-wiwa-1581703.html, accessed March 21, 2020.

4. M. Ratner and E. Ray, *Guantánamo, What the World Should Know* (White River Junction, VT: Chelsea Green, 2004), xv; S. Noyes Platt, "Intimate Violence: Artists' Responses to Illegal Detention and Torture, *Brown Journal of World Affairs* 19, no. 2 (Spring/Summer 2013): 163.

5. *Turning Point USA*, https://tpusa.com, accessed March 21, 2020.

6. A. Fazackerley, "'McCarthyism in the UK': Academics Fear Shaming for Leftwing Views," *The Guardian*, March 10, 2020, https://www.theguardian.com/education/2020/mar/10 /mccarthyism-uk-universities-academics-fear-shaming-for-leftwing-views?CMP=share_btn _tw, accessed March 21, 2020.

7. *Turning Point UK*, https://tpointuk.co.uk/, accessed March 21, 2020; Turning Point UK, *Education Watch*, https://tpointuk.co.uk/education-watch/, accessed March 21, 2020; P. Walker, "Tory MPs Back Youth Group with Apparent Links to US Far Right," *The Guardian*, February 4, 2019, https://www.theguardian.com/politics/2019/feb/04/tory-mps-back -rightwing-youth-group-turning-point-uk, accessed March 21, 2020.

8. G. K. Chesterton, *The Everlasting Man* (San Francisco: Ignatius Press, [1925] 1993), 63.

9. Chesterton, 56, 63.

10. "Honouring over 15 Million Victims of Slave Trade, UN Calls for End to Remnants of Slavery," *UN News*, March 2013, New York, NY, https://news.un.org/en/story/2013/03/435462 -honouring-over-15-million-victims-slave-trade-un-calls-end-remnants-slavery, accessed March 23, 2020; World Future Fund, "Death Toll from the Slave Trade: The African

Holocaust: 60 Million Dead at the Hands of White Christian Imperialism," *World Future Fund*, Alexandria, VA, www.worldfuturefund.org/Reports/Slavedeathtoll/slaverydeathtoll. html, accessed March 23, 2020.

11. S. Steinbacher, *Auschwitz: A History*, trans. S. Whiteside (London: Penguin, [2004] 2005), 42–43.

12. Steinbacher, 79.

13. Steinbacher, 30–31.

14. B. Hartman, "Donald Trump and the Dangers of Dehumanizing the Enemy," *Common Dreams*, November 2, 2017, https://www.commondreams.org/views/2017/11/02/donald -trump-and-dangers-dehumanizing-enemy, accessed March 22, 2020.

15. S. M. Hersh, "Torture at Abu Ghraib," *New Yorker*, April 30, 2004, https://www.newyorker .com/magazine/2004/05/10/torture-at-abu-ghraib; Platt, "Intimate Violence," 163.

16. J. Hirschfield Davis, "Trump Calls Some Unauthorized Immigrants 'Animal' in Rant," *New York Times*, May 16, 2018, https://www.nytimes.com/2018/05/16/us/politics/trump -undocumented-immigrants-animals.html, accessed February 20, 2021; R. Neate, "Donald Trump Doubles Down on Mexico 'Rapists' Comments Despite Outrage," *The Guardian*, July 2, 2015, https://www.theguardian.com/us-news/2015/jul/02/donald-trump-racist -claims-mexico-rapes.

17. C. Mims, "Electronics Makers Have Worst Labor Practices of Any Industry, Says Report," *MIT Technology Review*, January 9, 2012, https://www.technologyreview.com/s/426565 /electronics-makers-have-worst-labor-practices-of-any-industry-says-report/.

18. C. Posslac, "Liner Notes" (1994), *Górecki: Symphony Number 3 (Symphony of Sorrowful Songs) / Three Olden Style Pieces*, Zofia Kilanowicz, Soprano, Polish National Radio Symphony Orchestra (Katowice) conducted by Antoni Wit, Naxos, HNH International Ltd., [2001], 8.550822.

19. T. Lewis, "Ai Weiwei: 'An Artist Must Be an Activist,'" *The Observer*, March 22, 2020, https://www.theguardian.com/artanddesign/2020/mar/22/ai-weiwei-an-artist-must-be-an -activist.

20. "Barbara Kruger (American, born 1945)," *Artnet*, Berlin, http://www.artnet.com/artists /barbara-kruger/, accessed March 26, 2020.

21. A. Pownall, "Vivienne Westwood Protests Climate Change as Environmental Demon- strations Hit London Fashion Week," *Dezeen*, London, February 18, 2019, www.dezeen .com/2019/02/18/homo-loquax-vivienne-westwood-climate-change-london-fashion-week/.

22. K. Hamnett, *Best of British: Fashion Designers*, Farfetch UK Ltd., https://www.farfetch.com /editorial/best-of-british-fashion-designers.aspx, accessed March 26, 2020.

23. B. Stephenson, *Ritual: A Very Short Introduction* (Oxford: Oxford University Press, 2015), 55.

24. F. S. Michaels, *Monoculture: How One Story is Changing Everything* (Kamloops, BC: Red Clover Press, 2011), 99–100.

25. L. Fioramonti, *How Numbers Rule the World: The Use and Abuse of Statistics in Global Politics* (London: Zed Books, 2014), 138–143.

26. J. Gross Stein, *The Cult of Efficiency* (Toronto: Anansi, 2001), 139–140, 147–148.

27. C. S. Lewis, *The Abolition of Man* (New York: HarperCollins, 1944), 39–40.

CHAPTER 20

With apologies to John Masefield, author of *Sea-Fever*, in *Everyman's Book of Evergreen Verse*, ed. D. Herbert (London: J. M. Dent & Sons, [1902] 1981), 318, https://www.poetry foundation.org/poems/54932/sea-fever-56d235e0d871e, accessed March 1, 2021.

CHAPTER 21

1. United Nations, *UN Research Roadmap for the COVID-19 Recovery: Leveraging the Power of Science for a More Equitable, Resilient and Sustainable Future*, New York, November 2020, 15–16, https://www.un.org/en/pdfs/UNCOVID19ResearchRoadmap.pdf, accessed February 11, 2021.

2. United Nations, *UN Research Roadmap for the COVID-19 Recovery*, 14.

3. United Nations, *UN Research Roadmap for the COVID-19 Recovery*, 6, 9.

4. W. Sachs, "One World," in *The Development Dictionary*, 2nd ed., ed. W. Sachs (London: Zed Books, 2010), http://ezproxy.lancs.ac.uk/login?url=https://search.credoreference.com/content/entry/zeddev/one_world/0?institutionId=3497, accessed November 21, 2020.

5. J. Gray, "Secular Faith Has No Answer to the Coronavirus, *Catholic Herald*, May 15, 2020, https://catholicherald.co.uk/secular-faith-has-no-answer-to-the-coronavirus/.

6. S. Walker, *Design and Spirituality: A Philosophy of Material Cultures* (Oxford: Routledge, 2021), 121.

7. M. Dodge Luhan, excerpted from *New Mexico Magazine* (February 1936), quoted in H. Shukman, "Looking for Lawrence," *New Mexico Magazine*, November 1, 2012, https://www.newmexico.org/nmmagazine/articles/post/lawrencenewmexico-78512/#:~:text=In%20 the%20end%2C%20although%20Lawrence,Luhan%20gave%20it%20to%20the.

8. R. K. Broughton, J. M. Bullock, C. George, R. A. Hill, S. A. Hinsley, M. Maziarz, M. Melin, J. O. Mountford, T. H. Sparks, and R. F. Pywell, "Long-Term Woodland Restoration on Lowland Farmland through Passive Rewilding," *PLoS ONE* 16, no. 6 (June 16, 2021), 1, 16–18, https://journals.plos.org/plosone/article?id=10.1371/journal.pone.0252466.

9. S. Kierkegaard, *Fear and Trembling*, trans. A. Hannay (London: Penguin, [1843] 2005), 62, 70.

10. Kierkegaard, 72–74.

11. R. Williams, *Candles in the Dark: Faith, Hope and Love in a Time of Pandemic* (London: Society for Promoting Christian Knowledge [SPCK], 2020), 4–22.

12. Climate Change Committee, *Progress in Adapting to Climate Change:2021 Report to Parliament*, June 24, 2021, 21–24, 92, https://www.theccc.org.uk/publication/2021-progress -report-to-parliament.

13. R. Scruton, *Confessions of a Heretic* (London: Nottinghill Editions, 2016), 65–85.

14. Sachs, "One World."

15. S. Scheffler, *Death and the Afterlife* (New York: Oxford University Press, 2013), 33.

16. Climate Change Committee, *Progress in Adapting to Climate Change: 2021 Report to Parliament*, 164.

CHAPTER 24

1. Food and Agriculture Organization of the United Nations, *Agroecology Knowledge Hub*, Rome, https://www.fao.org/agroecology/overview/overview10elements/en/, accessed January 28, 2022.

2. W. Sachs, "One World," in *The Development Dictionary*, 2nd ed., ed. W. Sachs (London: Zed Books, 2010), http://ezproxy.lancs.ac.uk/login?url=https://search.credoreference.com /content/entry/zeddev/one_world/0?institutionId=3497, accessed July 15, 2021.

3. J. M. Bergoglio (Pope Francis), *Fratelli Tutti: Encyclical Letter on Fraternity and Social Friendship* (Vatican City: Libreria Editrice Vaticana, 2020), 43.

4. B. Pascal, *III Vanity—Pensées, Pensées and Other Writings*, trans. H. Levi (Oxford: Oxford University Press, [1670] 1995), no. 80, 21.

5. B. Pascal, *IX Diversion—Pensées, Pensées and Other Writings*, trans. H. Levi (Oxford: Oxford University Press, [1670] 1995), no. 171, 49.

6. A. M. S. Boethius (6th century), *The Consolation of Philosophy*, trans. P. G. Walsh (Oxford: Oxford University Press, 1999), bk. 3, 9:4, 53.

7. J. Elkington, "25 Years Ago I Coined the Phrase 'Triple Bottom Line.' Here's Why It's Time to Rethink It," *Harvard Business Review*, June 25, 2018, https://hbr.org/2018/06/25-years -ago-i-coined-the-phrase-triple-bottom-line-heres-why-im-giving-up-on-it.

8. S. C. Whitmore-Williams, C. Manning, K. Krygsman, and M. Speiser, *Mental Health and our Changing Climate: Impacts, Implications and Guidance* (Washington, DC: American Psychological Association and ecoAmerica, 2017), 14.

9. Bergoglio (Pope Francis), *Fratelli Tutti*, 12–15, 24, 39.

10. Gov.UK, *Plan Your Relationships, Sex and Health Curriculum—Information to Help School leaders Plan, Develop and Implement the New Statutory Curriculum*, London, September 24, 2020, https://www.gov.uk/guidance/plan-your-relationships-sex-and-health-curriculum #creating-a-policy-for-the-new-curriculum.

11. M. Busby, "Schools in England Told Not to Use Material from Anti-capitalist Groups— Idea Categorised as 'Extreme Political Stance' Equivalent to Endorsing Illegal Activity," *The Guardian*, September 27, 2020, https://www.theguardian.com/education/2020/sep/27 /uk-schools-told-not-to-use-anti-capitalist-material-in-teaching.

12. P. Connolly, *The Furrow*, St. Patrick's College, Maynooth, Ireland, December 1978, 93, quoted in B. O'Brien, "Under the Tyranny of the Majority," *The Tablet*, January 30, 2021, 4–5.

13. M. Gandhi, "203. Imam Saheb," in *The Collected Works of Mahatma Gandhi*, vol. 49, April 3, 1930–August 22, 1930, 204, https://www.gandhiashramsevagram.org/gandhi-literature /mahatma-gandhi-collected-works-volume-49.pdf, accessed July 18, 2021.

14. J. Randers, "Democracy Has a Hard Time Dealing with the Climate Threat," *extract*, January 15, 2015, updated June 29, 2021, https://www.extrakt.se/demokratin-oformogen -att-hantera-klimathotet/.

15. D. H. Lawrence, "New Mexico," in *Phoenix: The Posthumous Papers of D. H. Lawrence*, ed. E. D. McDonald (London: William Heinemann Ltd., 1936), 147.

16. K. Armstrong, *The Lost Art of Scripture: Rescuing the Sacred Texts* (London: The Bodley Head, 2019), 67.

17. J. M. Marincola, introduction to *The Histories*, by Herodotus (London: Penguin, 1996), xxvii–xxviii.

18. Ohiyesa a.k.a. Charles A. Eastman, *From the Deep Woods to Civilization: Chapters in the Autobiography of an Indian* (Boston: Little, Brown, and Company, 1916), 1–2.

19. K. Armstrong, *The Lost Art of Scripture: Rescuing the Sacred Texts* (London: The Bodley Head, 2019), 1–2.

20. Z. S. Strother, "Invention and Reinvention in the Traditional Arts," *African Arts* 28, no. 2 (1995): 26.

21. J. Comaroff, J. and J. Comaroff, quoted in Z. S. Strother, "Invention and Reinvention in the Traditional Arts," *African Arts* 28, no. 2 (1995): 24.

22. K. Armstrong, *The Lost Art of Scripture: Rescuing the Sacred Texts* (London: The Bodley Head, 2019), 45, 222. See also St. Augustine, *On Christian Doctrine, in Four Books* (Grand Rapids, MI: Christian Classics Ethereal Library, 397–426 CE; Public domain, n.d.), editor's summary, 3, and bk. 3, chap. 5, 53–54, http://www.ccel.org/ccel/augustine/doctrine, accessed May 25, 2019. See also St. Augustine, *Confessions*, trans. R. S. Pine-Coffin (London: Penguin, 1961), bk. 5, chap. 14, 108.

23. On ritual, see chapter 16; on community agriculture, see chapter 13, and on sports, see chapter 15.

24 J. Loughran, "EU Introduces 'Right to Repair' Rules for Electrical Goods," *Engineering and Technology*, March 2, 2021, https://eandt.theiet.org/content/articles/2021/03/eu -introduces-right-to-repair-rules-for-electrical-goods/.

25. Seneca (ca. 41 CE), *Dialogues and Essays*, trans. J. Davie (Oxford: Oxford University Press, 2007), 173–175.

26. See chapter 7.

27. A. MacIntyre, *After Virtue*, 3rd ed. (London: Bloomsbury, 2007), xxiii.

28. R. Williams, *The Way of St. Benedict* (London: Bloomsbury Continuum, 2020), 16.

29. W. Sachs, "Cosmopolitan Localism," in *The Development Dictionary*, ed. W. Sachs, 3rd ed. (London: Zed Books, 2019), 122–124.

30. J. M. McCarthy, "'Pan in America,' Modernism, and Material Nature," in *Green Modernism: Nature and the English Novel, 1900 to 1930* (New York: Palgrave Macmillan, 2015), 199–212.

31. E. Hemingway, *A Moveable Feast* (London: Arrow Books, [1936] 2004), 84.

32. H. Shukman, "Looking for Lawrence," *New Mexico Magazine*, November 2012, https://www.newmexico.org/nmmagazine/articles/post/lawrencenewmexico-78512/#:~:text=In%20the%20end%2C%20although%20Lawrence,Luhan%20gave%20it%20to%20the, accessed May 16, 2021.

33. S. Walker, *Design Realities* (Oxford: Routledge, 2019), 268–294. I included the following definition: "'Progressive Design Praxis' is a form of design practice that aims to change the situation for the better by striving to interpret, understand and apply the ethical values and notions of virtue found in the philosophical and spiritual traditions of one's culture."

34. W. J. Ripple, C. Wolf, T. M. Newsome, J. W. Gregg, T. M. Lenton, I. Palomo, J. A. J. Eikelboom, B. E. Law, S. Huq, P. B. Duffy, and J. Rockström, "World Scientists' Warning of a Climate Emergency 2021," *BioScience* 71, no. 9 (September 2021): 894–898, https://doi.org/10.1093/biosci/biab079; IPCC, "Summary for Policymakers," in *Climate Change 2021: The Physical Science Basis. Contribution of Working Group I to the Sixth Assessment Report of the Intergovernmental Panel on Climate Change*, ed. V. Masson-Delmotte, P. Zhai, A. Pirani, S.L. Connors, C. Péan, S. Berger, N. Caud, Y. Chen, L. Goldfarb, M.I. Gomis, M. Huang, K. Leitzell, E. Lonnoy, J.B.R. Matthews, T.K. Maycock, T. Waterfield, O. Yelekçi, R. Yu, and B. Zhou, 3–32 (Cambridge and New York: Cambridge University Press, 2021, https://doi.org/10.1017/9781009157896.001.

APPENDIX 1

1. E. T. Merrill, "An Old Roman Game," *Classical Journal* 11, no. 66 (1916): 365–366.

APPENDIX 2

1. U. Schädler, "Latrunculi: A Forgotten Roman Game of Strategy Reconstructed," *Abstract Games*, no. 7 (Autumn 2001): 11, https://www.abstractgames.org/uploads/1/1/6/4/116462923/abstract_games_issue_7.pdf.

APPENDIX 3

1. F. V. Grunfeld, *Games of the World: How to Make Them, How to Play Them, How They Came to Be* (Zurich: Swiss Committee for UNICEF, 1982), 59–60.

APPENDIX 4

1. F. V. Grunfeld, *Games of the World: How to Make Them, How to Play Them, How They Came to Be* (Zurich: Swiss Committee for UNICEF, 1982), 162–163.

Index

Page numbers in italics indicate figures.